LITERATURE AND PSYCHOLOGY

Literature
and Psychology

F. L. LUCAS

*Le cœur le plus serein en apparence ressemble au
puits naturel de la Savane Alachua; la surface
en paraît calme et pure, mais quand vous re-
gardez au fond du bassin vous apercevez un
large crocodile, que le puits nourrit dans
ses eaux.*

CHATEAUBRIAND

FIRST AMERICAN EDITION
REVISED

ANN ARBOR PAPERBACKS
THE UNIVERSITY OF MICHIGAN PRESS

First edition as an
Ann Arbor Paperback
1957

To Hilda Stekel

PREFACE

THIS book consists essentially of lectures given at Cambridge since the War; though a good deal enlarged and rewritten.

Two centuries ago Johnson questioned the value of lectures (apart from scientific demonstrations). He preferred books. So did Gibbon. None the less to-day, five hundred years after the invention of printing, Universities are more belectured than ever. Probably Johnson was (as so often) too sweeping; yet I believe he was (as so often) largely right. Only two of the lecturers whom I heard as an undergraduate helped me much—though, of course, the fault may have been mine. One dealt with a subject that needed lantern-slides; the other was that extreme rarity, a stimulating speaker. The rest I would rather have had in print—or not at all. Among many defences of this large-scale lecturing, only one that I have heard seemed cogent—'books', was the plea, 'are so formal'. True, they are. But, why should books be 'so formal'—unless the authors are owls? I still think that the modern University trusts too largely to spoken lectures; and that, where possible, they are more use printed. Often, I know, that is not possible. All the same . . . .

On the other hand, once it *is* printed, I think there are certain advantages in the lecture-form (which is my excuse for keeping it here). The tone of a lecture is, usually, not only less 'formal', it is also more exploratory, more provisional, less dogmatic. Again, the lecturer is curtailed by the clock—and most books are too long. He is speaking—and most books are too remote from living speech. Lastly, he cannot be *too* boring, or *too* obscure—

or he quickly reads the results in the faces, and the numbers, of his audience.

These lectures are not learned; they are not expert; but I hope some may find them not unhelpful, not only about literature, but (far more important) about life. For I could wish that, when I was young, I had been told some of these things, instead of having to learn by sharp experience. But then I own that current ideas of what really matters in education leave me speechless.

It is not at all that I think the ordinary reader should plunge into the oceans of psychoanalytic literature. That can be confusing, often dangerous; for neurotics, it can make treatment still more difficult; even for those not neurotic it can lead to muddle-headed superficiality or to weary and exasperated disillusion.

To read the bound volumes of *Imago* or *The International Journal of Psychoanalysis* for, say, the last twenty-five years leaves an impression of great unevenness and a feeling, if one dare say so, that many of the contributors would have been no worse for a little more scepticism. When I am told, for example, that the scene in the *Odyssey* where Nausicaä welcomes the hero escaped from the sea represents a birth-fantasy; that the princess represents Odysseus' mother; and that the ball she throws to her maidens turns out to be a phallic symbol ('"I knew it would," said Alice'), for such Homeric criticism I am afraid I can find only Homeric laughter. And when even Freud himself can write, as late as 1932, of learning 'on reliable authority' that from the night when a Zeppelin made a peaceful practice-flight over London, England resolved on war with Germany, it seems clear that even this very great psychologist was not infallible about the psychology either of the English or of 'reliable authorities'. I cannot think it was national prejudice—Freud was too great a man and had warm sympathies with that England which was to give him, as it turned out, his last refuge. I suspect it was merely that this psychological explanation happened to fit a theory. I do not recall this lapse out of any *Schadenfreude*, but merely as an example of the eternal perils of theorizing. Rapt disciples are too apt to forget the wisdom of Wesley's saying: 'I can call no man Rabbi.'

But that cannot alter my deep and lasting admiration for Freud's work. Quite apart from his splendid moral courage and from all he did for the science of the mind and its maladies, it seems to me vital for all who would guard their own mental health, and hand it on to their children, to know *something* of his discoveries—of such simple basic principles as are given in his *Introductory Lectures* (both series) and his *Outline of Psychoanalysis*, or in Stekel's *L'Éducation des Parents* and *Lettres à une Mère*.[1] It is well to know how little one knows about oneself; and to try to know more.

I am aware that in orthodox Freudian circles Wilhelm Stekel is regarded with some disfavour. Sometimes their Unconscious shows its dislike by even misspelling his name. But after the not inconsiderable test of reading some thousands of pages of Stekel's work, I have come to think him a better and finer mind than any other I have encountered in this field apart from Freud himself (not to mention Jung whose mysticism leaves me completely cold). I first met him personally in 1939, because someone near to me was suffering from a serious breakdown and a book of his I had just come upon in France seemed to me outstanding in its brilliance, honesty, and good sense. He was already old and failing in that March of

---

[1] I mention these French translations because they are excellent and more of us read French than German. But both books ought to be made easily accessible in English. Stekel's main work, *Störungen des Trieb- und Affektlebens*, in ten volumes, is intended only for the medical profession, not the ordinary reader. When quoting from it, therefore, I have not given references. Similarly with his *Technique of Analytical Psychotherapy*.

1939, a year after Hitler had hunted him from his beloved Vienna, and a year before he died: but in the first five minutes I felt that here was one of the most striking personalities I have ever known. (Indeed, in my memory he holds a place shared only by H. W. Nevinson.) To him this book owes a very great deal. I know this will get me into trouble with those that hunt him as a heretic. But that has to be faced.

I should like to express my gratitude to Mrs. Hilda Stekel, herself a brilliant psychotherapist, for many helpful criticisms and suggestions—though she is *not* responsible for my errors.

KING'S COLLEGE,
CAMBRIDGE.

CONTENTS

[11]

PART ONE

The Interpretation of Literature

I

Introductory:
Lady Macbeth, Oedipus, Hamlet

*To well manage our Affections, and wild Horses
of Plato, are the highest Circenses.*
SIR THOMAS BROWNE.

LAO TZU, says Taoist legend, rebuked Confucius for
expounding past literature—'All your lectures are concerned with things that are no better than footprints in
the dust. Footprints are made by shoes; but they are far
from being shoes.' How often, as one wanders among
the endless shelves of the University Library, or sets off in
the morning to lecture, that mocking voice drily whispers
across two thousand years, 'Footprints in the dust!'
And yet surely Confucius could have answered—'In
the deserts of existence, even footprints may help to
find "the Way". Only one needs, also, a sense of direction.' A sense of direction—this seems to me what our
criticism lacks, most of all.

Critics have, I feel, two duties—to interpret; and to
judge. Most of them prove far more successful at interpretation; and far more useful. Yet both tasks exist.
But I believe that critics often misinterpret, because they
simply do not know enough of human beings; and
misjudge, because they think too little of the effects of
literature on human beings.

Hence, in part, the irritated contempt felt by many
creative writers for critics and criticism—Landor's 'most
odious of small creeping things'; Tennyson's 'lice in the
locks of literature'; Musset's 'pharmaciens du bon goût';

[15]

Flaubert's 'leprosy of letters'—'ignominie mortelle qui lui ronge le visage'; Tchekhov's 'horseflies that hinder the horse from ploughing'.

Criticism there must be, spoken if not written. These great writers wrote criticism themselves—some of it excellent. And yet their loathing for critics was not merely piqued vanity. Partly, indeed, it may have sprung from a certain incompatibility of temper. Often the creator lives deep in dreams, the critic vigilantly awake; the one works largely by being passionate, the other by trying to be dispassionate.

In the words of Proust, 'il y a plus d'analogie entre la vie instinctive du public et le talent d'un grand écrivain, qui n'est qu'un instinct religieusement écouté, au milieu du silence imposé à tout le reste, un instinct perfectionné et compris, qu'avec le verbiage superficiel et les critères changeants des juges attitrés.' So the creators often dislike the critics as ardently as the critics pursue the creators; nightingales, I imagine, do not like owls, much as owls may like nightingales. (Hence the advantage to the critic of having been himself a creator—even though, like Sainte-Beuve, a poor one.) But, after all allowances for difference of temper and attitude, I do not think this general contempt of writers for critics has been wholly undeserved. Turn, for example, to the criticism of Shakespeare; you will find men pontificating about his characters with, apparently, less knowledge of human character than they must, one would think, have possessed at school; as if they had read every book except the Book of Life. One cannot talk rationally about human behaviour if one realizes so little how fantastically irrational it often is. (The same applies to many historians and biographers.) I do not pretend that I am going to floodlight these abysses. I bring only a pocket-torch. But I believe it the critic's business to learn more of men as well as books—of men in their

perpetual unreason; not in order to revel in that unreason like so much modern literature that seems to me
mere drunken Helotry; but in order to fight it, as our
eighteenth-century Age of Reason fought it, though with
a fuller understanding than theirs of what an uphill fight
it is. For to lose that battle may be to lose civilization
itself.

Sainte-Beuves, unfortunately, are rare—rarer even
than Victor Hugos. Probably it helped Sainte-Beuve
that he had once been a medical student. It may have
made him more scientific, less glib about generalizations.
Still more important, he not only had sense and sensibility, a style of his own, and a vast knowledge of literature, he had also a knowledge of human beings (with a
clear, if bleak, view of life). How does one learn about
human beings? First, by mixing with them. Not at
tea-parties; not in the salons of 'intellectuals'; there one
learns little. But in the business of life. One also learns
much of human beings (as Proust emphasized) by falling
in love with them; but that form of research (as Proust
also emphasized) is apt to be painful. If for a moment I
may be personal, I am deeply grateful, now, not indeed
to the Germans, but to destiny, that for ten years in all
they dragged me away from the seclusion of books and
Universities to war-service. A third of one's adult life is
a lot: yet the experience seemed well worth it.

But, further, our own age has had—thanks, above all,
to the indomitable persistence of Freud—the privilege of
gaining an insight into human nature that, previously,
no amount of personal experience, by itself, could ever
give. This is the reverse of welcome to some people.
To me it seems inestimable—possibly the best hope
(though that may not be saying a great deal) for the
future of our kind of civilization.

In the fifteenth and sixteenth centuries man discovered the New World. Since the seventeenth he has

[17]

been discovering new worlds of Science. (We call it
'the conquest of Science'—only it has become a little
obscure whether it is we that have conquered Science, or
Science that has conquered us.) But since the late
nineteenth century man has been discovering a new
world inside himself—in what we rather vaguely call
'the Unconscious'. As old Fuller put it, long ago: 'Who
hath sailed about the world of his own heart, sounded
each creek, surveyed each corner, but that there still
remains much *terra incognita* to himself?'

Earlier still the same thought troubled Sir John
Davies:

> We seek to know the moving of each sphere,
>   And the strange cause of th'ebb and flow of Nile;
> But of that clock within our breasts we bear,
>   The subtle motions we forget the while.
>
> We that acquaint ourselves with every zone,
>   And pass both tropics and behold the poles,
> When we come home, are to ourselves unknown,
>   And unacquainted still with our own souls.

That, in its turn, goes back to the tag of Seneca,
beloved by Elizabethan dramatists, on the great monarch
who dies—

> Notus nimis omnibus,
> Ignotus sibi.
> (Too known to all the world,
> To his own self all unknown.)

And even this derives from the 'Virtue is Knowledge' of
Socrates and that 'Know thyself' which stood inscribed
on the temple of Apollo at Delphi.

It is no doubt disconcerting that this *terra incognita* in
ourselves should now appear to be so largely inhabited by
savages. It is as if Prospero had discovered a wide tract of
his island to be dominated by an elusive and invisible
Caliban, beyond even *his* arts to control. True, Goethe

said long ago that he had never read of a crime he could not imagine himself committing; but minds as open as Goethe's are rare. And yet in the last thirty-five years we have painfully learnt for ourselves how thin is the crust on which civilized man treads above abysses of barbarism that our grandfathers never imagined in their most dyspeptic dreams. What twentieth-century psychology suggested, twentieth-century history has too bitterly confirmed.

In 1948 I was lecturing in Berlin. It was not merely

> Miles, and miles, and miles of desolation!
> Leagues on leagues on leagues without a change!

This horrible shambles of destruction, this rubble-heap of maddened conflict, was after all only a visible materialization of the frenzied conflict in the mind of a single Romantic, who had infected with his own crazy aggressiveness one of the most educated nations of the earth. Sanity is not a bagatelle. We master more and more each year the forces of this world we live in; they will only make our destruction the more utter, if we cannot learn to master also the hidden forces within ourselves.

More than ever, it seems to me, the proper study of mankind is man. If our world grows neurotic, all the more urgent need to understand neurosis. Much psychoanalytic theory may still be speculative and controversial; much harm, as well as much good, may be done by it; but its foundations are laid. It has given us a multitude of new data, however much rival schools may dispute their explanations. This seems to me the absorbing interest of psychological case-histories—here are *facts* more fantastic than any fiction. And as Montesquieu wisely said long ago: 'Les observations sont l'histoire de la physique; les systèmes en sont la fable.' I have myself watched how terrible a nervous breakdown can be; I have recognized, perforce, the actuality

of things that, till then, I should have waved away as
fantastic. Some of these traits of human nature may be
rare abnormalities; but many go on under our noses
every day, unnoticed by those who cannot, or will not,
see. Even in what used to be thought the relatively
simple business of bringing up healthy children, I find
one comes up perpetually against puzzles to which only
modern psychology provides a key. That psychology
may still be itself in its childhood; but even in its cradle
it can strangle more poisonous serpents than did any
infant Hercules. I believe that in the long run, unless
our world collapses, mankind will have owed yet more
to Freud than to Columbus, or Newton, or Darwin, or
Einstein; let alone Marx, whose work suffered precisely
because he remained (like many other reformers) so
crude in his psychology, so naïve, so incorrigibly blind to
the human lust for power, for inflicting pain, and even
for suffering pain. And yet such is the human reluctance
to face this that there are in the world to-day thousands
of persons—including brilliant scientists—ready to give
their lives (not to mention the lives of others) simply that
a system where the rich are powerful may be replaced,
as in Russia, by a system where the powerful are rich.
Of no travellers, indeed, is it so true as of 'fellow-
travellers' that to travel hopefully is happier than to
arrive. Small wonder that Marxists frown on Freud.

Even our own political idealists of the left, infinitely
more decent and civilized than the totalitarians, have
landed themselves and us in grave difficulties by this
same besetting blindness of reformers to basic human
nature. They felt that men should work for their
country or mankind without needing the meaner incen-
tives of carrot and stick. After all, in the days of
Dunkirk, what respectable being worked for reward?
But all our lives, perhaps fortunately, are not days of
Dunkirk. Preachments by politicians on the B.B.C.

remain less inspiring than the presence of Hitler at Boulogne. The Russians are at least not so Utopian. The Kremlin encourages the diligence of individual workers with very red carrots and still larger sticks. We may loathe their methods; but if we want to avoid mass-compulsion we must make it worth a man's while to work hard of his own free will—harder than his lazier or stupider fellows. (I happen to have work I like, and therefore tend to overwork; but, unfortunately, most of the world's work is, and must be, less attractive.) It is futile to preach changes of heart; the human heart does change—but in the slow course of generations, not over-night. And who knows whither? Freud would have given our social optimists colder comfort, but better counsel—men 'are *not* spontaneously fond of work, and arguments are impotent against their passions'.[1] Depressing? Reality, in the long run, is less depressing than illusions. The essential is to see that the rewards of efficiency are not excessive, nor the penalties of inefficiency cruel. As men are, rewards and penalties there must be; social security up to a point is excellent —but not too much. When Prince Eugène was warned that Lille was defended by a Marshal of France, he replied, 'I would rather it were defended by a Marshal of France than by a man who aspires to become one'. Prince Eugène was a sound psychologist. Too much safety can be very dangerous.

It matters to know about the earth, about the heavenly bodies, about economics: but it matters still more to know ourselves. It is now possible to know ourselves a good deal better. Much may remain dubious; Columbus, too, to the end of his life hugged many fallacies; but his New World was there.

I have suggested that psychological knowledge could help criticism; first, towards better understanding.

---

[1] *Unbehagen in der Kultur (Gesammelte Werke, XIV)*, p. 329.

Take as an example Lady Macbeth's washing of her hands:

> DOCTOR: What is it she do's now?
> Looke how she rubbes her hands.
> GENTLEMAN: It is an accustom'd action with her, to seeme thus washing her hands: I have knowne her continue in this a quarter of an houre.
> L. MACBETH: Yet heere's a spot. . . . Out damned spot: out I say. . . . Yet who would have thought the olde man to have had so much blood in him? . . . The Thane of Fife had a wife; where is she now? What, will these hands ne're be cleane? . . . Heere's the smell of the blood still: all the perfumes of Arabia will not sweeten this little hand. Oh, oh, oh. . . .
> DOCTOR: This disease is beyond my practise.

But it was not beyond Shakespeare's.

The ordinary reader sees this as a brilliant piece of imaginative symbolism, dreamed by a poet; he does not realize that hundreds of tormented souls are literally obeying similar obsessions at this very hour.

Now of course the symbolism of washing away guilt is familiar enough—as in baptism, or the Greek ritual of cleansing blood-guilt with the blood of swine. In poetry it has become almost a commonplace. Sophocles puts it into the mouth of his Theban king (*Oedipus Rex*, 1227-8):

> Not Ister, no, not Phasis would suffice
> To wash this palace clean of the pollutions
> It hides within.

Then Seneca expands Sophocles into typical Senecan rant (*Hercules Furens*, 1323-8):

> What Tanaïs, what Nile, what swirling flood
> Of Persian Tigris, what wild Rhine, what Tagus
> Rolling in turbid spate Iberian gold,
> Can wash this right hand clean?
>   Though cold Maeotis
> Should deluge me with all her Arctic waves,
> Though Tethys' Ocean overwhelmed these hands,
> The stain of crime will stay.

[22]

Shakespeare's Macbeth in his turn echoes Seneca:

> Will all great *Neptune's* Ocean wash this blood
> Cleane from my Hand? No: this my Hand will rather
> The multitudinous Seas incarnadine,
> Making the Greene one Red.

But Lady Macbeth's washing of her hands is not merely this sort of poetic imagery; it is not a piece of poetic imagination, like the Witches or Banquo's Ghost; it is a picture of real human behaviour.

Here, for instance, in all its grotesque detail, is the avowal of an obsessional neurotic. It has none of Shakespeare's poetry; but it is the raw material of that poetry; and, for me (others may differ), it leaves that poetry still more vivid and more real.

'To begin my morning washing I have to convince myself that the basin is clean. I fill it and let the water run away. Then I take a brush, dip it in hot water, and carefully rub the whole basin. Then I rub the brush with soft soap and lather the whole basin. (The soap has to be kept in a clean porcelain vessel.) Then I rinse again with water and make sure the basin is clean. (The basin must have no cracks or chipped places, because they always collect dirt.) Often I have to examine the whole basin with a magnifying-glass for cracks, faults, and dirt. Then I run clean water, which must only reach a certain height: if it happens to come higher, I cannot just let a little out—I have to empty it all and try again to get the exact level. Before I wash, I say the Lord's Prayer and cross myself three times. In saying the Lord's Prayer, I must not think of other things; otherwise I have to begin it all over again. Then follows the washing according to a clearly established ritual. First I dip my right-hand fingers—not the thumb—and wet my forehead, saying "Praised be Jesus Christ!" Then I pass them from right to left over my forehead. Then I do the same with my left-hand fingers, making sure not to dip them deeper than the right-hand fingers and to moisten my forehead in exactly the same places as before.

'I initiate the washing of nose, cheek, and chin in the same manner. Only then begin my real ablutions. I dip both hands, and raise the water to my face—but not a drop must fall. First I moisten my face ten times with both hands, then lather, then rinse ten times more, etc. etc.'

Such, beside Shakespeare's tragic splendour, is the crude tragi-comedy of real life. A neurotic like this may wash hands or face twenty or a hundred times a day. A therapist I knew had successfully treated an unfortunate whose work was wrecked by sudden and uncontrollable impulses, at any moment, to run and take a bath—

'Will these hands ne're be cleane?'

In another case a girl had been seduced by her stepfather. She developed a furious hatred both of him and of the mother who had now become her rival. But her death-wishes against that mother roused in her a no less frantic sense of guilt. Gradually she built round herself a barbed-wire entanglement of obsessions. Her terror of being 'infected' grew such that her fiancé, a doctor (and clearly a very Job for patience), had to go through endless disinfections of everything with which she could come in contact. For five months she slept only in one armchair; three weeks she spent in her room completely naked.

That Lady Macbeth is at the time walking in her sleep, makes the scene far more effective. But this too is true to life. In somnambulance, thoughts that the waking mind trampled down may assert control; as, for example, with a neurotic that haunted nightly in his sleep the gateway of a girl whom, waking, he affected to despise. The very dogs came to know him so well that, with creditable discretion, they no longer barked.

How did Shakespeare glimpse such things? By intuition? Possibly. Or had he seen, or heard of, such
cases? That need not be so improbable. We forget that
many Elizabethans saw far more of insanity than we.
Segregation was less organized. The repulsion, too, was
less. To their simple souls madness seemed amusing.
They thought it as natural to kill an hour or two by
watching unhappy lunatics in Bedlam, as their posterity
by watching unhappy animals in Zoos. Even the
marriage festivities of the Princess Elizabeth, James I's
daughter, were pleasantly enlivened by a masque of
lunatics. I find it hard to believe that Shakespeare drew
wholly from imagination either this scene or his picture
of Ophelia's madness; which so convincingly combines
childlike simplicity with a childish loss of inhibitions that
leads her to release, unashamed, the frankest imagery of
pent-up physical passion.[1] A hundred years ago all this
seemed too horrible to believe—'a state of mind', wrote
the agitated Joseph Hunter (1845), 'which, if it ever did
exist in nature, ought to be screened from every human
eye, nor should the sex be profaned by the remotest
suspicion of its possible existence'. To-day we have
grown more aware of the dangers of playing ostrich;
and 'the sex' less willing to be kept like white mice.

Does Shakespeare's truth to life matter artistically?
That depends on temperament. Some readers seem to
care not two pins about verisimilitude: others are like
Ibsen's Judge Brack in *Hedda Gabler*, ever ready to protest 'But people don't do such things'. For myself, I own
that, except in deliberate fantasias, I am irritated by
what seems false to life, or so abnormal as to be quite

[1] Compare the Bedlam-scenes in Dekker and Webster's *Northward Ho !*
IV. iii-iv, and Dekker's *Honest Whore*, Part I, v. ii. Also the Madmen in
Webster's *Duchess of Malfi*, IV. ii. Similarly, in seventeenth-century France,
la grande Mademoiselle is bored on a visit to the convent of Fontevrault ;
luckily her maids-in-waiting discover a mad nun in a cell—' Je pris ma
course vers ce cachot et n'en sortis que pour souper '. Next day the Abbess
' la régala d'une seconde folle '.

untypical. Siamese twins exist: but with very moderate attractions as *dramatis personae*. '*Incredulus odi.*'

For that reason I had always felt chilly towards the self-blinding of Oedipus in what some have praised as the sublimest of tragedies. Not only is the poking out of eyes physically disgusting, whether in Oedipus or Gloucester; in addition, this self-mutilation of Oedipus seems a needless fatuity that recalls the Abbé Maury's retort to the *Sans-culottes* yelling round him, 'À la lanterne!'—'Imbéciles, en verrez-vous plus clair?' Oedipus has committed a wholly unintentional crime; why add a deliberate folly? And a folly so excruciating? 'People do not do such things!' And yet, it turns out, they *do*.

The following case is recorded by Stekel. Its hero is no lord of Thebes, merely an unhappy kleptomaniac. In his childhood his mother had the engaging habit of taking him to hotels where she met her lovers; there she quieted the boy with alcohol. Not surprisingly, this failed to improve his character. He took to stealing. In those with a mania for stealing or buying, the objects taken may symbolize forbidden fruit—love denied. (We may recall how the Empress Elizabeth, unhappily married to Franz Josef, would buy castle after castle on her travels about Europe, so that an Imperial official had to bustle in her wake, cancelling her purchases.) Further, this neurotic, emotionally tied to his disastrous mother, first started falling in love with older women, of an age to resemble her; then, by a sudden reversal, with small girls. Life grew intolerable. After arrest for one of his thefts, he first tried to hang himself in prison, like Sophocles' Jocasta; then, like Sophocles' Oedipus, blinded himself—with glass-splinters. It was, indeed, a step long meditated, to end his sexual temptations. 'If thine eye offend thee . . .' He wished, he said, 'to make everything dreamlike'—in fact, like a mystic, to elude the burden of reality. And so he did not regret his blindness—he was

[26]

well satisfied to have found peace in this demented
expiation.

It has also to be remembered that blinding can be a
common symbol for castration. We may recall Cranmer
thrusting first into the flames the hand that signed his
recantation; and realize that with Oedipus also the
punishment was fitted to the crime. With like symbolism Van Gogh, after attacking his friend Gauguin
with a razor, cut off the lobe of his own ear.

In other words, the tale of Oedipus is not a far-fetched
primeval fantasy. It has unsuspected psychological truth
in details quite apart from the now familiar 'Oedipus-
complex'.

As a more detailed example of the light psychology can
throw on literature, let us take *Hamlet*. After all, where
find a better? The subject is, indeed, a little tired. But
it seems a new, and not unpromising, approach to try, instead of vaguely generalizing about 'human nature', to
find definite and detailed parallels to its hero's case in
biography and medical history.

Even more than Shakespeare's other work, *Hamlet* has
become a happy hunting-ground for maniacs. In every
act they have found enigmas; and have proceeded to
improve Shakespeare's 'difficulties' by impossibilities of
their own. We cannot all write *Hamlet*: but we can all
rewrite it.

It has been suggested, for example, that Hamlet was a
real lunatic. It has been suggested that he was a woman
—hence his natural embarrassments with poor Ophelia.
It has been suggested that Hamlet was himself 'an element
of evil in the state of Denmark'—'murdering his love of
Ophelia . . . taking delight in cruelty, torturing Claudius,
wringing his mother's heart, a poison in the midst of the
healthy bustle of the court'. ('Healthy bustle' is good.)
It has been suggested that he was James I, or Southamp-
ton, or both; and that James I was also represented

(how aptly!—James who used to turn pale at sight of a drawn sword!) by the warlike Fortinbras.

It has been suggested that the whole play is an allegory —a defence of Protestantism, or a defence of Catholicism, an attack on scepticism, or an attack on mysticism. It has been suggested that Hamlet himself represents Progress and the Search for Truth; Ophelia, the Church; Polonius, Absolutism and Tradition; Fortinbras, Liberty; and the Ghost (I particularly like this interpretation), 'the Ideal Voice of Christianity'.

But it is not merely a matter of cranks. Quite reasonable critics have turned this tragedy into a mystery-play; though, strangely enough, the ordinary audience and the common man do not seem tormented with these headaches that afflict the wise. And I think the ordinary audience is wiser. It may not be able to explain. But it instinctively feels the play is right. In fact, had there been no critics, I believe there would have been no 'difficulties'. For the first hundred years and more, hardly a soul seems to have realized what a wealth of pleasant and innocent speculation might be derived from the 'difficulties' of *Hamlet*.

After all, some of these stock problems are mere pedantry. They arise from thinking more precisely than audiences do think—from misunderstanding the psychology of the theatre. If you examine scene-painting through a magnifying-glass, naturally it looks rough.

How old is Hamlet? He is called 'young'; he is fresh from the University—yet arithmetic, based on Yorick's death and the grave-digger's tenure of office, makes him thirty.

The answer? That Shakespeare did not care a straw. Hamlet is somewhere between twenty and thirty; the plot demanded a young man, the weary wisdom of Hamlet's character suggested a man not so young. Who cares? Who need care, except the producer, and the person who makes up Hamlet's face? It is mere ignorance of the mentality of playwrights and playgoers to suppose they mind.

Was Horatio a Dane? He calls himself a 'liegeman to the Dane' and speaks of 'our King'—and yet he shows ignorance of Danish habits.

What a terrible impasse! What is a confidant for, if not to be obligingly ignorant of anything the author wants to tell the audience?

The theatre is a country with peculiar customs. As Andrew Lang put it:

> This is a realm where people tell
>   Each other when they chance to meet
> Of things that long ago befell,
>   And do most solemnly repeat
> Secrets they both know very well
>   Aloud and in the public street.

How, next, can Hamlet talk of the 'undiscovered country from whose bourn No traveller returns', when he has just interviewed an eloquent phantom, piping hot from Purgatory?

Because, says Professor Dover Wilson (to whom all Shakespeare-readers owe so deep a debt), Hamlet had now lost faith in the Ghost. But if he had undergone a change of mind so important, would not Shakespeare make Hamlet clearly say so? And note that shortly after, when debating whether to kill the King at his prayers, Hamlet expresses most definite views about Heaven and Hell, and how one gets there.

Such ingenuity seems needless. If we called back Shakespeare himself from the 'undiscovered country', I think he would be much surprised at being disturbed for so little. 'Why,' he might say, 'why should I spoil a fine tirade on Death because a few precisians have too good memories—or notebooks? I was writing a play, not giving evidence on oath. The stage is not the dock.' The 'difficulty', again, arises from a false psychology of the theatre.

Why does the King put up with the dumb-show, then boil over in the play-scene?

It has been suggested by Dr. Greg that the King had not in fact committed the murder in that way and the Ghost's tale to Hamlet was mere hallucination. This seems as elaborately perverse as Verrall on Euripides. What a brilliant dramatist who gets himself universally misunderstood for three centuries! Professor Dover Wilson, on the other hand, argues that the dumb-show was wantonly foisted in by the too enterprising players out of their own heads; but that the King never saw it, because he was too busy arguing with Polonius and the Queen.

This seems almost as unconvincing. It turns a thrilling episode into a superfluous addition by the players—doubly superfluous because Claudius fails even to notice it. What end, then, does it serve?

And it is not 'theatre'. No use expecting an audience both to watch the dumb-show (as they *will*) and to watch whether the King is watching it. The many-headed multitude is not so many-headed as all that. No use asking an audience to take microscopic subtleties— they will not see them. As well paint Cromwell's warts on a figure high as Nelson's column. Once more, false dramatic psychology.

Besides, where is the difficulty?

The King sees a poisoning very like one that he had himself performed. But, after all, on the Renaissance stage poisonings were common as blackberries. Hamlet did not have to invent a play suitable; he merely added a few lines to sharpen an existing drama, already pat to his purpose.

So the King says to himself: 'Odd! But probably coincidence. Anyway I had better keep a bold face, or I shall be fitting a very queer cap on my own head.'

But when his own crime is re-enacted, more circumstantially and now with spoken words, *then* his control breaks. He cannot stand a second blow in the same place. After all, a dentist's drill does not grow pleasanter with repetition. This astonishes those strong silent men, the critics—one would think they had committed half a dozen murders apiece and brazened them out in the face of all Scotland Yard. But I do not see why it should astonish anyone else.

But these difficulties require no new psychological knowledge. And they are not the real problem. This centres round Hamlet's character. Why did he delay? Was he mad, or only pretending? Why does he so grossly maltreat Ophelia? And here the explanation grows more intricate.

II

Hamlet

(continued)

*Why, looke you now, how unworthy a thing
you make of me: you would play upon mee;
you would seeme to know my stops: you would
pluck out the heart of my Mysterie; you would
sound mee from my lowest Note, to the top of
my Compasse: and there is much Musicke,
excellent Voice, in this little Organe, yet cannot
you make it. Why do you thinke, that I am
easier to bee plaid on, then a Pipe? Call me what
Instrument you will, though you can fret me,
you cannot play upon me.*   HAMLET, III. 2.

*Are the Commentators on Hamlet Really Mad
or Only Pretending to be?*

(Title suggested by Wilde for a work
he would write on the play.)

WHY Hamlet's delay? Theories abound. First, there
is the suggestion that there is no adequate explanation.
Surely a needless despair? And if the audience felt so,
would *Hamlet* be such a success?

Secondly, it has been suggested that the play had somehow to last five acts. In other words, if Hamlet does not
kill the King, it is because he has to kill time. Shakespeare becomes like a 'filibustering' senator in the United
States. Hardly plausible.

Thirdly, the delay has been explained by denying that
it exists. Revenge-plays in general, it is argued, employed this sort of delayed action; it was a mere convention to excite suspense, not a problem of character.
Yet one still asks why, in that case, Hamlet curses

himself for delaying and why the Ghost explicitly re-
proaches his 'almost blunted purpose'.

Fourthly, Hamlet's delay has been ascribed to practical
difficulties. Suppose he did kill Claudius, how justify
the deed to the Danish people?

The German critic Werder (1875), who was one of the
propounders of this view, was enormously pleased with his
solution. 'That this point', he says, 'for a whole century
should never have been seen is the most incomprehensible
thing that has ever happened in aesthetic criticism since
the beginning of its existence.' A good many incomprehensible things happen in aesthetic criticism; but
few of them surpass Herr Werder's contribution.

For here Shakespeare had surely done his best to make
his play fool-proof. To what end are we shown the
success of Laertes in rising against Claudius to avenge
his father's murder, if not to contrast that success with
Hamlet's inertia? If Laertes could do it, much more
could the popular Prince. Besides, why does Hamlet
never speak of these supposed practical difficulties? In
the old German Hamlet-play there *are* references to the
King's ever-present bodyguard; but not in Shakespeare.

Fifthly, there is the view that Hamlet's difficulties lie
not in his situation but in himself.

> The fault (deere *Brutus*) is not in our Starres,
> But in our Selves.

To most of us this seems obvious, so obvious that we
cannot for our lives understand how anyone could miss it.
But the real problem remains. What *is* this inner obstacle?

There is, for example, the familiar conception of
Hamlet as the typical man of thought who cannot act—
too much brain, too little will.

Mackenzie (1780) stressed his sensibility; Goethe in
Wilhelm Meister (1795) produced his famous comparison
of Hamlet to a costly porcelain vessel meant for flowers,
but shattered by an oak-tree planted in it. (Later,

however, Goethe himself seems to have felt this inadequate.)

Coleridge, again (1808), found in Hamlet something of himself—a subtle mind infirm of purpose. But it is not altogether easy to picture Coleridge boarding pirate-ships, or Fortinbras praising the soldierly promise shown by 'Trooper Comberbach'.

Schlegel (1809) went further. He considered Goethe's view too lenient; Hamlet, he says severely, is an example of definite weakness of will and self-deception.

Now this type of character is, indeed, not uncommon. Lord Fisher spoke of Lord Goschen very much as, on this view, Fortinbras might have spoken of Hamlet: 'Why should I waste my time looking at all sides, when I know that mine is the right one? The cleverest man· we ever had at the Admiralty was Goschen, and he was the worst failure of all. He was always looking at all sides and we never got anything done.'

But Fortinbras does *not* speak so of Hamlet. On the contrary.

This idea of the Prince as an ineffectual intellectual is still common; but that may be due to the commonness of ineffectual intellectuals. Thus Hamlet has been held up to German professors as an awful warning of the fate of the too academic. This may have been good for the professors. But is it true? Why does Ophelia talk of Hamlet as of a young Sir Philip Sidney?—

> O what a Noble minde is heere o're-throwne!
> The Courtier's, Soldier's, Scholler's Eye, tongue, sword!

Why? Because that is what Shakespeare meant his audience to think. There is much force in Schücking's principle that what Shakespearean characters say of themselves, or of one another, is often a deliberate hint to the audience—so much so, that these comments are sometimes markedly out of character; as when Iago praises the 'daily beauty' of Cassio's life. In a word, on the Elizabethan stage even consistency of character could be sacrificed to *clearness*. This curious convention alone should be a warning to us against all subtle interpretations cooked up in midnight oil. Sentences that the theatre heard in thirty seconds should hardly need to be wrestled with in the study for as many hours—except that some people apparently care less for grapes than for splitting pips. Shakespeare seems to have taken a much less optimistic view of the understandings of his audience than some of his critics.[1] Elizabethan scholars may forget, but Elizabethan playwrights had to remember, that truth uttered by the Player in a drama engagingly entitled 'The Hogge hath lost his Pearle [2]: 'I hope you have made no dark sentence in't; for, I'll assure you, our audience commonly are very simple, idle-headed people, and if they should hear what they understand not, they would quite forsake our house.' Certainly Shakespeare *can* be obscure in his poetic language; but I doubt if even he could afford to be downright misleading about plot or character. What Ophelia and Fortinbras say, is seriously meant. Hamlet is no Richard II.

Ulrici (1839) suggested that the delay was caused by Hamlet's *Christian* scruples about revenge. But why, then, does he never say a word about it? Here is a character who questions so many things in heaven and earth; yet the one crucial point this sceptic never questions—it seems, indeed, a slight flaw—is the rightness of revenge. (I suppose the answer is that the ordinary Elizabethan took revenge for granted.) The same objection applies to the kindred view that Hamlet's scruples were, not Christian, but legal!

Lastly, there is the theory that Hamlet was not a congenital waverer, but stunned by the shock of his

[1] See also the sensible comments on this point by H. S. Bennett in *Shakespeare and his Audience*, 1944.

[2] By Robert Tailor (*fl.* 1614).

mother's marriage. This view, which is in part as old as William Richardson (1784) and Herder (1800) and was taken up by Bradley, has the not unimportant advantage of being Hamlet's own.

> O God, O God!
> How weary, stale, flat, and unprofitable
> Seemes to me all the uses of this world! . . .
> But two months dead: Nay, not so much; not two. . . .
> > Within a Moneth! . . .
> She married. . . .
> But breake my heart, for I must hold my tongue.

These words from his very first soliloquy seem clear enough, would we but listen.

Yet we may still ask why was the shock—painful enough, no doubt—in this case so paralysing? That is not so easy to answer. It has been argued that to the Elizabethans marriage with a deceased husband's brother seemed more flagrant than to us. I believe this to be the flat contrary of the truth—certainly for Renaissance royalty.

After all, Queen Elizabeth's own father had done precisely the same. In April 1502 the death of Prince Arthur left Catherine of Aragon a widow of sixteen. Henry VII, himself newly widowed, actually proposed to marry his own daughter-in-law, though thirty years his junior. So much for the squeamishness of Renaissance statecraft. However, in June 1503 she was betrothed instead to her brother-in-law, the future Henry VIII, then a boy of twelve. It was not till a quarter of a century later that, captivated by Anne Boleyn and (to do him justice—for he could have easily kept Anne as a mistress) anxious for a male heir, Henry was seized with moral anguish.

We read the play so much through Hamlet's eyes that we may come to regard Gertrude's marriage to her brother-in-law as more shocking than by Tudor standards it was. But does it bother the other characters? Claudius states in public that the match is generally approved. If he was wrong, why does not Shakespeare make public disapproval as vocal as in *Lear*, *Macbeth*, or *Antony and Cleopatra*? Because public disapproval did not exist. Had Claudius felt the slightest qualm about closeness of kinship, he would hardly have gone out of his way to emphasize it by speaking of 'our sometime *sister*, now our Queen'. Hamlet is revolted; but if Claudius had been only Gertrude's cousin, would that have done much to reconcile him? I do not believe it.

It is the marriage itself that outrages him, far more than any consanguinity. Why? A professional psycho-analyst's interpretation has been given by Dr. Ernest Jones, following Freud himself.[1] Dr. Jones argues that if Hamlet does not explain his delay, it is because he cannot. And if Shakespeare does not explain it, it is because Shakespeare cannot either. The real reason lay beneath the consciousness of the dramatist himself.

Hamlet, says Dr. Jones, just cannot *will* to do what he sees he should do. All his utterances about his own cowardice, his doubts of the Ghost, his anxiety so to kill Claudius that he shall be safely damned—all these are mere evasions. (This I believe true.)

Claudius has committed two crimes—an incestuous marriage (only later found to have been preceded by adultery) and fratricide. But it is, above all, the marriage that matters to Hamlet: it appals him before he knows anything of the murder. (This too seems just.)

But now emerges the inevitable Oedipus-complex. Hamlet, says Dr. Jones, being a son, was in love with his mother and jealous of his father. This jealousy was repressed and, as so often, over-compensated into deep admiration.

But, Dr. Jones continues, he cannot kill his uncle, firstly because his uncle, in killing his father, has only

[1] *Essays in Applied Psychoanalysis*, 1923 ; *Hamlet*, 1947.

done exactly what Hamlet, at bottom, longed to do himself; secondly, because Claudius has now become a father-substitute and the moral prohibition against parricide reasserts itself.[1]

Perhaps you are thinking: 'If that is the sort of light psychoanalysis can throw on literature, let us go back to our darkness.' There I cannot contradict you. I too find it impossible to picture Shakespeare pitching at his audience a plot that neither he nor they could consciously understand. He was not a Surrealist, writing by free association whatever came into his head. Nor does *Hamlet* seem in the least to resemble dream-poetry like *Kubla Khan.*

The Unconscious may be the dark abyss whence rise the inspirations of genius; but I do not see dramatist and public descending to the bottom of it for an afternoon's entertainment. Clearly Shakespeare did not picture Hamlet as feeling hostility towards his father. Then surely for Shakespeare the play made sense without? How?

I cannot help thinking that modern psychology should be able to throw more helpful light than this. The trouble comes from trying to force literature into crude conformity with Oedipus-complexes. One can fully accept their existence, without being obsessed by them.

Let me give an example of this obsession from another piece of psychoanalytic criticism. In *Imago* for 1935 Johanna Heimann, writing of Elizabeth Barrett's *Sonnets from the Portuguese*, comes on the following passage in Sonnet V, where the poetess compares herself to Electra:

> I lift my heavy heart up solemnly,
> As once Electra her sepulchral urn,
> And, looking in thine eyes, I overturn
> The ashes at thy feet. Behold and see
> What a great heap of grief lay hid in me. . . .

[1] See also N. J. Symons, *The Graveyard Scene in Hamlet* (*Internat. Journal of Psychoanalysis*, 1928, p. 96); Ella Sharpe, *The Impatience of Hamlet* (ibid., 1929, p. 270); neither, to me, convincing.

Here, we are told, there is depicted 'in unerhört plas-
tischer Sprache' the collapse of the Oedipus-complex.
'The sonnet betrays that the death of her father (the
treading out of his ashes) is a pre-condition of her love
for Browning.'

This seems pretty far-fetched. And had the writer
only turned to the scene in Sophocles to which this
sonnet alludes, she would have found that there the
funeral-urn was not that of Electra's *father* at all, but
(supposedly) of her *brother* Orestes. The English poetess
is thinking simply of her grief for her own favourite
brother, drowned at Torquay. One could, it is true, find
few more typical cases of Oedipus-complex than the
unhappy Barrett household; but in this particular
passage the habit of seeing that complex always everywhere has led the critic into complete misunderstanding.

To return to Hamlet. That he was unduly tied to his
mother, I believe. After all, such a relation between son
and mother is neither rare nor hard to notice. After so
much theory let us turn back to practical experience—
the sort of thing Shakespeare might have observed for
himself. He held the mirror to life: we ought to be
able to find in life the kind of thing he mirrored.

First, the case of Baudelaire. His elderly father died
in 1827, when the poet was nearly six. For a year and
three-quarters the boy was intensely happy with his still
youthful mother. Even as a man of forty, he still recalled
regretfully that brief sunshine in his life—'C'a été pour
moi le bon temps.' Then Mme Baudelaire took the very
natural step of accepting the suit of a gallant and
distinguished soldier, the future General Aupick. But
the boy Baudelaire, with all the egotism of passion,
thought this monstrous of her, even in after-years—
'Quand on a un fils comme moi, on ne se remarie pas.'
Even if he invented the story that on the wedding-night

[39]

he threw the bedroom-key out of the window, his invention remains no less significant.

When he was nineteen or twenty the tension culminated in violence. At a dinner-party his step-father reprimanded him for an improper remark. Baudelaire retorted: 'Monsieur, vous m'avez manqué gravement. Ceci mérite une correction et je vais avoir l'honneur de vous étrangler.' He then advanced on the General, who promptly slapped his face. Thereupon the young poet had a nervous attack and was shipped off for a voyage to Mauritius (as Hamlet to England).

The whole story may seem fantastic. Life often is. Hence most of its tragedies. It is not hard to multiply examples of such passionate emotion binding son to mother or daughter to father.

Here are some typical case-histories recorded by Stekel. One patient, an obsessional neurotic, was travelling by sleeper. Lying in his bunk, he heard an inner voice order him to knock loudly at the door of the next compartment—'or your nurse will die'. In his embarrassment he tried issuing himself a counter-order: 'If you *do* knock, your *mother* will die.' No use. He got up and knocked, almost inaudibly. But the inner voice (one recalls the *daemon* of Socrates) was not so easily cheated. Twice more it forced him to go and knock. Nothing followed, except that he passed a night of sleepless nervous tension.

The trouble went back to an episode of his boyhood, when he was fourteen and his mother had a liaison with a well-known statesman. On one occasion the pair left his home by the same train; and the unhappy boy fancied himself boarding it, forcing his way into the sleeping-compartment, and stabbing the lover.

All this in later years he had completely repressed; he now thought of his mother as 'a saint'; but he had also become an obsessional neurotic and, like Hamlet, 'a doubter'.

In another instance[1] a woman with her twelve-year-old son had left her Don Juan of a husband in Russia and moved to Switzerland. There a neighbour began to pay court to the mother—much to the anger of the boy, who decried him as 'a fortune-hunter'. Returning from a stay in the South of France, the son found that his mother had married her suitor; and was as badly shattered as Baudelaire. He took to expensive illnesses, so as to increase his dependence on her. The step-father guessed his motive and taxed him with 'malingering'. (This was perhaps unjust; he may have been genuinely ill and unaware why.) His mother now gave him capital to live independently. This he promptly squandered. Independence was the very last thing he wanted. Further, he developed a phobia of being poisoned (from guilt at his own wish to poison his step-father).

In another case a girl of twelve, brought up in a cultured home, but tormented by quarrels between her parents, in which she sided with her father, one day found a love-letter in her mother's room. She wrote an anonymous note to her father, which led him to surprise the lovers and secure a divorce; after that she herself kept house for him till she was thirty-four; then married, but was frigid and unhappy; and, finally, fell in love with a music-master who bore her father's Christian name.

One more example. The mother of a twenty-one-year-old son became engaged. 'How do you feel about it?' 'Oh, delighted.' But this delight did not prevent a nervous breakdown. In his sanatorium the patient was noticed carrying a folded newspaper in his pocket. 'What is that?' 'A gun.' 'Whom do you want to shoot?' 'Him.' Stekel told the mother that she must choose

[1] Stekel, *L'Éducation des Parents*, pp. 108-10.

between her remarriage and her son's health. She sacrificed herself; and the son recovered.

In the light of all this I find a certain pleasant irony in Frank Harris's comment on Hamlet: 'Why did Hamlet hate his mother's lechery? Most men would hardly have condemned it, certainly would not have suffered their thoughts to dwell on it. . . . No one ever felt this intensity of jealous rage about a mother or a sister. The mere idea is absurd.' 'No one' and 'ever' are large words. Literary critics cannot afford to ignore psychology; though many of them still seem to think so. Frank Harris's remark throws an interesting light, not on Shakespeare, but on Frank Harris.

Such tragedies as I have just related arise ultimately from a failure to grow up, to grow out of the past, to surmount the dependence of childish years—and, sometimes, the shocks suffered in those years.

Hence Stekel's summary of the healthy mind—that it can 'surmount the past, utilize the present, prepare the future'. Those wise words are worth remembering. Far too often in the past both religion and literature have glorified the remorse or regret that broods with morbid iteration on sins committed or lovers lost. It is a perverted glorification. Lot's wife, turned to bitter sterility, remains an abiding symbol of what happens to those who thus look back—who cannot 'let the dead bury their dead'.

Other poets or story-tellers have recognized this fundamental truth. For Greek sanity, a wrong action was a ἁμαρτία, a mistake to be shunned in future; not a sin to be brooded over in sackcloth and ashes, as Augustine moans for page on page about the mediocre pears he once stole from a tree in boyhood. 'Man', says the stoic proverb of the Icelanders, 'must outlive man.' William Morris tells us that the men and women of his *News from Nowhere* sorrowed but a little while over unhappy love.

And Meredith, passing judgement on the married tragedy
of his autobiographic *Modern Love*, concludes:

> But they fed not on the advancing hours.

And again, more generally:

> Strain we the arms for Memory's hours,
> We are the seized Persephone.

The Bible, too, has divined this truth in relation to the
family, when it says that the daughter must leave father
and mother to become one flesh with her husband. It
sounds a mere platitude. But it proves sometimes less
easy than it sounds; and many a marriage comes to ruin
from the inability of one partner—or both—to break
from that magic-ring of the family circle, which remains
one of the most precious, yet (when abused) most
perilous, things in human life.

Therefore the most important gift that education can
bring a child is perhaps the power to be independent.
'Independent' does not mean cold, hard, loveless, or
aloof. But all of us have to be born and weaned a second
time—to be freed and detached from the body of our
childhood's home.[1] Ibsen knew that well enough when
he drew his child-wife in the *Doll's House*—the whole
theme of his play is the agony and tragedy of a woman
growing up too late. And it is a master-touch again that
the cold wife of Ibsen's Master-Builder clings above all
to the dolls still treasured from her childhood—that
childhood which she too has never outgrown.[2]

---

[1] Here may lie a certain danger of *too* paternal socialism in the Welfare
State. Many such reforms are admirable; but one can conceive a point
where, if overdone, they might lead a nation into a sort of infantile
regression, craving to be bottle-fed from cradle to grave.

[2] Ibsen's marvellous insight is illustrated by this case from real life.
A woman of past forty still talked and dressed childishly and suffered a
morbid horror of growing older. Coming in suddenly one day, her husband
found her with a doll under her arm, surrounded by other dolls and toys.
In his rage (he guessed that they were his rivals) he hurled them on the
fire. She fainted; and a four weeks' fever followed, which left her feeling

Poets, indeed, have often guessed an extraordinary amount of psychology, long before it became a science.

So too with Hamlet. His inhibited character, I believe, is simply and solely the not uncommon fate of a son who has not fully outgrown the tie that bound him in childhood and boyhood to his mother. I must, however, stress that in Hamlet's unhappiness there seem to me two vital factors, not one. First, there is the loss of a beloved person; second, there is the crash of a cherished ideal. This second is often no less bitter; it can be still bitterer. The death-agony of a dream may prove as poignant as that of a human being.

> That April should be shattered by a gust,
> That August should be levelled by a rain,
> I can endure; and that the lifted dust
> Of man should settle to the earth again;
> But that a dream can die, will be a thrust
> Between my ribs for ever of hot pain.[1]

Turn back to Hamlet's first soliloquy:

> Frailty, thy name is woman!
> A little Month, or ere those shooes were old,
> With which she followed my poore Father's body,
> Like *Niobe*, all teares. Why she, even she
> (O Heaven! A beast that wants discourse of Reason,
> Would have mourn'd longer) married with mine Unkle.

life empty and herself grown old. She then developed a kleptomania for dolls. Ellida in *The Lady from the Sea* is another victim of this clinging to the past; but her husband's love and wisdom save her, without the tragedy of Nora and Mrs. Solness.

The potency of childish impressions can indeed be amazing in its persistence. To quote one instance out of thousands, Ella Freeman Sharpe records the case of a middle-aged woman who could, by a sort of magic, rid herself of depression and anxiety by taking a bath in the afternoon; in part at least (so analysis revealed) because as a small girl she once angered her father by covering herself with sticking-paste—but after she had been bathed and dressed in clean clothes he kissed her again (*Internat. Journal of Psychoanalysis*, 1930, pp. 370-1).

[1] Edna St. Vincent Millay.

And now compare this passage of Stekel, not written with reference to Hamlet at all: 'We see hundreds of cases in which sons fall sick when circumstances compel them to sit in judgement upon a mother, and hundreds more in which the same thing happens to a daughter who finds cause for thinking lightly of either father or mother. . . . When I look back upon the long series of obsessional diseases that I have published and observed, I see that invariably the parents have failed to practise what they preached to their children.'

I have somewhere read of Fox, the eighteenth-century statesman, that he had ordered the demolition of a kiosk in his grounds; at the wish of his schoolboy son, who wanted to watch, he consented to postpone it till the next holidays; but, after the boy had gone, thinking he would forget, Fox let the work go forward. Returning, the boy reproached his father: 'You broke your word.' Regardless of expense, Fox ordered the kiosk to be rebuilt, then pulled down again for his son to see, just as he had promised. That seems to me the act of a very wise man —a far finer story than anything about George Washington and cherry-trees.

Stekel quotes also the case of a boy of twelve who found in a desk a letter from his mother to a lover and developed an obsessional neurosis. He was apparently cured, and allowed to go back to his family. But this proved a mistake; the wound had not been fully healed; and he ended in a permanent breakdown.

After all, it is not so hard to see why such disillusionment can be devastating. The poets have long known this supreme torture of conflicting love and loathing. There is the anguish of Catullus:

> Odi et amo. Quare id faciam, fortasse requiris.
>   Nescio. Sed fieri sentio—et excrucior.
> (I loathe, yet love. You ask how this can be.
> I cannot tell—I feel. 'Tis agony.)

[45]

There is Coleridge's:

> For to be wroth with one we love
> Doth work like madness in the brain.

To the beloved the lover has transferred part of himself —his ego-ideal; and now he must see it shattered. He has incorporated the beloved to become part of himself; and that part of himself he must now hate (which is the basis of melancholia).

If you wish, then, for happiness, above all avoid divided wishes and mental conflicts, where all your energy goes in fighting one part of yourself with the other—just as the worst wars of all are civil wars. Even the minds of dogs can collapse under it—you may recall Pavlov's ingenious method of tormenting the poor beasts by alternately throwing on the screen a circle, followed by food, and an ellipse, followed by nothing. As the ellipse was made harder and harder to distinguish from a circle, it is not perhaps very surprising that under this mental conflict some of the victims grew completely hysterical. (At times one wonders if Soviet diplomacy deliberately models itself on Pavlov.)

After all, it has never been thought a pleasant end to be torn asunder by wild horses. And that, in effect, is here happening to the mind. The first result is naturally inability to take any line of action—like Hamlet. It is as if two powerful locomotives put on full steam, in opposite directions, at opposite ends of a train. At first the train may be unable to move at all; then, it may be wrenched asunder. So with the human character.

Though it is now many years since it was written, I still know few more fascinating books than Dr. Morton Prince's *The Dissociation of a Personality*, with its description of a girl split mentally, by a like inward conflict, into three different persons; and, later, into more than three.[1]

Hamlet is in the stage of paralysis. Here too he corresponds exactly to descriptions of obsessional neurotics, written without Hamlet in mind at all: 'The impulsive ego is at war with the "cultural" ego. The illness is a protest against cultural demands, manifesting itself as a rebellion against work and every social obligation. . . . The obsessional parapath rebels against duty ("that odious word, duty").' And again: 'These patients are gambling with themselves. They waste so much time on their obsessions that they have not enough left for the fulfilment of their social obligations, their life's task. Everything is staked on the last card. Then the miracle will happen. What they do now is but preparatory. . . . They are always getting ready, but they never do anything. Strindberg's phrasing fits the obsessional neurotic to a T. "Life is like the tuning of an orchestra—which never begins to play."' And yet again: 'In Faust, the typical doubter, Goethe gives a striking portrait of an obsessional parapath.' And finally: 'The most important thing is to make these patients aware of their daydreams. They are dreaming the romance of their life. . . . They satisfy their affective hunger by playing with time (they are never ready, always in a hurry, full of doubt, etc.); and if accused of laziness they try to exculpate themselves on the plea of illness.' Rossetti well knew that state of mind:

> Unto the man of yearning thought
> And aspiration, to do nought
> Is almost in itself an act. . . .
> Yet woe to thee if once thou yield
> Unto the act of doing nought!

[1] Cf. F. Wittels' account (*Imago*, 1934, p. 320) of a girl, split between father and mother, who conducted long conversations with her left thumb, as 'Jimmy'; and had to say aloud to herself: 'Heute ist Freitag, es ist Sommer, und die Sonne scheint. Ich bin wirklich und heiße Peggy. Ja, Peggy heiße ich wirklich.'

Balzac called it 'smoking enchanted cigarettes'. One of life's central problems is how to hold the balance between extraversion and introversion. For the man who never dreams may grow as sterile as the excessive dreamer grows futile.

Here, it seems to me, we have the exact Hamlet-type. Note that he is an *only* son. (Neuroses seem far less common in the larger families of the poor.) Until the tragedy of his mother's remarriage we are clearly meant to suppose that he was an active, healthy young man— not in the least a Coleridge. Presumably, if we may talk for a moment as if he were the real person he seems, he was still too much tied emotionally to his mother. But, had his father lived, such a person might have matured at last under the influence of Ophelia, and transferred that part of his emotional energy to her. Or he might still have remained mother-dominated and there would have been just one more unhappy marriage.

The advantage of this view—that Hamlet is the victim of a too close mother-love, lacerated by the loss *both* of her *and* of faith in her—seems to me that it credits Shakespeare with no special knowledge beyond what his own keen eyes and ears could have gathered. After all, the Elizabethans and Jacobeans were not without interest in psychology. As Professor Dover Wilson has pointed out, verbal parallels in Shakespeare's writing suggest that he had read Timothy Bright's *Treatise of Melancholy* (1586). And there is a good deal of shrewd observation in Burton. Something like the Hamlet-type not only reappears in various malcontents and melancholics of the Elizabethan stage, but is closely reproduced, with striking verbal echoes of *Hamlet*, in Overbury's character of 'A Melancholy Man':

A Melancholy Man is a strayer from the drove: one that nature made sociable, because shee made him man, and a crazed disposition hath altered. Impleasing to all, as all to him; straggling thoughts are his content, they make him dreame waking, there's his pleasure. His imagination is never idle, it keeps his mind in a continuall motion, as the poise the clocke: he winds up his thoughts often, and as often unwinds them; *Penelope's* web thrives faster. . . . Hee carries a cloud in his face. . . . He thinkes businesse, but never does any: he is all contemplation, no action. He hewes and fashions his thoughts, as if he meant them to some purpose; but they prove unprofitable, as a peece of wrought timber to no use. His spirits, and the sunne are enemies. . . . Lastly, he is a man onely in shew, but comes short of the better part; a whole reasonable soule, which is man's chiefe preeminence, and sole marke from creatures sensible.

The Elizabethans could not scientifically investigate what produced such types; but they knew them. And Shakespeare seems to have made a shrewd guess how they could be caused. Later critics have exclaimed, like Judge Brack, 'But people do not do such things.' Like Judge Brack, they were wrong.

It is now perhaps easier to answer the further question: 'Why is Hamlet so brutal to Ophelia?' The fall of a maternal ideal, which causes Hamlet's tragedy, causes hers also. In *every* woman he sees his mother. 'Frailty, thy name is woman!'

> Such an Act . . . takes off the Rose
> From the faire forehead of an innocent love,
> And makes a blister there.

There is a curiously exact counterpart of this in *Troilus and Cressida*. In *Hamlet* the false mother casts a shadow on the innocent mistress; in *Troilus*, the false mistress on the innocent mother:

TROYLUS: Let it not be beleev'd for womanhood:
   Thinke, we had mothers . . .
ULISSES: What hath she done, Prince, that can soyle our mothers?
TROYLUS: Nothing at all—unlesse that this were she.

Such thinking is clearly quite irrational (there are all sorts of women, Imogens as well as Cressidas); but it happens, unfortunately, to be perfectly human. Remember too, for it seems to me nearly certain, that Hamlet realizes that in her innocent weakness Ophelia has lent herself to her father's espionage.

Yet actors are apt to baulk at the brutality of this piece of truth to life. They cannot bear—and it does credit to their kind hearts, if not to their heads—such cruelty to an innocent girl. But neurosis can be pitiless. On this point Desmond MacCarthy in his *Drama* has written admirable sense: 'I have never seen a Hamlet who played this scene with Ophelia as it acts itself in the theatre of the attentive reader's mind. . . . Tree used to return to kiss the tresses of the prostrate Ophelia; Kean, it is said, used to play the scene as though Hamlet were counterfeiting brutality in order to conceal the tenderest passion; Wilkes, so Davis says, "preserved the feelings of a lover and the delicacy of a gentleman". Mr. Barrymore let his voice tremble to a sob, when he told Ophelia that "he did love her once". It may be traditional, but it is a bad tradition. . . . In this scene, it is the pathos of Ophelia that should hold the stage, and the error of all "Hamlets" has been to draw our sympathies towards "the lover". Do they want pathos? Is there not more in the pain of a girl, uneasy at being used for a purpose she does not understand? . . . Yet our actors play this scene as though it were a lovers' quarrel! One which might be ended by Ophelia saying soothingly, "Darling, you *know* you love me!"'

Readers of Alfred de Musset's Life may recall how he too, even before taking refuge in habitual drunkenness, used to make life a purgatory for his mistresses—not for George Sand only—by alternations of tenderness and of savage bitterness like Hamlet's. And here also the trouble seems, at least in part, to have gone back to an episode of his own life (embodied in his *Confession d'un Enfant du Siècle*), when his faith too in womanhood was

[50]

suddenly shattered. It was at a dinner-party; he dropped his fork and, stooping to pick it up, saw the foot of the adored mistress opposite him resting on that of the young man next her.

Here is a further case from life. An aristocratic and intelligent medical student so tormented his mistress with his jealousy that, like Ophelia, she tried suicide. She left him. But, with that relentless recurrence which marks neurotic destinies, he reconstituted the same situation with another mistress; like Musset, he too was fascinated, yet furious, to hear her talk about her past love-affairs. His interrogations became so exacting, that she was driven to invent. And all the while his own disintegration continued, as he sank to reckless extravagance, and even fraud.

How did it begin? Treatment revealed that as a child he had come upon his mother in the arms of the family-coachman. He had forgotten that episode too terrible to remember; but not the embittered distrust of all women it engendered. At length, by learning to face it, he was cured and enabled to work again.

There is more than platitude in those lines of Juvenal:

> Maxima debetur puero reverentia, si quid
> Turpe paras; nec tu pueri contempseris annos,
> Sed peccaturo obstet tibi filius infans.

(None can too much revere his son—let *that* restrain
The sin you plan—his childhood is not for your disdain;
Remember, when you are tempted, his young years—and
  refrain.)

III

Hamlet

(concluded)

A type of hero-legend

O father, father. . . .
Tear all my life out of the universe,
Take off my youth, unwrap me of my years,
And hunt me up the dark and broken past
Into my mother's womb: there unbeget me;
For till I'm in thy veins and unbegun,
Or to the food returned which made the blood
That did make me, no possible lie can ever
Unroot my feet of thee.

T. L. BEDDOES, *Torrismond.*

WE have considered the problem—'Why does Hamlet delay?' I do not believe we are meant to attribute it to external difficulties, nor to Christian or legal scruples, but to something in Hamlet himself—not the congenital weakness of an ineffectual intellectual, but the sudden paralysis caused by the loss of a loved maternal ideal.

In short, I do not believe, with Dr. Jones, that Hamlet is torn between love and hate of his father, but between love and hate of his mother. Not only has he lost her; she has also destroyed his faith in her, in other women, in humanity, in life itself.

If we are to speak in terms of the Oedipus-complex, we can only say that its mother-love is conspicuously present in the play, but its father-hatred concentrated wholly upon the new step-father, Claudius. Of any hostility between Hamlet and his real father there is no more trace than of hostility between Orestes and Agamemnon, who hardly even saw each other.

In general I must own to extreme scepticism about this supposedly universal law that in the relation of son to father there is *always* an element of jealous dislike. The potentiality may always be there; but more than that? I have watched for its appearance (I need hardly say, with some apprehension) in my own small son. The appointed age has come and passed. For his mother, indeed, he shows adoration enough to satisfy Freud himself; but of anti-paternal feeling not a sign—unless it be in three or four tiger-dreams. Orthodox Freudians can always explain that I was the tiger and that the dreams expressed a guilty fear of retribution for hostile wishes. They may be right, but the net result appears negligible. On the other hand I most freely admit having seen how easily different treatment could have aroused the fiercest resentment and jealousy in this small person; and we shall see later how clearly the Oedipus-situation does emerge in the type of folk-legend to which the *source* of Hamlet belongs. But in that type of legend, as we shall see, the ambivalent love-hate of son for sire often expresses itself by splitting the paternal figure into two— one loved, like Osiris, or Numitor, or the elder Hamlet; one hated, like Set, or Amulius, or Claudius. Indeed the orthodox Freudian explanation of *Hamlet* is itself partly inconsistent with the orthodox Freudian explanation of the Hamlet *legend*.

Lastly the question has been raised—'Was Hamlet really mad?' Its very crudity betrays a curious ignorance of the infinite gradations between mental health and derangement. Was Hamlet certifiable? Obviously not. He is a very different case from Ophelia. Was he neurotic? Surely. He shows a familiar type of alternation between melancholy depression and wild elation—between the melancholia that annuls hope and the mania that, for a moment, annuls despair. His feigning of madness as a stratagem comes from the original story; but in Shakespeare it grimly harmonizes at moments with his real mood. Half maddened by grief and rage, Hamlet finds it a bitter relief to act the madman. And this very uncertainty keeps the audience breathless.

After all it is nothing new for actors curiously to mix art and life, make-believe and reality. That was one reason for Plato's condemnation of all acting as demoralizing. Ancient tradition tells how the famous player Pōlus, chanting the lament of Electra over the supposed ashes of her brother, once gave a supreme performance by carrying on the stage the real ashes of his own son. It is said, again, that Talma, sobbing over *his* dead son, found himself listening to himself, to perfect his knowledge of how such grief should be played. Hamlet is not mad; but he is sufficiently unstrung to find his hysterical rôle an outlet.

In Saxo, and presumably in Kyd's *Hamlet* (if Kyd's it was), the madness was wholly feigned, the conflict wholly external; Shakespeare's signal advance lay in transferring the deepest conflict to within Hamlet's soul and making the assumed madness far more poignant because at times it is not far from becoming real.

In short, could we question Shakespeare himself, I can imagine he might say: 'I knew nothing of your theories. I never cared much for theories. But I have seen, and known, what can happen to a young man when a woman whom he idolized—mother or mistress—turns out to have feet of clay. (I drew it again in Troilus.) The fall of that ideal can break him. He can become like an animal with a shattered spine, a clock with a broken spring. He can no longer will—what is the use?—except in emergencies, when he has no longer time to brood over the futility of everything, the falsity of everyone.

It is an interesting state of mind. I have been through it. You recall my sonnets? It seemed worth a play. That is all.'

In short, Shakespeare turns out to have been a better psychologist than most of his critics. Is that surprising? Poets who work more with their emotions and in closer touch with their Unconscious, may easily be wiser than philosophers and scholars who live in a dry atmosphere of logic and rationality. In the same way the poet Euripides proved a better psychologist than the philosopher Socrates. 'Virtue is knowledge', said the philosopher. 'For how could a man knowingly choose what is worse for him?' 'But that', answered the poet, 'is exactly what *can* happen.' So he drew his Phaedra; and in the mouth of his Medea he put that famous cry, as she decides to sacrifice her own children to her revenge:

> I see the evil I am bent on doing,
> But passion is stronger than all prudence is.

The poet had realized, as the philosopher had not, how a mind can be divided, a personality split in two—or more than two.

So much for the 'difficulties' of *Hamlet*. The more one thinks of the play, the more natural, the more convincing, the more inevitable this masterpiece seems to become. It is indeed masterly, not only in its psychology, but in the architecture that underlies what may seem a certain carelessness of form.

Let us turn back, for a moment, from psychology to poetry. The primary theme is the relation of child and father. The plot gives us no less than four children who have lost their fathers—Hamlet, Ophelia, Laertes, and Fortinbras. By that loss two are spurred to action; two are broken—the two who feel they have been betrayed by those they loved.

For what, after all, is the essence of this play which

[55]

remains, for many, the greatest in the world? Not merely a study of a young man with melancholia; I believe it is, in one word—loyalty. I feel that this was the human quality that Shakespeare, like Homer before him, came in the end to value most of all—loyalty like that of Achilles or Hector, Odysseus or Penelope, Romeo or Antony, Hamlet or Othello, Cordelia or Imogen.

What is rotten in Denmark? What causes the whole tragedy? The disloyalty of a queen, the disloyalty of a brother. And it is the horror of their disloyalty that breaks Hamlet.

His mother has failed him. The girl he loved fails him. For that poor well-meaning doll (whom Coleridge, in one of his curious aberrations, thought Shakespeare's idea of an ideal wife), instead of behaving like a Juliet or an Imogen, dutifully lends herself to bait her father's hook and help him spy on her own lover. Even friendship fails him. For Rosencrantz and Guildenstern smile only to betray. Circle beyond circle, the spider's web of falsity is twisted round him—Polonius preaching honesty ('to thine own self be true') to the son he is about to set spies on in Paris—until, in pursuit of this favourite pastime, the old sage gets himself spitted behind a curtain; Laertes preaching honour to the sister over whose grave he is to rant his rhetoric, before he goes smiling to assassinate his prince with a poisoned sword. Even when Polonius is dead, there are other traitors quick to fill his place—Osric cringing exactly as Polonius had cringed, while he well knows that the venomed rapier waits.

Even the scene with the players, whose connection with the plot may seem tenuous, wakens the same hollow echoes—this sixpenny hireling can howl out his heart for Hecuba, as Laertes for Ophelia—and yet 'what's Hecuba to him?'

Only Horatio is left, among the treacheries of Elsinore.

It is not enough. What wonder that such words as 'honest', 'honesty', 'wholesome' recur through the play like an agonized refrain?

The great masters, like Homer and Shakespeare, seldom preach; it is far more effective to imply. In this way the hearers draw their own conclusions—and value them the more because they seem their own. They absorb the poet's values unconsciously; and the more deeply because unconsciously.

Mr. T. S. Eliot has argued that 'the play is most[1] certainly an artistic failure'. 'We must simply admit that here Shakespeare tackled a problem which proved too much for him. Why he attempted it at all is an insoluble problem.' Had Mr. Eliot said '*seems to me* an artistic failure', no one could deny the truth of what he said, or his right to say it. But to say blankly that *Hamlet* '*is* most certainly an artistic failure' is surely a little confident. One recalls Rogers's remark on Croker's review of Macaulay's *History*—that Croker had 'intended murder and committed suicide'.

Why is the play an 'artistic failure'? Because, says Mr. Eliot, Hamlet's emotion has no 'objective correlative'. In plainer English, Gertrude is too trivial an object for so much passion and despair. Doubtless, by similar reasoning, Cressida is no 'objective correlative' for the passion and despair of Troilus. Would that tragedy be any more tragic if Cressida were less trivial? Is not the tragedy precisely that she *is* trivial? Does that make it 'Much Ado about Nothing'? Gertrude, too, is trivial? But she was Hamlet's mother. Not a wholly trivial relationship. Proust has written shrewdly of the type of person who fondly imagines that a man (instead of wrecking himself like Charles Swann for a trivial person like Odette) 'ne devrait être malheureux que pour

---

[1] Not 'almost', as I have seen it misquoted by an admirer where Unconscious wished, no doubt, to make this drastic judgement milder.

une personne qui en valût la peine; c'est à peu près comme s'étonner qu'on daigne souffrir du choléra par le fait d'un être aussi petit que le bacille virgule'. Such astonishment does not seem any more intelligent in criticism than in the real world.

Hamlet remains, I think, a masterpiece, first, because it is intensely moving as drama and poetry; secondly, because it is intensely true to life; thirdly, because the values it implies are also intensely important to life.

That is why no critical cavils have been able to cast down Hamlet himself from that throne in men's imaginations which remains unshakably his, whatever thrones he was denied by fate in Denmark. That is why down-at-heel touring-companies, when all else failed, have as a last resort billed *Hamlet*. That is why for generation after generation, for writer after writer, its hero has become one of the eternal human types— for Turgeniev, who in the nineteenth century, portrayed him in a famous essay as the man of thought, contrasted with Don Quixote, the man of action; or for Paul Valéry, who in 1919 saw him as the embodiment of European man—'Maintenant sur une immense terrasse d'Elsinore, qui va de Bâle à Cologne, qui touche aux sables de Nieuport, aux marais de la Somme, aux granits d'Alsace—l'Hamlet européen regarde des millions de spectres. . . . Nous verrons enfin apparaître le miracle d'une société animale, une parfaite et définitive four- milière.'

To-day the ramparts where walks the modern Hamlet run from Hamburg to Trieste. Still more millions of spectres are there. And the menace of a yet vaster ant-heap.

It is this richness of meaning, as well as of poetry, that seems to me to make *Hamlet* superior even to what some have thought the greatest work of man—the *Oresteia* of Aeschylus. It is a better story—the murder of a mother becomes to-day, I feel, too savage, too uncivilized, too pointless.[1] So already Euripides felt. And much of the debate in Aeschylus' third play, the *Eumenides*, is marred by too primitive genetics—the curious controversy whether the mother or the father is biologically the real parent of a child.

There remains, however, another interesting contrast between *Hamlet* and *Oresteia*. Orestes duly takes vengeance on his mother with little of the heart-searching of Hamlet; it is only after the deed that *his* mental pangs begin, symbolized by the pursuing Erinyes. But in their grim and gloomy figures the modern reader can find a symbolic truth that may or may not have been dimly felt by Aeschylus himself. These dark powers of the Netherworld, these incarnations of the scourging conscience, are changed at last, in the third play of the trilogy, to beneficent goddesses, the Eumenides—'the Kindly Ones'—when the whole struggle between them and Apollo, the radiant Intellect, has been made conscious and analysed before the Goddess of Wisdom in the clear air of her city, Athens. It might well serve as a parable of the supreme lesson of psychoanalysis—face your conflicts; bring to light the terrible memories that have stalked so long, masked, through the Netherworld of your soul; and what seemed the hideous nightmares of a morbid sense of guilt can give place to the kindly light of a balanced Ideal that sees life calmly, tolerantly, forgivingly—as in their wisest moments Homer, Chaucer, and Shakespeare saw it.

The miracle of Greek mythology is that again and again it provides for the forces of Life the most perfect poetic symbolism the world has known. So that Nietzsche could find in Apollo and Dionysus two vivid symbols of the Classic and Romantic elements in art;

[1] For a strangely close parallel to the matricide of Orestes from American real life see F. Wertham, *Dark Legend*, 1947.

and Freud could find in Oedipus or Narcissus eternal types for certain tangles of the human consciousness. In this same way the *Eumenides* of Aeschylus may serve as an allegory of modern psychoanalysis in general.

So much for *Hamlet*. It is indeed ironic that the hero whose last words were 'The rest is silence' should have provoked more babel than any other character in literature: that he, for whom Horatio wished 'flights of Angels' to sing him to his rest, should have been battled over by so many legions of bedraggled cherubim in the shape of critics. One is ashamed to add to the number. But I have only tried to suggest that no explanation is needed, for those who know a little of life; and to use our new knowledge of the human mind to show how much better Shakespeare already knew it than those who have so superciliously tried to set him right.

Note

IT is worth turning, for a moment, to that folk-psychology of earlier eras which is embodied in legends of the type of Hamlet's source—tales where the young hero triumphs over his elders. Here, as Otto Rank has pointed out, the Oedipus-complex plays a far clearer part.

For example, Oedipus is exposed by his father on Cithaeron and saved by a shepherd; he grows up and kills his father.

Perseus is set adrift with his mother, by her father, in a chest; he drives ashore on the isle of Seriphos, grows up, and kills his grandfather.

Cyrus is exposed by his mother's father, and saved by a herdsman—or, in another version, by a dog that suckled him; he grows up and dethrones his grandfather.

Zethus and Amphion, the legendary founders of Thebes, are exposed; they are saved by shepherds, grow up and kill their great-uncle.

Paris is exposed by his father on Ida; he is fed by a she-bear, grows up, and causes the destruction of his father and of Troy.

Romulus and Remus are exposed by their great-uncle; they are suckled by a she-wolf, grow up, and kill him.

Theseus is left by his father Aegeus with his mother Aethra in

Troezen; he grows up, comes to his father in Athens, kills his uncle Pallas and later, by forgetting to hoist the white sail on his return from Crete, causes his father to kill himself.

The legend of Moses departs from the usual type. Instead of a royal infant found and saved by a humble person, we have a child of humble birth found and saved by an Egyptian princess. But the finding of a child in a cradle on the water looks, as Freud points out, very like a disguised version of bearing a child (water is a regular dream-symbol of birth or death). And the very name Moses is Egyptian, so that this story shows traces of wide changes from its first form.[1]

The general likeness between all legends of this type remains remarkable; as if, long before history, the struggle of the younger generation in the *Urhorde* against its elders had left, as Freud suggests, a lasting stamp on human imagination.

Now often it is in revenge for his father that the hero kills his elder kinsman. Thus Horus avenges his father Osiris on his uncle Set; Jason avenges his father Aeson on his uncle Pelias; Aepytus of Messene avenges his father on his step-father; Orestes also; Romulus and Remus avenge their grandfather on their great-uncle; and Amleth avenges his father on an uncle who is also his step-father. As we have seen, this latter type of story seems to split the paternal figure into two—one loved, one hated—to correspond with the ambivalent love-hate of son for sire. Just as in the tale of Cinderella the maternal figure is split between kindly godmother and cruel step-mother.

In fine, there is already much primitive psychology in the ancient source of Hamlet as well as observed psychology in the masterpiece that Shakespeare made of it.

[1] See Freud, *Moses and Monotheism*, 1939.

IV

Lear, Othello, Macbeth

In tragic life, God wot,
No villain need be ! Passions spin the plot:
We are betrayed by what is false within.

MEREDITH.

THIS same primitive clash between generations is the theme of Shakespeare's most primitive tragedy—*Lear*. *Hamlet* is the story of a son ruined by a mother; *Lear* the story of two fathers ruined by their children.

It does not, indeed, seem to me nearly so profound or penetrating a play. *Lear* contains, unlike *Hamlet*, several characters who are, Aristotle would have felt, vile and excessively vile, without that demonic poetry which half redeems Iago: the plot has at times the naïveté of a fairy-tale; and the author's own mind seems at times to lose the magnificent balance it maintains in *Hamlet*, *Macbeth*, *Othello*, or *Antony and Cleopatra*.

And yet, whatever view one takes of the place of *Lear* among Shakespeare's plays, its psychology turns out to be less fantastic, I think, than it looks. It is a tragedy of family relations—Lear and his daughters; Cordelia and her sisters; Gloucester and his sons; Edmund and his brother. First, Lear and his daughters. Here Freud, in his essay *Das Motiv der Kästchenwahl*,[1] has suggested an interpretation of the legend that, I must admit, leaves me sceptical. He compares, reasonably enough, the legend of Psyche and her two sisters, of Aschenputtel (Cinderella) and hers, of Paris and his three goddesses;

[1] *Gesammelte Werke*, X. pp. 24-37.

and also the choice of Bassanio between the three caskets (familiar symbols for the feminine) in *The Merchant of Venice*. He suggests that in all these legends the three women are the Three Fates or Norns, and the one chosen is Death. And he points to the pale lead of Portia's casket:

> thou meager lead,
> Which rather threatnest than dost promise aught,
> Thy palenesse moves me more than eloquence.

Since in dreams all may go by opposites, Freud argues that here the man's choice of Death can symbolize Death's inevitable choice of man; by a similar interchange of contraries, in the choice of Paris the Goddess of Love replaces Death; and in *Lear*, when the old king carries off the dead Cordelia, this disguises the real situation in which Death carries off the doomed king. He has indeed found only Death still left for him; the years of woman as mother, woman as mistress, are past and gone. Hence the deep effect of Shakespeare's tragedy on our unconscious minds.

I am afraid I should find it just as convincing to explain *Lear* as a solar myth. More interesting, I think, is the question—can psychological experience justify this old father's quarrel with his favourite daughter over the mere wording of her affection? Or the icy ruthlessness of Goneril and Regan towards their father and sister?

It may be argued that it is idle to demand probability of a folk-legend; but this is a play, not a fairy-tale. And yet Lear's contention with Cordelia seems as fantastic as a lover's quarrel. Perhaps, in a way, that is precisely what it is.

The following case-history may help.[1] The patient, an American of fifty-three, once a robust athlete, arrived pale and thin in the consulting-room, with his weight fallen from 73 kilos to 53. Once he had been a successful

[1] Stekel, *L'Éducation des Parents*, pp. 139-45.

business-man, happily married—too happily, indeed, so that he paid only grudging attention to his two sons and his daughter. He gave them an expensive education; he rewarded and punished; but his leisure, Sundays and holidays, was always devoted to his adored wife.

Then came the Slump. He retired, hoping for consolation in a calm domestic happiness with home and children. But *they* had not forgiven his early indifference. Children, it seems, will sooner forgive even tyranny in a parent than apathy.

His sons had left home. His daughter, though still there, remained icily unresponsive. And to this ageing man her coldness grew intolerable—for now she recalled to him what his wife had been in the days of their youth.

> Thou art thy mother's glasse and she in thee
> Calls back the lovely Aprill of her prime.

He grew jealous of his daughter's friends, of her music, of all her interests. What did she give him but a grudging walk in her company once a week, with hardly a word spoken? And yet he was still unaware why he was in general so miserable and so ill. He dreamed— 'Twenty-six could end your troubles. But twenty-six will not help.' He was mystified. The number 26 meant nothing to him. 'Does the date 2/VI mean anything?' Yes, that indeed was his daughter's birthday. *She* was the helper he craved in vain. When he had been brought to face his own conflict, and his daughter had travelled from home, he was at last able to recover his lost balance of mind and body.

Such cases when parent is tied to child, though less prominent in psychological literature than their converse, where child is tied to parent, remain common enough, alike in modern reality and ancient legend. In story after story we have a king who imposes dire penalties on the suitors of his daughter. The lovers of

Atalanta who could not outrun her were put to death by her father, Iasus. King Oenomaus allowed his would-be sons-in-law to take his daughter Hippodameia in a chariot, gave them a start while he sacrificed a ram to Zeus, then drove after and killed them; until Pelops bribed the old king's charioteer to take the linch-pins from his chariot-wheels, so that Oenomaus crashed and was killed, breathing as he died the first of those curses that were to dog the House of Pelops, down to Agamemnon and Orestes.

More memorable still, to me, is the story of Icarius and his daughter Penelope. When she wedded Odysseus, Icarius tried to keep the young pair with him at Sparta. But Odysseus, as we might guess, would not give up his Ithaca. Then Icarius implored his daughter to remain. Even when Odysseus set her in his chariot and drove north out of Lacedaemon, the insistent father pursued Penelope along the road with his entreaties. At last Odysseus said to her, 'Choose'. In silence she veiled her face. Then Icarius understood what, gentler than Cordelia, she would not say; and, resigning himself to necessity, set up by the wayside a statue of Modesty— the same, Pausanias fondly believed, as he saw there fourteen hundred years later, in the second century A.D. Such was the Greek genius for embodying eternal truths in stories almost as eternal in their grace.

Similarly, in real life Charlemagne could not bear to let his daughters marry; nor could Mr. Barrett of Wimpole Street. Mr. Barrett may seem a Victorian monstrosity. But his case is not so rare; there are only too many mothers that find no girl good enough to marry their sons; and every now and then we read of some father who has unaccountably committed suicide just at the period of his daughter's wedding.

I do not wish to overstate; but I suggest that the first fatal scene between Lear and Cordelia becomes more intelligible, and more pathetic, when we see in it a lovers' quarrel, though neither of them knows it. Lear is jealous.

> Why have my Sisters Husbands, if they say
> They love you all ? Haply when I shall wed,
> That Lord, whose hand must take my plight, shall carry
> Halfe my love with him, halfe my Care, and Dutie.
> Sure I shall never marry like my Sisters,
> To love my father all.

Indeed Dr. Paunez of New York has coined for such situations in real life the term 'Lear-complex'.

Once more we are faced by the hidden pitfalls which civilization has introduced into the human family. Parents too fond may tangle their children in emotional leading-strings; parents not fond enough can breed in their children a rankling resentment. Life is not easy. The only solution is a fondness that does not clutch, an affection that is freedom.

> The wild hare of love
> Is alert at his feet.
> Oh the fierce quivering heart!
> Oh the heart's fierce beat!
>
> He has tightened his noose,
> It was fine as a thread;
> But the wild hare that was love
> At his feet lies dead.

Those lines of Susan Miles were not written of father and daughter, mother and son; but they well might have been. That was the tragic error committed by the parents of John Ruskin.

There is no less psychological truth in the relations of Gloucester with his son Edmund, who can never forget that he is illegitimate:

> Thou Nature art my Goddesse, to thy Law
> My services are bound—wherefore should I
> Stand in the plague of custome?

Edmund's ruthlessness to his father, his rancour towards his brother, his scorn and hate of all established authority are much more typical—less melodramatic—than most critics realize. It is, of course, usual enough for sons to react against their fathers anyway; but with an illegitimate son there is (very understandably) a far stronger motive for hating the parent who has disgraced both the child's mother and the child itself; and for hating also the society that inflicts that disgrace.

Let us take an actual example that in fiction we should dismiss as overdrawn. A Viennese dentist had a natural son. The boy grew up ignorant of his parentage. But when he reached manhood, he discovered the secret, went to the dentist as a patient, and shot his long-lost father in his own consulting-room. Many of us may, it is true, have felt similar impulses towards our dentists; but we seldom carry them out.

Noticeable also is the tendency for a revolutionary attitude towards society to be closely linked with the revolutionary's attitude to his own father. (I am speaking now of sons in general, legitimate or not. And I wish to make it quite clear that I am speaking only of things that are liable to happen, not of universal laws.) An amusing instance is provided by the son of a left-wing father, in France, who was passionately right-wing till his father died; *then* promptly switched round and became left-wing himself. A similar case, I believe, from history is our own Henry V—a far more intriguing, complicated, and sinister character in reality than Shakespeare's fifteenth-century Rupert Brooke. It seems fairly well established that the historic Henry V *was* riotous in his youth; it is certain that the antagonism between him and his father, Henry IV, grew at times acute; what is less known is that after that father's death, he became not merely a reformed character, but a ruler whose austerity was the astonishment of his age—a figure

far grimmer than Shakespeare's king of Agincourt—
more like another Cromwell, not only in strictness, but,
unfortunately, in cruelty also, even by the standards of
his day; a leader, just indeed, but pitiless. One gets the
impression that, like the French politician I have just
mentioned, the young Henry may have played libertine
from antagonism to his father; and when that father
died, swung back to a fundamental austerity of temper
not uncommon in masterful characters. For such aggressive masterfulness can be turned against oneself as well
as against the world. So it was with the ascetic Charles
XII of Sweden.

For similar antagonism between son and father one
has only to look at our own Hanoverians in the eighteenth
century, or Frederick the Great, or the Prince de Ligne,
or Mirabeau. More striking still is the penalty that
Henry II paid for unfaithfulness and rigour towards his
queen—one after the other, as they grew up, his sons
made open war against him—Henry, Richard, Geoffrey,
John; until the last and best-loved broke his heart. The
Oedipus-complex has been overworked; some of us have
grown sick of the very name of it; but it exists; and
those who ignore it can pay bitterly.

I can recall a distinguished colleague in the war who
was in certain things subordinated to me. It soon grew
clear from his comments on those above us, especially
our commanding officer and the Prime Minister, that he
suffered from a resentfulness that bore no relation to
reality. By taking great pains to avoid anything re-
motely suggesting parental authority it proved possible
to get through those years without incurring—at least,
audibly—the violence of his anathemas. Perhaps in the
far future when such elementary psychology grows more
widely spread, the ordinary audience that hears some
zealot blowing up with all his bellows the fires of class-
hatred, instead of being deceived, or dismayed, or dis-

gusted, will burst into peals of knowing laughter. When apparently rational men find their spiritual home in Moscow or Berchtesgaden, the answer to the riddle often lies simply in reaction from the homes of their childhood.

> Yes *Cassius*, and from henceforth
> When you are over earnest with your *Brutus*,
> Hee'l thinke your Mother chides, and leave you so.

Let us not too hastily condemn Shakespeare's Edmund and his treatment of his father as overdrawn. Shakespeare was no novice in the human heart. There has been in our time a tendency to praise Shakespeare as a mere wizard of words, whose conjuring with phrases conceals commonplace ideas and mediocre psychology. I do not think he cared very much about general ideas; but I have come to think he knew a good deal more about human nature than some of us suspected—than some of us knew ourselves.

Meanwhile there is yet another psychological trait in *King Lear*—the callousness of Goneril and Regan towards their younger sister, and of Edmund towards his legitimate brother. This too may seem to a purely rational mind—or one that fondly imagines itself so—rather theatrical. Perhaps it is; but not because it is untrue to life. Long before Shakespeare, popular psychology recognized the intense hatred that can be felt by elder brothers or sisters towards younger, in stories like those of Joseph, or Cinderella.

Even with the most scrupulous parental justice elder children may hate intensely the younger arrival who inevitably deprives them in part of the attention and tenderness they monopolized before. Every year there is a steady number of cases where this jealousy leads to the actual murder of a younger child by an elder—just as queen-bees do with their sisters and Turkish sultans used to do with their brothers.

Let me tell you the tragi-comic story of the lady with the cats. This patient at the age of eight or nine became jealous of a baby-niece. She had heard from her nurse the horrific tale of a clergyman's cat which used to sit at table with its master; but one day the bishop came to dinner; a cat could not possibly be allowed to sit at table and look at a bishop; so it was excluded. The cat, however, was of a revengeful disposition; that night it stalked into the poor clergyman's bedroom and stifled him by the ingenious method of thrusting its tail down his throat.

Shortly after hearing this tragic tale the child came on a black cat sleeping in the baby-niece's pram. She fainted.

From that time she was haunted by cats as Orestes by the Furies. Even when grown-up, she would burst into wild screams on finding a cat at the foot of her bed. She developed a power to smell cats whose presence no one else had even guessed. She would come home and refuse to enter because there was a cat. No assurances to the contrary could shake her. At length search would reveal some miserable kitten cowering under the stairs.

She tried every means of overcoming this aversion. She even kept a cat in a cage in her room. No use. The very mention of a cat was enough to make her vomit.

Her travel-journal contained only references to cats— 'St. Gothard Hotel—white angora.' She married and was hoping to become a mother: she met a cat and miscarried.

Why? In her jealousy she had entertained death-wishes against the infant-niece. When she found the black cat sitting in the pram, it seemed the very incarnation of her guilty hope that the child might perish like the unfortunate clergyman in her nurse's story. (There were other complications also—such as her father's fur-coat—that need not concern us here.) Hence a lasting

[70]

horror of cats as symbols of her death-wish—a horror that made her literally sick.

So much for this fantastic hatred which *can* burst out between brothers and sisters, and has given birth to so many stories and tragedies, including those Greek plays that turn on the detestation of Atreus for his brother Thyestes, whom he feasted on his own children's flesh; or of Eteocles and Polyneices, whose abhorrence was stronger even than death, so that on the funeral pyre itself the flames from their two bodies, in unconquerable loathing, turned different ways.

Lear, then, is a concentrated tragedy of the jealousy between parents and children, between sisters or brothers; above all, of a father's morbid possessiveness towards a favourite daughter. As drama I cannot myself, as I say, rank it with *Hamlet*; but my object has been, not to stress a personal preference, but to justify some of the psychology of the play from real life. It is *not* so naïve as it looks.

Nor is a fuller grasp of such things irrelevant to our own lives. It would be grotesque to give the impression that I regard the family as a sort of den of cannibals where every member either loathes or perversely loves every other. On the contrary, I do not believe a state can be happy where happy families grow few and rare. They are its firmest foundation. Healthy happiness at home in early years can perhaps do more than anything else to produce sane and balanced men and women. But these dangers do exist. The family is, in both senses, one of the most *primitive* features of human society.

The human individual contains a menagerie in his Unconscious. The only wise course is neither to ignore the menagerie nor to be frightened of it; but to control it, without being either shocked by it or overmastered. As the Chinese proverb says, 'He that rides on a tiger, cannot dismount'. We cannot, either. We cannot kill

the primitive within us, without being poisoned ourselves by its corpse. That is the doom of asceticism;
which produced grim enough consequences in the Dark
and Middle Ages. It is not asceticism the world needs,
but good sense and loving-kindness.

It seems a grim paradox that the faith whose first
tenet is love should have stained its history with so much
hatred and atrocity. But the paradox is only apparent.
The same repressed aggressiveness that turned inward to
flagellate itself, turned outward to rack and burn others.
'Oh that I may enjoy the wild beasts that are prepared
for me!' wrote Ignatius of Antioch on his road to Rome
and martyrdom. But the tortures that the masochist
welcomed for his own flesh could be employed as
sadistically on the heretic. The Renaissance unwisely
despised the Middle Ages; some moderns seem to me to
admire them no less unwisely; it was hardly one of the
healthiest periods of the human mind.

Let us turn next, very briefly, to *Othello*. Here is
a tragedy both of jealousy, like Lear's, and of a noble
character broken, like Hamlet's, by the idea of a woman's
disloyalty.

The psychology as a whole remains much clearer and
more straightforward—for jealousy in love is unfortunately too common to seem so much a mystery. But,
here again, there is one psychological touch so deft and
true that it is worth dwelling on. I mean that warning
cry of Desdemona's father, Brabantio:

> Looke to her (Moore) if thou hast eies to see:
> She has deceiv'd her Father, and may thee.

It is no mere angry fancy of Brabantio's that a daughter's
relation to her father may foreshadow her relation to
her husband. 'He who would have a happy love',
Stekel has written, 'should consider the father of the
woman he loves. He will see his destiny.' Destiny, I

feel, is often more complicated than that. But I have myself seen it happen. A daughter that has felt an antagonism to her father is liable to repeat that antagonism towards lover or husband—especially her first lover. Or a daughter who has been too much punished may grow masochistic—to crave violent handling from her husband likewise—little though she may understand herself.

Let us turn aside for a moment to a less important Shakespearean play—*The Taming of the Shrew*. It is apt to seem farcical. And yet take this case from real life. A woman of thirty-four, married to a quiet husband, was completely cold to him. One day he lost patience and struck her. Then, suddenly, the ice in her melted. Why? Because she had often been severely punished by her parents as a child; in secret, she craved it still.

This, of course, is nothing new. Everyone has heard of Russian wives in old days complaining that their husbands did not love them because they did not beat them. It becomes clear enough that beating children *can* be extremely bad for them—despite Solomon in all his wisdom. Indeed, it is far more dangerous, in certain cases, than parents or schoolmasters realize. Patmore in his *Unknown Eros*, to take another literary example, has still a curiously Russian outlook, when he speaks of the happy wife:

> By Eros, her twain claims are ne'er forgot;
> Her wedlock's marred when either's missed;
> Or when she's kiss'd, but beaten not,
> Or duly beaten, but not kiss'd.
> Ah, Child, the sweet
> Content when we're both kiss'd and beat.

Here indeed Patmore's *Unknown Eros* would have been better had its true nature remained a little less 'Unknown' to his own consciousness. This poet who wrote an Ode to 'Pain' and would humorously say that whenever he heard too much of humanitarians, he went down to the stable and whipped the dogs all round, was playing with far darker forces than he realized. And Swinburne also. Dolores is decidedly not a goddess to worship, nor de Sade a master to follow.

On the other hand, while the child that has been beaten may still crave for violence in mature years, the child that grows up with resentment against a parent may make marriage an opportunity for revenge—no matter at what cost to happiness.

For instance, the son of a certain industrial magnate determined to marry a prostitute—a Magdalene whom he would, of course, redeem. Not surprisingly, this romance turned into tragedy. The poor woman tried her honest best to live down her past; but the young man himself could never forget it. After all, his real motive had been, not to help her, but to annoy his father. One cannot base a life-partnership on passion for annoying one's father. The end was suicide.

One wonders if Shelley's marriage to Harriet Westbrook was not partly caused by a similar desire to wound a detested parent. In another case a young girl of Socialist opinions wished to marry a workman. Her parents objected. She threatened suicide and they gave way. But this marriage, too, was unhappy. And having threatened to kill herself if she could not get her will, the unfortunate girl finally killed herself, because she had got it—because her real motive was not love of her husband, but hate of her parents.

But life is infinitely various. Women have married beneath them, not to vex their parents, but for a quite different reason. They have watched in their homes from early years that struggle for domination between husband and wife which is one of the deadliest poisons on which a child can be bred. Such children vow that *they* at least will not be the under-dog; and so they may be impelled to fall in love with a social inferior, as Roman ladies with gladiators, or the Princesse de Chimay (like Browning's Duchess) with a gipsy, or Christina of Sweden with her equerry Monaldeschi, or D. H. Lawrence's Lady Chatterley with her gamekeeper. There can, of course, be other motives; but an important one may be the secret hope that social superiority will help in 'the struggle of the sexes'. For that struggle is always threatening. Did not Rilke's mother liken the marriage-service to a prayer before battle?

Moral—if, when you marry, you *must* quarrel, at least do not quarrel before your children. It is a worse crime than many that are on the statute-book. I once had a pupil, a gifted pupil, who was shattered by it—by a split in his own personality reflecting that split between the parents he loved.

Now there is no ground for supposing that, as Brabantio threatens, we are to imagine Desdemona capable of abandoning her husband as she abandoned her father. But there *is* enough worldly wisdom, enough truth to life, in Brabantio's remark, to sink disquietingly, if unconsciously, into the mind of a cleverer man than that fine character Othello. And, after all, Desdemona does prove in the upshot not the frankest of Shakespeare's heroines—there lurks in her character a little grain of well-meant deception, which helps to cost her own and her husband's life.

Then there is Iago. What are his motives? Jealousy about his wife? That sounds largely pretext. Jealousy of Cassio's promotion? Partly. An Italian love of conspiracy for conspiracy's sake, as a fine art—of playing chess with human lives? Partly. As Michelet says of Pope Nicholas III: 'Conjuration au dehors, conjuration au dedans. Les Italiens se croient maîtres en ce genre ... pour ce peuple artiste, une telle entreprise était une œuvre d'art où il se complaisait, un drame sans fiction, une tragédie réelle.'

[75]

There is much truth in this picture of a sadistic sort of art. But, in addition, I cannot but remember what Stekel has called 'the Judas-complex'.

In such a case the dominant motive *can* be a love turned to hate (intimately linked as love and hatred are). A man who loves his master and feels himself less loved than others, can be provoked to passionate resentment and betrayal by that jealousy alone. It is a mere suggestion here—but Iago's case is not so dissimilar. Stekel had a patient who afterwards admitted that he had prowled for weeks about the doctor's house with a loaded revolver, meaning murder. He was so jealous of the other patients—'I loved you so much'. (Evidently an analyst's life does not lack excitements.) *Othello* may conceivably include more kinds of jealousy than one. I should add, however, that this vague suggestion does not seem to me on the same level of probability as the theory that Hamlet's tragedy is the fall of a maternal ideal. That seems to me patent; this, on the contrary, is too subtle for any audience—merely something that Shakespeare himself might have dimly felt. As such, I should be the last to suggest that it is important.

Next, *Macbeth*. With Lady Macbeth's obsessional washing of her hands we have already dealt. But this play as a whole—even more than *Hamlet*, *Lear*, or *Othello*—is essentially a tragedy of Poetic Justice. 'Poetic Justice' is, however, in general a rather misleading term. We employ it with a sardonic implication—'Yes, the poets punish their villains; but real life is less well arranged.' Often that is only too true; but, as we shall see, 'Poetic Justice' remains by no means so rare in the actual world as the bitter nuance of the phrase implies. Not because some God out of a machine punishes the sinner; but because the sinner is often driven to punish himself. In the words of a fine fragment of the lost *Melanippe* of Euripides:

Dream you that men's misdeeds fly up to Heaven
And then some hand inscribes the record of them
Upon God's tablets; and God, reading them,
Deals the world justice? Nay, the vault of Heaven
Could not find room to write the crimes of earth,
Nor God Himself avail to punish them.
Justice is *here on earth*, had ye but eyes.

Macbeth is not only the story of retribution falling on
a murderer; it is the story of a murderer who drags that
retribution on his own head. The Witches, like the
Erinyes of Aeschylus, are not just stage-machinery; they
are profound symbols of those obscure forces in the mind
that so often make men court the ruin that must expiate
their sense of guilt. A neurotic is apt to have not less,
but more intense, pangs of conscience than what we call
'normal' men. And it is amazing how sometimes the
most modern conscience can still instinctively embody
the dreaded forces of retribution in forms that repeat the
legends of long ago.

Take, for example, the Greek myth which tells how,
when Atreus fed his brother Thyestes on his children's
flesh, the sun in horror hid his face. What hyperbole!
And yet medical history records the case of a modern
woman whose sense of guilt was such that she dared not
go out of doors except, literally, when the sun had
hidden his face—in thick cloud. The patient had been
to doctor after doctor and to no less than eighteen
analysts. When she was five, her mother died and
her father, marrying again, had a son, to whom she was
apparently devoted. One day she found the little boy
dead in his cradle; she screamed 'Alfred is dead', and
for a long while nothing could calm her. This was now
thirty years ago. Under analysis the patient mentioned
that she had once falsely boasted of strangling a lover.
His name? 'As I expected—"Alfred".' 'Now I felt
able to say to her,' Stekel continues, '"You killed your

brother and you suffer from photophobia because the sun brings everything to light. . . ." I had expected a violent reaction, but there was no such thing. Wide-eyed, she looked at me and said: "Could you forgive me if I had?"'

'Poetic Justice', Popular Legends, Romance

I have been cunning in mine overthrow,
The careful pilot of my proper woe.
BYRON.

WE have seen Macbeth lured by the equivocations of the Witches to commit new crimes that will make certain his punishment for the old. But this idea is far older than Shakespeare—it is older even than Homer.

When men grow insolent with prosperity and trample on the prayers of the weak, then into their palaces, into their inmost souls, there comes, says Homer, the dark figure of Ate. Who is Ate? Ate is human infatuation, the blindness that darkens those who sin through pride. And she does not only blind; she drives her victims to compass their own doom. 'God maddens first the man He would destroy.'

There is an identical idea in Icelandic saga, when Torfi says: 'I deem that by now the Holm-men, through their evil deeds, have lost their luck and *will not see things as they are*.' It recurs again in the *Arabian Nights* (of evil sorcerers): 'malgré la puissance de leur sorcellerie et de leur science maudite, ils ne savent point prévoir les conséquences des actions les plus simples, et ne songent jamais à se prémunir contre les dangers que distinguent les hommes du commun. Car, dans leur orgueil et leur confiance en eux-mêmes, ils n'ont jamais recours au Maître des créatures, et leur esprit reste constamment obscurci d'une fumée plus épaisse que celle de leurs fumigations, et leurs yeux sont voilés d'un bandeau, et ils tâtonnent dans les ténèbres.'

So fell Napoleon. And twice in a half-century we have seen the rulers of Germany do the same.

What really happens?

It seems that the process may work in two ways. First of all, there are few men in civilized communities who can completely free themselves from conscience—from the ghostly voices of their childhood's parents and teachers, the imagined voices of their fellow-men, condemning certain kinds of action. Nietzsche might write *Beyond Good and Evil* and deride the feebleness of compassion: yet this sage who said one should never approach woman without a whip, took touchingly gentle precautions lest his ideas or his books should upset the ladies in his Pension at Sils Maria; and on the day his reason failed, this denouncer of pity flung his arms round the neck of a suffering cab-horse.

No, it is not so easy for the tree to tear up its roots. And, as I have said, neurotics are characters with more, not less, conscience than other men. Hence, indeed, the violence of the inner conflicts that make them neurotic.

So too a psychopath like Macbeth, even when his crime has succeeded, may kindle an obscure civil war within himself. It may be fought out only by forces struggling dimly in the twilit levels of his consciousness —'where ignorant armies clash by night'. But when a house is divided against itself, we know it may be near its fall. A man's once clear judgement can become blinded, not only by pride, but by secret self-division. So Macbeth is blinded by the Witches.

Secondly, and not less important, there may even be a secret impulse to seek punishment and so expiate the crime. Man's aggressiveness can turn against himself. Lady Macbeth actually takes her own life. Indeed, there is reason to believe that many suicides are self-retribution for previous death-wishes against others.

Long ago Aristotle pointed out that the tragedy where a man blindly destroys himself is more poignant than the tragedy of ruin brought by outside enemies. It acquires a tragic irony. But such tragic irony of self-destruction is not a mere stage-device; it would be far less dramatic, if it were; it is based, often, on a deep psychological reality. 'We are betrayed by what is false within.'[1]

Often it is as if inside a man's own self there sat Minos, Aeacus, and Rhadamanthys, holding implacable judgement on the actions of his life; as if within him there ruled a Mosaic law exacting an eye for an eye and a tooth for a tooth. Again and again 'character is destiny'.

Here are a few more examples of 'Poetic Justice' from real life. A child of six has a phobia about being run over—because it wished that fate for its mother's lover. A son has a phobia of being poisoned (as I have already mentioned), because he wished to poison his step-father. Then there is the grotesque case of an Indian doctor studying in Vienna, who used the freedom of Viennese life to indulge in adventures which the code of his own country condemned. After these escapades he used to develop an irritation of the skin, which vanished again when he abandoned them. He was punishing himself (and perhaps also rendering himself unattractive). Much disconcerted by this explanation, he asked anxiously how to grow a robuster conscience; only to be told that this was impossible. Human beings are not like birds, but

---

[1] Critics still blindly persist in translating the tragic ' peripeteia ', on whose importance Aristotle in the *Poetics* lays such stress, as ' reversal of fortune ', quite undeterred by the nonsense that ensues. A ' peripeteia ' occurs when human blindness produces exactly the opposite of what it hoped and planned ; as when Othello destroys what he loved best. Often this blindness is the result of guilt, as when Macbeth or Antony or Coriolanus compasses his own ruin. Thus in Tragedy the ' peripeteia ' always involves Tragic Irony ; often, Poetic Justice. (Further examples in my *Tragedy*, ch. iv.)

like trees; they cannot change their roots; nor their fundamental conscience.

Or, again, a man will leave a love-letter in his coat-pocket where his wife will find it. Forgetfulness?—no; an unconscious impulse to be found out, a sort of gesture of confession. A husband had an affair with his sister-in-law. His wife caught pneumonia; while administering oxygen, he 'accidentally' let the oxygen escape; and during the delay of bringing another cylinder his wife died. On the exact anniversary (as I have said, the Unconscious seems a great stickler for anniversaries) he was attacked by asthma, which made him gasp for breath as his dying wife had gasped.

Another patient was tormented with asthma and a choking cough. As a child, it turned out, he had once amused himself by feeding a cat with meat tied on a string so that the animal choked to death. He had become in adult life, by a useful over-compensation of his childish sadism, a member of a society for preventing cruelty to animals. But his unconscious conscience had somehow been provoked to demand its eye for an eye, its tooth for a tooth. He must choke as the poor beast had choked.

Two friends married two sisters. Later, one of the husbands developed asthma. He dreamed, too, he was swimming in a torrent, sinking and drowning. 'After a fortnight,' says Stekel, 'I bluntly told him that there was something on his conscience; and that unless he could disburden himself by confiding in me, he could not possibly get well. He said there was nothing; but as he lied, his voice trembled.' At last, after bursting into tears and sobbing for nearly an hour, he admitted a liaison with his friend's wife, his sister-in-law. It was on the anniversary of their first love-making that the asthma began.

A son found his mother hanging by a cord from a

window. Relations between them had been savagely
embittered; and he contented himself with walking,
humming as he went, to call his father. It was too late.
Subsequently he developed curious epileptic attacks, in
which his own head hung forward, just as his dying
mother's had hung; and on these occasions both his
arms became anaesthetic even to the prick of needles—
a lack of feeling that fitted the crime of his own
callousness.

Again, an Englishman of thirty-three had suffered ten
years from anxiety, loss of will, incapacity to work. He
made an unpromising start to his analysis by begging
first for ten days' rest. In other words, he did not really
want to be cured, but to run away. He was told,
'to-morrow or not at all'. It now emerged that in 1914
he was exploring in Australia. War came, but he
hesitated about returning to England—then occurred his
first breakdown. In 1915 he at last came home and
joined the army; but, after four weeks' training, he
produced a second breakdown. He then contrived to
keep himself on sick-leave for the rest of the War.
Fourteen days before the Armistice his brother, home on
leave, called him 'coward and shirker'; and there was
an angry scene. On Armistice-day itself his brother was
killed, as he had secretly hoped; for he was that brother's
heir. But his own conscience was *not* killed. The
Erinyes were there. He finally broke off treatment
and fled.

Even where there is no *apparent* sense of guilt (though
it may well have been present) it is amazing how the
prophetic soul can foreknow, years beforehand, what it
will one day do. 'Character is destiny.'

The Swiss psychologist Flournoy, treating a young man
with a phobia of heights, extracted from him a promise
to give up climbing. Years later the doctor chanced to
read in a newspaper that his ex-patient had gone to

sleep near the edge of a precipice and fallen over. He had thought his secret leaning overcome, and resumed mountaineering. But the impulse was still there.

The poems of Verhaeren, again, as Baudouin[1] points out, are full of railways:

> Rails qui sonnent, signaux qui bougent,
> Appels stridents, ouragans noirs . . .
> Parce que ceux qui les montaient, glissent à terre,
> Soudainement, parmi les morts.

In November 1916 Verhaeren fell under a train in Rouen station. Coincidence? Perhaps.

Or, simpler still, there is Reik's case of a young Englishman who entered his consulting-room and talked without ever removing his pipe—because he was an embittered masochist who employed impudence as a short-cut to getting himself humiliated. There are people who run to be slapped.

In Ibsen's *Hedda Gabler*, when the neurotic heroine shoots herself with those symbolic pistols of her father the general with which she had tried to persuade her lover to commit suicide; or in Ibsen's *Rosmersholm*, when Rosmer and Rebecca at last fling themselves into that mill-race whither Rebecca in her love for Rosmer had once goaded Rosmer's wife, the ordinary spectator is apt to feel that both endings, especially the second, are perhaps too theatrical and artificial, as contrasted with the realistic brilliance of both plays as a whole. Like the critics of *Hamlet*, they know too little of the mysterious reckonings of life. I never understood the end of *Rosmersholm* till I had read enough psychology to realize its grim truthfulness; down to minute details like Rosmer's avoidance of the fatal footbridge above the mill-race even at the very opening of the tragedy. Yes, in spite of Judge Brack, people do 'do such things'.

It may be too fanciful; but I have sometimes wondered

[1] *Psychoanalysis and Aesthetics*, p. 145.

if even Hitler's fate was not partly self-engineered—if he did not commit his supreme folly of invading Russia (followed by endless smaller follies) partly because something in him actually craved for retribution and destruction. (Hitler's conduct, however, is complicated by the secret hatred he seems also to have developed for the German people.) A similar unconscious impulse may have driven Oscar Wilde so persistently to court his own ruin.

In these examples of psychology from some of the world's great dramatists—the Greeks, Shakespeare, Ibsen—whether by intuition or observation, their drawing of character turns out again and again to be truer than ordinary men or critics could guess. But after all one expects dramatists to know character. That is their business. It is even more surprising how much psychology is hidden away even in folk-legends and fairy-tales and popular traditions. Narcissus, for example, has found a second immortality in psychoanalysis. We thought he was a fantasy about a flower. But he too is a reality. 'You won't believe me,' remarked to Stekel one of this numerous posterity of Narcissus, 'but I *envy myself.*' What aptness, what wit in the original Greek story that not only symbolized so vividly this type of self-lover, but for mistress gave him Echo—the sound of his own voice!

Then there are folk-stories in which disaster follows if a person looks back—Lot's wife, Orpheus and Eurydice, Odysseus and Leucothea. It has been suggested—and here I have doubts, while admitting the possibility—that these legends embody an early realization of the fatal effect of looking back to the past and growing absorbed by it, instead of keeping the gaze fixed on present and future.

There seems less doubt that the stories of giants which still beguile our nurseries are largely based on childish fantasies about grown-ups (hence that ponderous stupidity which so often characterizes the creatures) and on day-dreams of triumphing over these large, dull monsters, like Jack the Giant-killer![1] Baudelaire caused much scandal by a poem, *La Géante*—a fantasy of a giant mistress.

> Parcourir à loisir ses magnifiques formes;
> Ramper sur le versant de ses genoux énormes,
> Et parfois en été, quand les soleils malsains,
>
> Lasse, la font s'étendre à travers la campagne,
> Dormir nonchalamment à l'ombre de ses seins,
> Comme un hameau paisible au pied d'une montagne.

The critics were mystified as well as horrified—'je jure mes grands dieux,' cried the reviewer in *Figaro*, 'que je copie textuellement, je serais fort empêché d'ajouter un mot à de telles choses.' Very possibly Baudelaire did not understand it himself. It remains, I think, one of his more foolish poems (they are many): but there is occasion for pity rather than horror in this homesick dream of the happy days of childhood when to his small self his mother seemed a giantess. (Just as places or things we have not visited since childhood so often seem to have grown strangely smaller than our memory of them.)

Similarly it has been suggested that the Paradises, Golden Ages, and Eldorados of legend are ultimately the trailing clouds of glory which childish years acquire in retrospect. The memory of the lost childhood of the individual becomes a dream of the lost childhood of the race.

Take, again, the story of the Sleeping Beauty. This has been explained by Stekel—here again I feel it best to suspend judgement—as a dream-symbolism of girlhood

---

[1] Cf. the story of Polyphemus (where the blinding, as with Oedipus, suggests castration) with its childlike evasion—' " Nobody " did it '.

passing into womanhood. The princess lies captive among
the ties that bind her to her childhood and her family,
shut off from life by the growing hedge of thorns: but
at her lover's kiss the enchantment breaks, the world
re-lives, and she turns, as Nature wills, from past to
future, from the home of childhood to the new home
that waits for her.[1]

> And on her lover's arm she leant,
>   And round her waist she felt it fold,
> And far across the hills they went
>   In that new world which is the old:
> Across the hills, and far away
>   Beyond their utmost purple rim,
> And deep into the dying day
>   The happy princess follow'd him. . . .
>
> But any man that walks the mead,
>   In bud, or blade, or bloom, may find,
> According as his humours lead,
>   A meaning suited to his mind.[2]

No doubt, it is sometimes dangerously easy to find such
'meanings'. Yet I own that here I can find no other;
and I shall never henceforward be able to think of this
ancient fantasy of the nursery without this interpretation
which adds to it, I think, a new and more poignant
reality. Across the ages the Sleeping Princess and Ibsen's
Nora clasp hands.

Then there are the fairy-tales and legends where
human beings change into animals; especially men into
wolves, witches into hares or cats. Such stories come

---

[1] In *Imago* for 1933 Steff Bornstein gives a more elaborate interpretation,
comparing the sleep of Briar Rose in her lonely room to the isolation, often
in cell or hut, imposed by savage tribes for months or years on the girl
initiated into womanhood. He suggests that the fatal prick of the spindle
corresponds to the defloration, often artificial, which sometimes accompanies
the ritual; and that the burning of all spindles by the king her father
implies that paternal jealousy we discussed in relation to King Lear. In
either case the story is a symbol of girlhood growing up.

[2] Tennyson, *The Sleeping Beauty*.

from many times and lands. It is enough to recall Nebuchadnezzar or Circe, the werewolf stories of antiquity and the Middle Ages (Herodotus, Virgil, Petronius, the *Volsunga Saga*, *Bisclavaret*), down to Horace Walpole's account in his letters of the wolf of the Gevaudan, which remarked with justified complacency to a peasant, as it leapt across a river, 'N'est ce pas assez bien sauter pour un homme de quatre-vingts ans?'

When Webster in his *Duchess of Malfi* (v. ii) makes his Duke Ferdinand, melancholy with the guilt of his sister's murder, imagine himself a wolf with the hair turned inwards, we are apt to exclaim 'What imaginations these Elizabethans had!' But such zoanthropy is no fiction. Janet had a woman-patient who in her attacks believed herself a lioness and bit up photographs; Freud's Little Hans identified his father with a horse and a giraffe; cases treated by Stekel barked like a dog or crowed and scratched like a cock. Indeed this knowledge is nothing new. Saint-Simon sardonically records how the Prince de Condé imagined himself a dog, rolled on the bed of the Maréchale de Noailles, and duly preserved *les bienséances* at prayers in the King's room by throwing back his head and barking only *mutely*. As a malicious *chanson* put it—

> Quelle fortune! n'être ni loup ni lapin
> Pendant le cours d'une lune!
> Quelle fortune!

Sometimes the delusion becomes collective—villagers believing themselves turned into wolves, nuns into cats, revivalists into dogs. But these will be better dealt with later, when we come to the *Bacchae* of Euripides and the remoter twilight of totemism.

All such cases seem to involve a regression of the adult mind to a childish state, where (like a totemistic savage) it loses its sense of the gap between human and animal, and the sadistic, even cannibal, impulses of the primitive world reawaken. In particular, Webster's association of Duke Ferdinand's lycanthropy with a state of melancholia turns out to be quite correct.

Similarly, even the Vampire and the Ghoul are not creatures only of fantasy. There actually exist in each generation a certain number of unfortunates for whom (to adapt Ronsard):

> L'Amour et la Mort n'est qu'une mesme chose;

whose necrophily can love only the dead, even if it has to dig them from the grave. Dr. Epaulard published a work (1901) dealing with twenty-three such cases. Here , is neither time nor place for lurid details; but it becomes clear enough on studying them that the same aberration in more or less sublimated form haunts a good deal of literature, especially Romantic literature. It recurs in writers like Bürger (*Lenore*), 'Monk' Lewis, Beddoes, Poe; in stories like Boccaccio's *Pot of Basil* or Keats's *Isabella*; or in the persistent, unhealthy fascination of the legend of Salome.

Again there is the popular superstition of the *Doppelgänger*,[1] the double of oneself, to meet whom may be a sign of coming death. Writers have used it repeatedly —Jean Paul Richter, Hoffmann, Chamisso, Heine, Lenau, Andersen, Dostoievsky, Strindberg, Poe in *William Wilson*, Wilde in *The Picture of Dorian Gray*, Maupassant in *Le Horla*, Stevenson in *Dr. Jekyll and Mr. Hyde*, H. H. Ewers in *The Student of Prague*. Rossetti, too, on his honeymoon in Paris with the doomed Lizzie Siddal was driven by his inner demon to draw from her and himself that sinister sketch of two medieval lovers encountering their *Doppelgänger*, which he called 'How They Met Themselves'.

[1] Cf. O. Rank, *Der Doppelgänger* in *Imago*, 1914, p. 97. Also Aubrey's story of Sir R. Napier, shortly before his death, refusing a bed at an inn on the ground that there was a corpse in it. Assured that there was none, he looked again—and saw it was himself. See too p. 122 below.

In real life this is not an uncommon type of hallucination; it occurred to Goethe, Jean Paul Richter, Hoffmann, Maupassant; but perhaps the most famous sufferer from it was Alfred de Musset. It seems to consist in a projection outwards of half the personality—sometimes the better self (in *King Robert of Sicily* it is an angel), sometimes the worse. Rank suggests that it originates in the Narcissism of the infant, which first loves a shadow-image of itself, but later may come to hate it. Sometimes the 'ego' in alliance with the 'super-ego', projects outward its baser, sensual self; sometimes the 'ego' surrendering to the impulses of the 'id', sees the 'super-ego' as an external and reproachful shape.

Then there is that figure of a more literary tradition —Don Juan; who corresponds in the Latin world to Faust in the Teutonic—the rebel of sense beside the rebel of knowledge. In a way he recalls the ancient Ixion who loved the Queen of Heaven, but embraced only a cloud of illusion from which chimerical monsters were begotten, and found himself bound in Hell to the wheel of eternal recurrence. Actually, the typical Don Juan is often a character tied to mother or sister and so latently homosexual. Hence if he wanders for ever without rest (like the Wandering Jew, another popular embodiment of the eternal quest for happiness), straying from woman to woman, it is because he unconsciously seeks a fulfilment no woman can ever give. Happiness seems his; but always at that moment the stone hand of the Commander, of the avenging Father, knocks at his door to bear him down to Hell. (Similarly among women there is a 'Messalina-type' suffering from a like unconscious abnormality.)

One may indeed say of the original Don Juan that he incarnates the Freudian, sexual rebellion of Son against Father, where Lucifer represents a more Adlerian revolt against the Father's power.

[90]

A somewhat similar type of eternal frustration recurs in the Icelandic Saga of Cormac, and again in Proust's great novel. Cormac was indifferent to his love, Steingerd, whenever she was free and ready to respond; it was only whenever she became another's that his desperate love reawakened. Similarly Proust's Marcel loved Albertine only when his jealousy was aroused by a sudden stab of suspicion about her having belonged to another in the past. Typical also are the recurrent trios in Rousseau's life—with Mme de Warens and Claude Anet, with Mme d'Épinay and Grimm, with Mme d'Houdetot and Saint-Lambert.

Here too the root of the evil lies in fatally repeating a childish situation. Then between the child and his mother stood the father; now between the man and his mistress there must still stand some 'shadowy third'. He can only crave for what is another's.

Such an obsession may take forms still more bizarre. Stekel mentions the case of a 'Witwensammler'—a collector of widows. 'The intensity of his passion was in proportion to the recency of the bereavement. Young or old, pretty or ugly, he did not care, provided they were widows. His real pride was in widows he had won on the very day of the funeral.' The extraordinary scene in Shakespeare's *Richard III*, where Gloucester wins Anne Neville, whose husband and father-in-law he has murdered, by courting her as she follows the body of that father-in-law to its burial, remains to our eyes grotesque. Not even the parallel case of the eccentric I have just mentioned, wooing widows on the day of the funeral, can, I feel, justify it artistically; but once more it illustrates how few fictions can (or dare) equal the strangeness of reality. Which is why novels in general, unless superlatively written, seem to me a feeble waste of time compared with biography and psychology.

Just as there are men hounded through life by this

neurotic craving always to shatter the happiness of others, morbidly driven to desire the love only of women already beloved by someone else; so, naturally, there is a corresponding type of Siren-woman, who can covet only the husbands or lovers of her friends. In either case this disastrous type of person is really groping back towards the trinity of infancy—father, mother, child; and so goes through life constructing infinite series of triangles, each angle of which is only too likely to prove, in defiance of Euclid, both agonizingly acute and wearisomely obtuse.

Yet another variety of fatal reversion to the situations of childhood is what one may call 'Petrarchan passion'— where the lover wishes only to love the unattainable, as a moth a star—content to yearn from far off; to watch, perhaps, only a lighted window or the shadow on a blind, without ever making an effort to approach and win 'la princesse lointaine', in whom the parent unattainably loved in childhood is incarnate once more.

Brill[1] records the somewhat different case of a doctor who was bewitched by hearing a woman sing the 'Spring Song' from *Samson and Delilah*. Timid though he was, he did actually meet and marry her. Soon afterwards she died; but he was just as happy with records of her voice as he had been with the living woman.

Such things may seem 'poetic'. Platonic longings have enriched the world's literature. But one may doubt if they are really so admirable; though sometimes, where circumstances forbid a closer relationship, such sublimation may be the only compromise. All the same, there remains, I feel, much healthy good sense in Ronsard's irritation against Petrarch.

> A voir son escrit
> Il estoit eveillé d'un trop gentil esprit
> Pour estre sot trente ans, abusant sa jeunesse
> Et sa Muse au giron d'une vieille maistresse;

[1] *Psychoanalytic Psychiatry*, p. 202.

> Ou bien il jouyssoit de sa Laurette, ou bien
> Il estoit un grand fat d'aimer sans avoir rien.
>   (To read his page,
> Too nobly-bred a heart he seems, too sage,
> To waste for thirty years his manhood's flower,
> Ay, and his Muse in a faded Mistress' power;
> Either he won his Laurette, or his brain
> Was addled, thus to love so long in vain.)

Or in the words of our own Sir Robert Ayton (1570-1638):

> He that can love unloved again,
> Hath better store of love than brain;
> God send me love my debts to pay,
> While unthrifts fool their love away.

We may recall, too, the impatient pride of Wilfrid Scawen Blunt:

> What is this prate of friendship? Kings discrowned
> Go forth, not citizens, but outlawed men;

or the satiric laughter of Wilhelm Busch:

> Und die Liebe per Distanz,
> Kurzgesagt, mißfällt mir ganz.

It is probably wiser in love to be neither too patient nor too impatient, neither too easily deterred nor too persistent—as Meredith was too persistent in proposing, it is said, no less than seven times to his first wife, Peacock's daughter. Such iron endurance may win the admiration of romantics. But it too has its dangers. By this dogged iteration the conscious mind may be worn into assent; yet the intuitive resistance may still be there. Instinct in such a case can prove wiser than intellect; for, in the end, it is likely to prove stronger. (The lover, too, may unconsciously resent those past refusals; as Byron with Lady Byron.) Little wonder, then, that Meredith's first marriage failed. Once more it becomes clear that life offers liberal facilities for unhappiness.

> The paths of love are rougher
> Than thoroughfares of stones.

Another, and a very different, variety of what I have called 'Petrarchan love' also goes back to childhood's idealizing affection for a parent. But here the unhappy victim lives split between ideal love for an idealized woman on the one hand and, on the other, physical relations with women despised or half-despised. Or it may happen, with similar results, that a love-hate for a mother may lead her son alternately to place her image on a pedestal and to drag it vindictively through the mire. In either case love and passion can become hopelessly sundered. Such was the fate of Sainte-Beuve. It recurs in Meredith's sometime friend Rossetti—the tragedy of whose marriage, Lizzie Siddal's suicide (1862), was, I suspect, adapted by Meredith and added, as a conclusion, to his own marriage-story, *Modern Love* (published very shortly after the Rossetti tragedy, at a time when the two poets were intimate). Always in Rossetti one is conscious of this double relationship between idealist and sensualist, rending his life in two with the same divided impulse as dragged Dante from Beatrice to light loves and hunted Byron from Lady Byron to the slums of Venice, and back from the slums of Venice to La Guiccioli. So in Rossetti there recur, with constant alternations, the two types of woman—Saint and Siren, Mary Virgin and Mary Magdalen, Beata Beatrix and Jenny, Blessed Damozel and Sister Helen. In his poetry the result is often moving; but in real life such a rifted personality can prove, as it proved for him, a curse.

> My love I call her, and she loves me well:
> But I love her as in the maelstrom's cup
> The whirled stone loves the leaf inseparable
> That clings to it round all the circling swell,
> And that the same last eddy swallows up.[1]

On the other hand, lest this analysis of various types of

---

[1] D. G. Rossetti, *The Orchard-pit* (an unfinished poem, of which a complete prose-draft survives).

romance may seem to some depressingly unromantic, it is to be remembered that human beings are not only less ideal, very often, than they imagine—they are sometimes more so. The better self is partly unconscious, as well as the worse one. Not infrequently it will happen that those who have sacrificed a genuine love for mere money or worldly considerations pay the penalty in neurosis. The heart too can take its revenges, sometimes in strangely hidden form. The moral of much modern psychology, I feel, is not 'Be prosaic', but— 'Be honest'.

VI

Romanticism

The world of dreams is better far
Above the light of the morning-star.
                WILLIAM BLAKE.

Le vent qui vient à travers la montagne
Me rendra fou.
                VICTOR HUGO.

FROM these maladies of human romance we may
pass to Romanticism itself—though the word has been
so tumbled about, battered out of shape, and generally
misused that the heart sinks at the very name of it.
Yet it remains, I think, one of the literary questions on
which psychology can throw most light.

What is Romanticism? The revolt, some have said, of
Emotion against Reason. But in what sense were Swift
or Johnson or Voltaire or Mozart lacking in emotion?
Romanticism, said Goethe, was diseased. But how are
The Ancient Mariner or *The Lady of Shalott* diseased?
'Romanticism', said Hugo, 'is the grotesque.' But
how is *La Belle Dame sans Merci* grotesque?

Heine said it was 'the reawakening of the Middle
Ages'. But in what way are *Werther* or *Wuthering
Heights* medieval? Pater described it as the addition of
'strangeness' to beauty. But 'Monk' Lewis or Mrs.
Radcliffe have little beauty. Brunetière dismissed it as
a blind wave of literary egotism. But is *The Ancient
Mariner* egotistic?—it is a sermon against egotism.

Lascelles Abercrombie explained Romanticism as the

opposite of Realism, 'a withdrawal from outer experience to concentrate on inner experience'. But think of the realism of Scott's humbler characters, or the carpets rising along the gusty floor in *The Eve of St. Agnes*; of the realism mingled with extreme romanticism in Balzac, Stendhal, Dickens; of the Pre-Raphaelites with their concentration on minutest detail, like the beads of melted snow on Sir Galahad's steel shoes in the poem of William Morris.

It is of course possible to argue, as has been ably done by Professor Lovejoy in America, that 'Romanticism' is a hopelessly woolly term fit only for slaughter; and that one should speak only of 'Romanticisms.' [1]

For example, argues Professor Lovejoy, there was a Romantic false dawn in the England of the seventeen-forties, when Batty Langley and Sanderson Miller tried, with temporary success, to revive Gothic architecture. This was helped by the admiration for Chinese gardens already started by Sir William Temple as far back as the sixteen-eighties. For the essential quality praised in Chinese gardens was their irregular beauty—what its partisans imagined the Chinese to call by the harmonious name of 'sharawadgi'—the kind of 'sweet disorder' Herrick loved. Hence *le goût anglo-chinois* in gardening, which played its own part in preparing for the Romantic Revival of the seventeen-nineties.

Another quite different influence in English Romanticism was Shakespeare, whom critics like J. Warton (and indeed Milton) praised because he was 'wild' like 'Nature'.

On the other hand, Professor Lovejoy points out that German Romantics like F. Schlegel started from quite different principles—not from a worship of irregularity and wildness, but from the idea that Ancient Art had been a static, limited thing, whereas Modern Art should

[1] A. O. Lovejoy, *Essays in the History of Ideas*, 1948.

be dynamic, evolutionary, progressive, aiming at greater universality, and therefore finding nothing common or unclean; on the contrary, including even the abnormal and monstrous, and refusing to be cramped by any rules or laws. Thus for Schlegel, Shakespeare himself was great, not because 'wild', but because universal. (But note, even here, the over-riding of rules or laws.)

Then, again, there was the earlier French Romanticism of Rousseau, Bernardin de Saint-Pierre, and Chateaubriand, with their primitivism, their admiration for the patriarchal community, for the pastures of the Alps, the exoticism of the Tropics, the forests of America.

And, lastly, there was also the later French Romanticism of Victor Hugo and his group in the eighteen-twenties and thirties, influenced both by foreign Romanticisms and by the Middle Ages.

This complexity is still further complicated by the worship of 'Nature'—a long-suffering and tormented term for which the microscopic eye of Professor Lovejoy has tabulated no less than sixty-one different meanings. I think he has split this unhappy word into more splinters than he need. But it *is* true that 'Nature' became so vague a divinity that Romantics as well as Classicists could claim to be virtuously obeying her laws.

For the Classicist, Nature enjoined simplicity, uniformity, economy, regularity. Natural reason and natural goodness were the same in modern Paris or ancient Athens, in civilized Europe or primitive Polynesia. Therefore the artist should aim at the natural and the general, and avoid the local, the individual, the eccentric. Only so would he follow (as the wise Ancients had followed her):

> Unerring Nature, still divinely bright,
> One clear, unchanged, and *universal* light.

Indeed the Deity of eighteenth-century Deists and the

Nature of eighteenth-century Classicists tended to merge in one. For Deism was 'natural' religion, to be reached by the 'natural' reason, everywhere, at all times, without need of revelation.

But it was just as easy for the anti-Classicist to argue that Nature was, universal indeed, but *not* uniform; irregular, *not* regular; spontaneous, *not* artificial; evolutionary, *not* traditional. For Johnson, one blade of grass might be like another blade of grass; but, for the microscope, no two blades of grass ever were, or could be, the same. In fact, Nature provided specious (and quite futile) arguments for both sides in the aesthetic battles of the eighteenth century, as readily as the Bible had provided texts for both sides in the religious battles of the seventeenth. No Odysseus ever had so persistent a passion for his Penelope as the human mind for false analogy.

231240

But I still think, despite the useful sweeping of this Augean Stable by the Herculean broom of Professor Lovejoy, that there *is* a common factor in all Romanticisms—and that this factor is psychological.

Freud has pictured the life of the human ego as subjected to three main forces: the 'id', the primitive impulsive part of us that mutters in its caverns 'I want that'; the 'super-ego', or 'ego-ideal'[1] the conscience, that cries out 'It is pleasant; but wrong'; and the reality-principle that warns us, 'It looks pleasant; but it is a snare and a delusion'.

> Too sweet is the rind, say the sages,
> Too bitter the core.

This may be only a rough, schematic picture of the

---

[1] It must be remembered that Freud pictures the 'id' as an *unconscious* source of our primitive impulses, and the 'super-ego' or 'ego-ideal' as a *partly unconscious* embodiment of our ethical standards (parental and social). F. Alexander has suggested keeping the term 'super-ego' for the unconscious element, 'ego-ideal' for the conscious.

truth; but over a wide field it works *as if* something of the sort were true; it can help without becoming dogma. It seems possible to suggest (much simplifying the complexity of a situation where the voices are partly conscious, partly not) that in literature Realism corresponds to a dominance of the reality-principle; Classicism, very roughly, to a dominance of the 'super-ego'; Romanticism, also very roughly, to a dominance of impulses from the 'id'.

In other words, it is misleadingly incomplete to picture a duel between Classicism and Romanticism. This literary conflict is not really a duel; it is part of a three-cornered conflict between Classicism, Romanticism, and Realism.

On the whole, then, our primitive impulses lead us towards Romanticism; our sense of reality towards Realism; our social sense towards Classicism—the art of men who honour a code and a tradition. Naturally there are many other contributory causes that vary with time and place. But a fundamental part seems played by these three fundamental factors of the human mind; and the basis of all Romanticism becomes clearest if approached from the side, not of literary or social history, but of psychology.

Sometimes Romantics have called in Realism as an ally against the unreal conventions of Classicism; sometimes Classicists have appealed to Realism against the fantastic dreams of Romanticism. For the danger that lies in wait for the Classical Muse is of becoming a blue-stocking and a governess; the danger that besets her Romantic sister is of becoming a drunken libertine.

The best literature, I believe, tends to keep a balance of all these forces—as Homer, Chaucer, Shakespeare, Ronsard do. But such balance is difficult—how difficult can be seen even in a brilliant intellect like Napoleon, with his classic love of order and lucidity, his feeling for the tradition of Roman Church and Roman Empire and the drama of Corneille rather than Shakespeare; but also with his sometimes unbalanced realism, which underestimated the power of ideas and ideals; and his sometimes excessive romanticism, which lost itself in megalomaniac dreams or in the vapours of *Ossian*. The first, the classic side of him, helped to produce the Code Napoléon; the second, the too cynical realism, led to acts like the shooting of the Duc d'Enghien; the third, the too intoxicated romanticism, drove him to Moscow and his gambling refusal of reasonable terms, even in 1813. Yet this many-sidedness has also produced part of Napoleon's fascination and the wildly conflicting portraits drawn of him. He has *some* appeal for almost all men.

The same three elements, more happily mixed and balanced, are conspicuous in another figure, whose greatness need not be unduly dwarfed for us by our good fortune in being his contemporaries—Winston Churchill; classic in his hate for vapours and jargon, romantic in his passionate sense of the English past, supremely realist as a minister of war.

In art, however, this balance remains especially difficult, since artists are often neurotic by temperament, and often tempted from the pursuit of perfection by that Circe of novelty who can change them to beasts.

It now becomes clearer, I think, how Romanticism could be described in so many ways; which all contain truth, yet not enough truth. Sometimes Romanticism *was* a 'triumph of emotion over reason' because, though 'Classical' writers like Swift, Johnson, or Voltaire were just as passionate as many a Romantic, and in their practice very far from reasonable, they did in theory believe in common sense and sound tradition. Sometimes Romanticism *was* 'grotesque'; for what emerges from the Unconscious often is so, like one's dreams, in contrast to the Ancients' insistence on ideal beauty and dignity—or at least on not *mixing* ideal and grotesque. Sometimes Romanticism cultivated the childlike or the savage, in nostalgia for a less inhibited life; sometimes it cultivated the Medieval, for the Middle Ages were more childlike than Antiquity or modern times; sometimes it devoted itself for similar reasons to Christianity or mysticism. Often it produced great work; often its excesses led to the morbid or the mad. The history of Romanticism remains, I think, one more illustration of the immortal Greek platitude 'Nothing too much'.

Similarly Classicism, within limits, could be admirable —as in the Parthenon, or the best of Sophocles, or Horace, or Racine, or Johnson:

> Though deep, yet clear: though gentle, yet not dull:
> Strong without rage: without o'erflowing, full.

But in the eighteenth century its atmosphere grew stale and stuffy as a smoking-room in a club—even if it was a very select club.

Realism too, within limits, could be admirable, in the spirit of Bishop Butler's: 'Things and actions are what they are and the consequences of them will be what they will be; why then should we wish to be deceived?' It could become less admirable in the pedantic unimaginativeness of Bentley emending Milton's

> No light, but rather darkness visible.

to

> No light, but rather a transpicuous gloom.

(For how else could 'sights of woe' have been visible through it?)

There is the admirable realism of Homer or Shakespeare or Ibsen; the less admirable realism of Swift or Zola or Aldous Huxley, which, because truth is often unpleasant, too often assumes that a collection of un-

pleasantnesses *must* be truth—when it is really regressing
towards that stage of infancy which finds fascination in
its own bodily by-products. (Since then Mr. Huxley has
regressed still further into a mysticism which seems to
me mere *nostalgie de la matrice*.)

The original impulse of Romanticism was sound. From
the more primitive energies within us comes the artist's
creative power; from the twilight of preconsciousness
rise his visions and his dreams. The inhibitions of
Classicism had become like a tourniquet; the whole body
of poetry was threatened with gangrene. But it was
unfortunate, though inevitable, that the new movement
early developed signs of mania—as in Blake. 'Exuber-
ance is beauty'; 'damn braces, bless relaxes'—these are
thrilling war-cries, no doubt; but one cannot live by war-
cries. The next step led straight into nonsense—'sooner
murder an infant in its cradle than nurse unacted desires'.
How many infants had Blake murdered? The shrewd-
ness of some of Blake's aphorisms, the beauty of some of
his lyrics cannot conceal, except for idolaters, a streak of
craziness.

In its extreme forms Romanticism becomes essentially
a revolt against reality and against society; a rejection of
the world of facts and duties for dream and drunkenness;
where, as for the small infant, thought is omnipotent and
impulse is unrestrained. 'Thinking makes it so'; but
this supposed 'Allmacht der Gedanken', typical of child
and savage, remains a dangerous half-truth.

Indeed, of the more tiresome type of minor Romantic
there are few better summaries than Lavater's description of Fuseli: 'His look is lightning, his word a storm,
his jest death, his vengeance hell. At close quarters he is
rather trying.'

Take, for a moment, that important forerunner of the
Romantic Revival, Rousseau. His neurotic extravagances
dumbfounded his rational contemporaries — Diderot,

Grimm, Voltaire, Hume. How should they, with their ideal of 'good sense', have understood this strange genius?—who was a narcissistic self-lover; a masochist perpetually looking for pain; an exhibitionist, who exhibited himself full-length on paper also; the victim of an unconscious homosexuality, against which he had unconsciously to protect himself by quarrelling violently with his best friends; a character in some ways so permanently infantile that he found happiness as the adorer of a mother-substitute, Mme de Warens (herself a neurotic who asserted her desire for domination by taking lovers, yet remaining frigid), and left his children to be foundlings (for he was too infantile to accept a father's responsibility—and his own father, he felt, had abandoned him by marrying again).

It is, no doubt, common enough—especially in modern times—for genius to be in some ways neurotic. Johnson, for example, was a fetichist who would stoop down at dinner-parties and twitch off ladies' shoes; an obsessional neurotic who had to touch posts in the street. But though Johnson had his oddities, he did not *abandon* himself to them like this Rousseau whom he would so gladly have sentenced to transportation. Up to the end of a long life he remained a dogged fighter for his ideals of good sense and 'no cant'. That lifelong resistance to the irrational, in the teeth of his unbalanced impulses, typifies the contrast between Classic and Romantic.

Grinker and Spiegel's *Men under Stress* (studies of nervous cases among U.S. air-crews) has illustrated the very practical value of an ego-ideal under the still greater strains of modern war. Almost every airman in battle was frightened; but it was often the possession of a strong (yet not *too* rigid) ego-ideal, built up in early years, that saved him from collapse. The men of the eighteenth century had to an unusual degree the ideal of rationality. Indeed they often had it too much. To-day, on the other hand, we could do with a good deal more of their staunch belief in the value of good sense.

In contrast, no one has more eloquently summed up the Romantic attitude than Baudelaire: 'Il faut être toujours ivre. Tout est là; c'est l'unique question. . . . Mais de quoi? De vin, de poésie, ou de vertu, à votre guise. Mais enivrez-vous.

'Et si quelquefois, sur les marchés d'un palais, sur l'herbe verte d'un fossé, dans la solitude morne de votre chambre, vous vous réveillez, l'ivresse déjà diminuée ou disparue, demandez au vent, à la vague, à l'étoile, à l'oiseau, à l'horloge, à tout ce qui fuit, à tout ce qui gémit, à tout ce qui roule, à tout ce qui chante, à tout ce qui parle, demandez quelle heure il est; et le vent, la vague, l'étoile, l'oiseau, l'horloge vous répondront: "Il est l'heure de s'enivrer! Pour n'être pas les esclaves martyrisés du temps, enivrez-vous; enivrez-vous sans cesse! De vin, de poésie, ou de vertu, à votre guise."'

This emotional dipsomania may not be quite so mad as it sounds. To look coldly in the Sphinx-like face of reality for too long does paralyse. But the best remedy may be, not wine, but other saner consolations—work, action, affection. It is not hard to see whither in literature a doctrine like Baudelaire's was bound to lead; and why Goethe came to call Romanticism 'diseased' (to-day he might have preferred to say 'neurotic'); and why he turned away from his own youthful Romanticism as firmly as Wordsworth turned away from his own youthful neo-Classicism. For more than a century after the Revival, Romantics were to learn by painful experience, like Jane Austen's heroines, that sensibility is no substitute for sense. Unluckily for them, they mostly took longer to learn than Marianne Dashwood.

Many of these writers were in fact rather too anxious to recapture 'the visionary gleam', the 'clouds of glory' of the Heaven that 'lies about us in our infancy'. But

Wordsworth, as we know—as even his contemporaries
knew—had an imperfect knowledge of children. He
omitted a good deal. His Philosopher Child remains a
fantasy like the Noble Savage.[1] (Indeed, infants are in
many ways savages; and savages, large infants.) Yet
Wordsworth's picture is incomplete rather than untrue;
and he at least did not make vain attempts to unlive the
'years that bring the philosophic mind'. Many Romantics, however, did attempt precisely that.

> O wüsst' ich doch den Weg zurück,
> Den lieben Weg zur Kinderzeit!

And much of their work shows the neurotic tendencies
that are the inexorable penalty of refusing to grow up.[2]

First, there is the infant's Narcissism. We may recall
Brunetière's summary of Romanticism as 'literary
egotism'. Writers have seldom at any period been
notable for modesty: but seldom have they equalled the
vanity of Romantics like Blake, Rousseau, Chateaubriand,
Wordsworth, Byron, Lamartine, Hugo, Vigny, or Musset.
I dislike generalizations without instances: here are a
few.

Blake (of one of his poems): 'The Grandest Poem
that this World contains.'

Rousseau: 'Moi qui me suis cru toujours, et qui me
crois encore, à tout prendre, le meilleur des hommes.'

---

[1] Or, to-day, the Noble Worker. It is, in the long run, no kindness to
human types to stick them on fancy pedestals. They end by falling off.

[2] The dangers of clinging to the infantile are vividly symbolized in a
dream recorded by one of Hilda Stekel's patients. 'I am asleep in a
room with the doctor, where is also a five-years child. Suddenly it weeps
and howls to be taken into the doctor's bed. . . . Then I realize the child is
myself. I nestle happily against the doctor. But my second self grows
furious. I jump out of bed, seize the child, and pitch it through the window.
I can hear it hit the stones beneath, and now I know it is dead and will
never rise again. The doctor says I was very cruel. But I answer that the
child was crueller still to me.'

More and more there is borne in on me the vital need to accept
external reality, time, and change—to distrust all *excessive* flights from
these into childishness or mysticism.

'Je crois que jamais individu de notre espèce n'eut naturellement moins de vanité que moi.'

Chateaubriand: 'Si Napoléon avait fini avec les rois, il n'en avait pas fini avec moi.'

Alfred de Vigny (to the friend who thought his speech at his reception into the Academy had perhaps been a little long): 'Mais je ne suis pas fatigué.'

Victor Hugo (to a young man who said he had been reading Goethe and Schiller): 'Mais à quoi bon? Je les résume tous.' Of a young poet: 'He will never write well; he did not turn pale on meeting me.' (Hugo, indeed, allowed his mistress to compare him favourably with the Founder of Christianity and to look forward to a time when mankind would date its chronology, not from Christ, but from Victor Hugo.)

D'Annunzio (on his first visit to Sarah Bernhardt): 'il s'arrêta à quelques pas d'elle et dit, comme inspiré: "Belle! Magnifique! D'Annunzienne!" Après quoi il dit: "Bonjour, Madame."'

This Narcissism of the infant goes with a great deal of aggressiveness. I have no wish to libel childhood. No one has had more occasion to feel its extraordinary charm than I have. But the barbarian is there. And yet childish nature is so fluid, and its hidden depths so disguised (partly by our unwillingness to see), that Freud's view of human infancy at first provoked as frenzied resistance as Darwin's view of human origins. Why? Is it not really more creditable to have risen from apes than to have fallen from demi-angels?

Now a similar infantile aggressiveness in the Romantics often showed itself in a rebellion against all accepted restraints. Writers made daisy-chains of 'les fleurs du mal'. 'Je voudrais', cried young Romantics, 'm'enivrer de coupables délices.' Swinburne indulged in puerile fantasies of having seven towers, one for each day of the week, in which to commit by turns the Seven Deadly

Sins (what a bore!). Rollinat cultivated this fashionable
'Satanism' even in his dog, by beating it when it behaved
well and giving it sugar when it did not.[1]

It was only to be expected that this general aggressiveness should lead in its turn to sadism, the craving to
inflict pain on the object loved; and to masochism, which
is aggression turned inwards, till men crave to suffer pain.
Dr. Mario Praz in his *La Carne, La Morte, e il Diavolo
nella Letteratura Romantica*, which traces in astonishing
detail the influence of the Marquis de Sade himself on
writers of this period, has quoted the observation made
even at the time by Sainte-Beuve: 'Byron et de Sade
(je demande pardon du rapprochement) ont peut-être été
les deux plus grands inspirateurs de nos modernes.' Hence
those sinister figures, often half hero, half villain, who
stalk in historic gloom through pre-Romantic and
Romantic pages, from Mrs. Radcliffe to Emily Brontë—
those fatal women, *belles dames sans merci*, from Keats's
Lamia to Pater's Monna Lisa or Wilde's Salome. So
before the eyes of Baudelaire:

> Resplendit à jamais, comme un astre inutile,
> La froide majesté de la femme stérile.

On the whole, these Sirens—daydreams of a masochistic
imagination—seem, in the long decadence of Romanticism, to replace more and more the male ogres of its
earlier phase; and this too is what we should expect.
For masochism seems to be a secondary development
from sadism (so that masochistic cases under treatment
may pass back through a sadistic stage on their way to
health). Why? Because, it seems, the sick soul that
craves sadistic satisfaction is often tormented by a guilty

[1] For fuller details of this chapter of human imbecility see my *Decline
and Fall of the Romantic Ideal*, ch. ii. Much of the argument in this
chapter has already been given in that book. But one needs little psychology
to learn that in this world it is necessary to repeat truths to get them
listened to; after which the hearers often end by thinking they knew
them all along.

fear of punishment; it may acquire a habit of running to meet the suffering that will expiate its sin, rather than bear the suspense of awaiting it; until, at last, this penalty of indulgence, now paid beforehand, can become an indulgence in itself. (We may recall Samuel Butler's ironic suggestion that if the headache came before the drinking, instead of after, drinking would become virtuous; for the masochist, it is often as if he actually put this into practice; until finally the headache itself becomes the pleasure.) So cunning is the human mind at building tortuous and twilit labyrinths in which it plays its ghostly part as Minotaur, or victim, or both at once.

There is no question of condemning Romantic art simply because, like much medieval religion, it found inspiration at times in sadism and masochism. These are ugly names for ugly things, yet none of us is without traces of both. The fault of the Romantics lay in growing too obsessed by them. Thus *La Belle Dame sans Merci*, slightly masochist though it is, remains for me Keats's best poem—its bitterness is free from those traces of syrup which make sticky and cloying a good deal of his earlier poetry. But Flaubert's *Salammbô*, despite magnificent passages, was largely a folly; Wilde's *Salome*, despite exquisite sentences, largely *une pourriture*. Flaubert was very true to life when he made his Madame Bovary pursue her own pathetic damnation by nightlong reading of 'tableaux orgiaques avec des situations sanglantes'. (Her Rouen was not yet blessed with cinemas.)

> C'est l'Ennui:—L'œil chargé d'un pleur involontaire,
> Il rêve d'échafauds en fumant son houka.
> Tu le connais, lecteur, ce monstre délicat,
> Hypocrite lecteur—mon semblable—mon frère.[1]

Swinburne's work, again (for instance, *Chastelard, Anactoria, Phaedra, Dolores*), shows many symptoms of

[1] Baudelaire.

this malady; and it reappears to mar the close of Flecker's *Hassan.*

Another neurotic strain in Romanticism was its pre-occupation with incest—not a subject much discussed by the normal civilized person. But to our primitive ancestors it was, on the contrary, a matter of violent struggle, as can be seen from the legends on which Aeschylus based his *Suppliants* and Sophocles his *Oedipus.* It is indeed one of the defiles through which our species has had to struggle on its way from brute to man. And in periods of decadence this theme has a way of raising its head again—as in the *Hippolytus* and *Aeolus* of Euripides (who treats the subject with a passion foreign to his fellow-dramatists); in Jacobean playwrights like Ford and (to some degree) Webster[1]; and again in the Romantics—in *The Mysterious Mother* of that pre-Romantic, Walpole; in Chateaubriand's *René*; in Byron's *Manfred* and *Parisina*; in Shelley's *Laon and Cythna* and *The Cenci*; in Ibsen's *Ghosts, Rosmersholm,*[2] and *Little Eyolf*; in D'Annunzio's *La Città Morta.*

Thus in its beginnings Romanticism was an idealistic anarchism; but, inevitably, the anarchy tended, especially in France, to eat up the idealism; and the decadence of the movement sank towards a Satanic chaos, where

---

[1] This theme is obscurer in Webster than in Ford : but it is there. It appears between Romelio and Jolenta in *The Devil's Law-case,* and between Cesario and Clarissa in *The Fair Maid of the Inn* (attributed to Ford, Massinger, and Webster). But these are of minor interest beside *The Duchess of Malfi,* where Duke Ferdinand's rage at his sister's re-marriage otherwise lacks motive for its extreme frenzy. As, indeed, his brother the Cardinal feels (II. v. 86) :

CARD. : Are you starke mad ?
FERD. :   I would have their bodies
    Burnt in a coale-pit, with the ventage stop'd,
    That their curs'd smoake might not ascend to Heaven :
    Or dippe the sheetes they lie in, in pitch or sulphure,
    Wrap them in't, and then light them like a match.
(Cf. IV. ii. 300-6.)

[2] Rebecca displaces Beata in Rosmer's heart as she had once displaced her mother in her father's.

writers grown half infantile defied common sense and
social sense alike. It was as if European literature
between late eighteenth and mid-nineteenth centuries
passed largely through a fit of Dionysiac intoxication,
sometimes beautiful, sometimes degraded; until this
reaction against eighteenth-century rationalism produced
in its turn a further reaction into nineteenth-century
Realism. To some extent this was a reversion to
eighteenth-century reason; but other qualities that great
century had prized did not so easily return—its sense of
dignity and grace and composure, its aristocratic contempt for *mauvais goût* and *mauvais ton*. It is not hard
to see social and economic reasons why.

Like a Nile flood, Romanticism brought both a golden
harvest and a crop of monsters. Dealing with its psychological side, I have necessarily paid more attention
to the monsters. But these need not blind us to the
harvest. There was a healthy Romanticism also. Few
writers of any age have been more sanely vigorous than
that passionate Romantic, William Morris—largely, I
think, because he was a passionate Realist also, and
balanced his dreaming brain with the busy hands of a
master-craftsman. But one has only to turn from him
to his master Rossetti, or his friend Swinburne, to breathe
again a sultrier and unhealthier air. The Romantic
rebellion was inevitable; it was needed; it was valuable:
but again and again the Romantic rebel sank from
Prometheus Unbound to Lucifer—or lower.

Indeed it seems that we can already see something of
a forerunner, and a type, of Romanticism in Milton's
Satan, that primal Rebel, that incarnation of the revolt
of the Son against the Father, of the imperious ego
against the restraints of necessity and the laws of society:

> O Heav'n that such resemblance of the Highest
> Should yet remain, where faith and realtie
> Remain not!

Let us turn back to him for a moment. What was Milton's own attitude to the Prince of Hell? For this problem, too, illustrates how lack of psychology can lead critics to misinterpret. It has been argued that Satan is really the hero of *Paradise Lost*; it has been as passionately denied. But surely both parties have absurdly oversimplified the question. 'If Milton', writes Dr. Bowra, whose criticism one must always respect, 'felt unconscious sympathy for Satan, it is surprising that he should have also felt horror for his hatefulness.' This seems itself a most astonishing comment. There is nothing in the least unusual about such a doubleness of attitude (or 'bipolarity', for those who love technical terms). Writers have stated that simple truth long before Freud—Catullus, torn between love and hate of his Lesbia; La Rochefoucauld, in his observation that violent love can more easily turn to loathing than to indifference; Mr. James Stephens in a poem of years ago—*Hate*:

> My enemy came nigh;
> And I
> Stared fiercely in his face:
> My lips went writhing back in a grimace,
> And stern I watched him from a narrowed eye:
>
> Then, as I turned away,
> My enemy,
> That bitter-heart, and savage, said to me:
>
> '—Some day, when this is past;
> When all the arrows that we have are cast;
> We may ask one another why we hate? . . .'
>
> But I fled quickly: fearing, if I stayed,
> I might have kissed him, as I would a maid.

Turn to a typical case-history. Here is a wife that loves her husband so terribly, she cannot let him take his hand from hers. Every ten minutes of the day she has a compulsion to utter the prayer: 'Dear God, keep my husband and children safe.' And yet this is not how normal lovers behave. Slowly, under analysis, the truth comes out—the secret wish that she dared not face, the small voice in her that she drowned as with a roll of drums—the hidden hope that her husband might indeed be run over and so leave her free. 'Methinks the lady doth protest too much.' In the same way many a rabid anti-clerical will turn out to be suffering inwardly the fears and scruples of an excessive pietism.

So Milton, I feel, was inwardly divided, with sympathies on both sides. With his conscious intention he stressed Satan's folly and painted his swift, sure degradation towards toad and snake. And yet who can read the first two books of *Paradise Lost* without seeming to catch a tremor of enthusiasm in Milton's voice as he describes the dauntless resolution of his great Rebel—as dauntless as some of the fallen regicides of England's Commonwealth?

After all, it is nothing new for a character to run away with its creator. We cannot control our dreams; we can only partly control, or seem to control, our daydreams. So Dido seduced Virgil. His theme demanded that his readers should sympathize with his hero, the ancestor of Rome; not with the foundress of Carthage, Rome's deadliest enemy. Yet in that great fourth book of the *Aeneid* the ghosts of Euripides' Phaedra and Medea, of the Medea of Apollonius (and who knows what other memories from Virgil's own earlier years?) rose up around this forsaken Queen; till, unawares, Virgil made his Trojan hero odious and, for the moment, stultified his whole epic. None the less he had produced its most moving episode.

So too Shakespeare with Shylock. Shakespeare did not set out to write Zionist propaganda. Indeed his hero and his heroine and his hero's benefactor all beckoned him into the opposite camp. And yet somehow, with his

imaginative sympathy, Shakespeare caught so vivid a
vision of the world as seen through the eyes of this
persecuted Israelite, that the balance of his play suddenly
tilted like a ship whose cargo shifts under the beating of a
gale; till spectators of the Trial Scene cry out, like the
young woman overheard by Heine in the theatre, 'the
poor man is wronged'. Similarly, I believe, with
Falstaff; whose genial girth grew till it overshadowed
his not too generous prince, and whose 'perpetual gaiety'
so bewitched our older critics, like Morgann and Coleridge, that they brought fantastic arguments to prove
him brave and highly intellectual. Modern criticism,
leaping to the opposite extravagance, tries to blacken
Falstaff and to whitewash Prince Hal. But surely matters
are not so simple. Poets' purposes are not so steadfast
and straightforward—they can often become cross-purposes. One may create a character, like a child; but
live characters, like live children, may not prove easy to
control. Again and again our criticism proves too
ignorant of the human mind.

Therefore it seems to me perfectly possible that part of
Milton—most probably without his knowledge—identified itself with this unfilial Son of God, especially at the
opening of *Paradise Lost*; just as another part of him
identified itself with the filial Son of God in *Paradise
Regained*. Rebel to the backbone—rebel against his king,
against the Presbyterian tyrants who tried to replace that
king, against the censors of the press, against the deniers
of divorce—passionate and splendid voice of freedom that
he was—we yet know that Milton was himself a tyrant
to his children and his schoolchildren. This is surely
clear, without blackening his character like Mr. Robert
Graves in his novel on Milton's first wife. Aggressive
authority—aggression against authority—both were there.
The real trouble is not, I feel, that Milton made his rebel
angel too sympathetic, but that he made his Almighty

Father so unsympathetic—a pompous personage against whom many of us would have gladly joined any revolt that offered the least chance of success.

Under the banner of the Rebel Angel would certainly have marched many of the Romantics—among them, Blake and Burns, Shelley, Byron, and Alfred de Vigny.

VII

Blake, Shelley, Dionysus

The wise want love; and those who love want wisdom;
And all best things are thus confused to ill.

SHELLEY.

THE Romantic revolt was needed. But it became a revolution. And, like almost all revolutions, it went too far. For humanity, as Erasmus said, is like a drunken rider falling off his horse alternately to left and right.

And so, although the Romantic Movement did great things, its decline was often swift and its fall was sometimes far.

> Ma jeunesse ne fut qu'un ténébreux orage,
> Traversé çà et là par de brillants soleils;
> Le tonnerre et la pluie ont fait un tel ravage
> Qu'il reste en mon jardin bien peu de fruits vermeils.
>
> .   .   .   .   .   .
>
> Ne cherchez plus mon cœur; les bêtes l'ont mangé.[1]

We have seen how Romanticism looked back to that Miltonic Satan (himself influenced by the Satan of Marino) who has left his traces on heroes like those of Mrs. Radcliffe or of Byron, or the Karl Moor of Schiller's *Robbers*, and who seemed to Baudelaire the most perfect type of male beauty. Characteristically the first famous utterance of sympathy for Milton's Rebel Angel came from that pre-Romantic, William Blake.[2] No doubt it is

[1] Baudelaire.
[2] Compare also Burns on his 'favourite hero': 'I have bought a pocket Milton which I carry perpetually about with me, in order to study the sentiments—the dauntless magnanimity; the intrepid, unyielding

exaggerated to say, in Blake's words, that 'Milton was of the Devil's Party without knowing it'—it might have been better to say, not 'Milton', but 'part of Milton'. But this recurrent link between Romantic revolt and filial resentment against the Father grows clear enough in Blake himself. Enough to quote a foolish but illuminating poem of his—'To Noboddaddy' (that is, the 'Daddy' who is yet 'Nobody'):

> Why art thou silent and invisible,
> Father of Jealousy?
> Why dost thou hide thyself in clouds
> From every searching Eye?
>
> Why darkness and obscurity
> In all thy words and laws,
> That none dare eat the fruit but from
> The wily serpent's jaws?
> Or is it because Secrecy gains females' loud applause?

Here is enough filial rebelliousness for the most Freudian mind. (In a more veiled form the same feeling towards the Eternal Father had produced the Mariolatry of the Middle Ages.) 'The Devil's account', says Blake, 'is that the Messiah fell, and form'd a Heaven of what he stole from the Abyss.' Yet one cannot build one's habitation on the Abyss. Blake might dwell with pleasure on the idea that Raphael died of dissipation; but to die of dissipation cannot be really very amusing. And though in our own age of controls we may feel a certain sympathy towards anarchism, anarchy has one serious drawback—it only becomes feasible by removing to a desert island. And a desert island, even if liberally populated with angels, would scarcely have satisfied Blake himself. He seems to have safeguarded his theories by a certain caution in practice. Some later Romantics were less cautious. They paid.

independence, the desperate daring and noble defiance of hardship, in that great personage, Satan.' (To William Nicol, June 18, 1787.)

The shoe of civilization often pinches and lames. The Romantics set about loosening its laces. Their next step was sometimes to kick the shoes off. But on the stony thoroughfares of modern life that will not work, either. We cannot go back to our own childhood, nor to the childhood of our race.

A vivid example of the suffering that attempts to do this can cost, is provided by a more famous Romantic than Blake—by a poet whom Francis Thompson called (too narrowly) 'the eternal Child'. Shelley took over Blake's sympathy with Satan; even on Dante he lavished the curious praise of being the 'Lucifer' of his age. For Shelley detested alike his earthly and his Heavenly father. By the standards of his time that poor, bewildered, limited gentleman, Sir Timothy Shelley, seems to have been, at first, a quite fond and well-meaning parent; but his punishment for begetting a genius was to have toasts drunk by his son, even at school, 'to the confusion of my father and the king'. 'I think', wrote Shelley later, 'were I compelled to associate with Shakespeare's Caliban, with any wretch—with the exception of Lord Courtney, my father, Bishop Warburton, and the vile female who destroyed Mary—that I could find something to admire.' And again, in a letter to that father himself: 'Think not I am an insect whom injuries destroy . . . had I money enough I would meet you in London and hollow in your ears Bysshe, Bysshe, Bysshe . . . Bysshe till you're deaf.'

Hence his efforts to find a substitute father in Dr. Lind, then in the awful Godwin. Even behind the Jupiter of *Prometheus Unbound* lurks still poor Sir Timothy. Aeschylus had in the end reconciled Prometheus with the Almighty Father. But that past compromise revolted Shelley—Jupiter must be hurled to the bottomless pit. Milton cast down his great Rebel to irrevocable ruin; Shelley cast down God. In Aeschylus, on the other hand, the end had been reconciliation; there are advantages in the good sense of Greece.

But for Shelley there could be no reconciliation with that paternal spectre, even beyond the grave. I cannot believe that Shelley's own feelings are absent from the cry of his Beatrice Cenci:

> Sweet Heaven, forgive weak thoughts! If there should be
> No God, no Heaven, no Earth in the void world;
> The wide, grey, lampless, deep, unpeopled world!
> If all things there should be—my father's spirit,
> His eye, his voice, his touch surrounding me!

At this point many may say: 'I love Shelley's poetry; I am not interested in his neuroses.' That is quite legitimate. No one is compelled to take an interest in the neuroses of genius; but no one is forbidden, either. Further, if one wishes to understand Romanticism and its decadence, here is part of the answer. Finally, I feel that Shelley's poetry is weakened by a certain lack of sanity, which poetry need not lack and the greatest poetry, for me, does not lack. It seems worth asking, more closely, why.

A good deal of new light emerges from the recent Life by Professor N. I. White [1] (who, quite legitimately, refuses to be drawn into psychological interpretations). He makes clearer than ever how tragically Shelley too was entangled with his family. When his mother planned to marry his favourite sister Elizabeth, who had collaborated in his early work, to his own friend Graham, Shelley was so furious that he wrote to his mother accusing her of pushing the match to conceal her own adultery with the young man—'If it is unjust, prove it.' We are used to the eccentricities of genius, especially of Romantic genius; all the same. . . . It implies an abnormal jealousy about mother and sister alike. Next he formed a passionate scheme for marrying his sister to his

[1] See also *New Shelley Letters*, ed. W. S. Scott (1948).

far more intimate friend Hogg. It failed. But that was not the end. When Hogg tried to make love to Harriet, it was not Shelley himself, it now appears, who would have objected, so much as Harriet herself. Stranger still, Shelley actually agreed that Hogg should share Mary Shelley. Mary herself was willing; only circumstances prevented. Yet at the fourth attempt this odd impulse in the two friends to possess a common love did realize itself—though only after Shelley's death. For Hogg lived with Shelley's last idol, Jane Williams, from 1827 till his own death in 1862.

There is also another bizarre impulse that fatally recurs through Shelley's life. Most lovers find that two make perfect company; but certainly not three. Yet Shelley seems never happy without an adopted sister to complete the triangle. First, Eliza Westbrook had to be imported into his marriage with Harriet; then Elizabeth Hitchener. When he had left Harriet, he was still impelled to send her that extraordinary invitation to join him and Mary in Switzerland. Then Mary in her turn had to be supplemented by Claire Clairmont,[1] Emilia Viviani, Jane Williams. Life cannot have been easy for Mary when, for example, in the raptures of *Epipsychidion* Emilia became the sun, herself merely the moon—even if this sun was speedily eclipsed. But uneasy lies the head that marries genius.

The probable explanation of all this is not difficult to find, especially in conjunction with works like *Laon and Cythna* and *The Cenci*. Shelley, it would seem, failed to surmount the primitive loves and hates of childhood. It is far less rare than most realize for a boy's passion for his mother to transfer itself, often unconsciously, to a sister (in whom that mother reappears in younger

[1] Professor White argues against the view that Shelley's illegitimate child, whose existence recent research has ferreted out of the Naples archives, was Claire Clairmont's. I do not find his arguments convincing. But, after all, what does it matter now?

form). After all, it has been a theme for drama from Euripides' *Aeolus* and Ford's *'Tis Pity* to Ibsen's *Little Eyolf* and D'Annunzio's *Città Morta*. And readers of Dorothy Osborne will recall how her brother Henry was so passionately possessive about her that his letters, she says, would have been taken by any stranger for love-letters to a mistress and he revolted at the idea of her marrying for love—whence his frantic antagonism to the suit of William Temple.

Here is a modern instance. A medical student of twenty-five suddenly broke down and could not work. He went to a psychologist who was presumably an Adlerian, as he attributed the crisis to excessive ambition. One day the patient announced that he proposed to commit suicide. The psychologist replied that he was being ridiculous and just trying to excite pity. The young man retorted by going home and duly shooting himself. However, the wound was not fatal. After recovery he was brought to Stekel. It emerged that he came from a happy home; the only other child was a sister now married. 'How did you feel about your sister's wedding?' 'I was wildly gay—no one had ever seen me so happy.' 'What was the date when you shot yourself?' 'December 6th.' It was the first anniversary of that wedding.

Analysis revealed that he had secretly hoped the marriage would prove unhappy. It did not; on the contrary, a few days before his attempted suicide his sister had told him she was going to have a child. He felt himself separated from her for ever. And despair overwhelmed him.

In the end he was brought to realize his real attitude of mind and—the vital point of psychotherapy—to face and *accept* reality. He was cured, resumed his work, and married happily.

But in less fortunate cases this fixation on mother or

sister can lead to homosexual tendencies, though the
sufferer may not realize them himself. Hence, I believe,
not only was Shelley driven constantly to supplement his
love-affairs by adding a sister-substitute; he and Hogg
were also impelled to try to share the same passion, as an
unconscious substitute (this impulse is common enough
—there is, for instance, a similar story of Beaumont and
Fletcher) for a direct relationship. No doubt, Shelley
rationalized his own motives into a protest against the
tyranny of current convention: but that is not wholly
convincing. The curious form taken by this protest still
needs to be explained.

It was possibly this same homosexual tendency in
Shelley which kept him restlessly searching, through his
brief life, for a feminine ideal that he never permanently
found, though he so often dreamed he had found it—in
Harriet Grove, Harriet Westbrook, Elizabeth Hitchener,
Cornelia Turner, Mary Godwin, Claire Clairmont, Sophie
Stacey, Emilia Viviani. Like one type of Don Juan, he
could never discover the woman he really wanted because part of him, unconsciously, was seeking something
'passing the love of women'.

It ceases to be surprising that a mind so torn with
conflict should have suffered so, to the point of attempting
suicide; or that those conflicts should have haunted him
with nightmares and hallucinations. After the supposed
nocturnal attack on him in Wales he sketched his
assailant on a screen; this screen he subsequently burnt,
but a copy of his sketch is reproduced by Professor White;
it shows a figure with horns! (Presumably he had seen
his own worse self, projected as a *Doppelgänger*.) Again,
shortly before his death he walked in his sleep with a
fantasy of strangling Mary; which suggests that part of
him had turned against her also.

Little wonder, too, that one with so much to struggle
against should have found his perfectionist optimism

darkened at times by utter despair. A new pathos
gathers round lines like those in the *Triumph of Life*:

> Into this valley of perpetual dream,
> Show whence I came, and where I am, and why—
> Pass not away upon the passing stream.

'The eternal Child'—this refusal to grow up was,
indeed, his tragedy (as in a different way it was Swinburne's). Yet in spite of it he could earn from Byron
(whose work and life were similarly haunted by the
obsession of incest) that impressive praise—'the best and
least selfish man I ever knew'.

That Shelley was, in some ways, sick in mind, as Keats
in body, does not alter this. Dig up the roots of any tree
and you will find them a good deal less sightly than leaf
and blossom. It is the fruits, not the roots, that matter.
Supposing his neurosis had been spared him, or had been
cured, would he have been as good a poet? Or a better
one? I do not know. He might have caused less
unhappiness in his lifetime; but he might have given
less happiness after his death. My aim here is not to
pass moral verdicts, but to try to understand.

It has seemed worth dwelling on Shelley's personality,
first because such things are interesting to those who
wish 'rerum cognoscere causas'; secondly, because it
appears typical of the maladies to which Romanticism
was predisposed—this is one more example of what may
come of living too much according to the gospel of
William Blake; thirdly, because, I believe, his poetry
becomes clearer—and more poignant—after it.

Yet I understand now, also, the instinctive distrust I
have always felt for Shelley's ideas. I think one glimpses
at once, if one is sensitive to such things, how neurotic
those ideas are. For many, I know, that only increases
their appeal. It would, perhaps, be unduly cynical to
sum up Shelley's Utopia as a world where all persons

in authority and all elderly gentlemen (except a few benevolent white-haired hermits) are knocked on the head, so that the young may then fall into each other's arms in rotation, singing Hymns to Intellectual Beauty, and refreshing their enthusiasm with meatless dishes. But his world remains, I feel, a daydream world. 'He has no eyes', said William Morris. It seems to me true. Saintsbury and Cazamian have judged Shelley the greatest of modern lyrists; that, for me, is fantastic: but it remains a matter of taste, not of argument. Yet it seems arguable that mankind has been better enriched by other poets who, with equal beauty (in many eyes, at least), have achieved a deeper and saner view of life.

To the devout this will, no doubt, seem damnably faint praise. I can only plead that some famous judges have been far unkinder to Shelley's fame. To say nothing of Hazlitt, Carlyle, and Arnold, there is Patmore's comment: 'Most of his poems—even his most celebrated, as *Prometheus Unbound*—is all unsubstantial splendour, like the transformation-scene of a pantomime, or the silvered globes hung up in gin-palaces. He is least unreal when he is wicked, or representing wicked people, as in *The Cenci*.' It was perhaps a little cruel of Patmore thus to exploit Shelley's own comparison of himself to a gin-palace. But the simile may remind us that there is a presiding spirit of Romanticism still older and more appropriate than Milton's Satan—Dionysus; and that there are Romanticisms far earlier than those of the eighteenth and nineteenth centuries—a Romanticism in the Alexandrian literature of declining Greece and of Roman imitators like Catullus and Propertius; another Romanticism (beginning with writers like Apuleius) through the centuries that saw the decline of Rome into the Middle Ages.

After all, this remains one of the fundamental problems in life, in art, in politics—how to be stable without growing stagnant. That is 'stable' which can stand. But Time will not let us stand still—it keeps us moving. For a moment—in the Athens of Pericles, the Rome of Augustus, the China of the T'ang, the France of Louis XIV, the England of the Augustans—life seems clear; passionate still, yet balanced. But this balanced world of Sophocles or Horace, of Po-chu-i or Racine, cannot endure. Either storms sweep it suddenly away, or calm breeds a decadence that wastes it in a long decline. Plato's abiding city remains a dream: St. Augustine's also. As at ancient Delphi, Apollo, it seems, must reign by turns with Dionysus. In politics, perhaps the happiest solution of this problem of combining balance with growth, stability with elasticity, has been provided by the England of the last three centuries with its continuous 'revolution by due course of law'. Only after reading the history of less happy lands does one realize how much more than mere rhetoric lives in the words Shakespeare gave his dying John of Gaunt. English government and English poetry seem to me, with all their faults, two of the greatest contributions to civilization that any nation has ever made.

We cannot, as individuals, choose the sort of age we are born in. But we can decide what sort of temper and attitude towards life seems to us best—and at least aim at it, for ourselves and our children. That is why I dwell on these aberrations of uncontrolled Romanticism —not from the mere curiosity of historian or biographer, but because I believe passionately in the value of balance for a happy and useful life. Let us enjoy the Sirens' singing; but remember their claws.

In art this balance, this gift of serving both Apollo and Dionysus, is, as I have said, more difficult still. The artist tends by nature to be passionate, primitive, Dionysiac. The conflict that was to take so many forms in the last two thousand years has never been better symbolized than by one of the first of all European Romantics, Euripides.

The old poet of eighty had turned his back on a mocking, embittered Athens and removed to the Court of Macedon, in the still half-savage north. There he saw revealed, as never before, that wild, primitive energy which civilization has to tame—yet dies if it tames too rigidly. For the garden-rose *must* grow grafted on a wild-briar root; yet the briar is always trying to thrust up its own shoots into the light and turn all back to green thorns again.

In *The Bacchae*—that epilogue to his long experience, and farewell to life—Euripides shows the rigid King Pentheus trying to repress a fanatic enthusiasm which he abominates for its loosening of all law, its ecstatic denial of sober reality. Yet it proves perilous to strive with eternal forces. Pentheus is torn piecemeal by the Maenads; as, eight centuries later, Hypatia was to be torn piecemeal by other fanatics, at the instigation of the Christian bishop of Alexandria. Dionysus has many incarnations.

Euripides could himself well understand this struggle. For the Romantic in him was joined with a Realist and a Rationalist as well. But I cannot share the view that sees in *The Bacchae* his recantation of his lifelong rationalism. Are we to suppose that this most compassionate of Greek dramatists meant his audience to admire a deity that drove a mother to rend in ghastly communion the flesh of her own son? It seems to me simply that in Macedonia Euripides realized at last the terrible strength of the primitive in man—how mad to ignore it, how vain to wave it away. The problem of finding outlets for this violence that millions of years have bred in us through the ceaseless struggle for existence challenges us still to-day, more urgently than ever.

Perhaps we are no nearer its solution. We are only learning anew that this violence can be made more dangerous still by too much repression, as by too little; by thwarting human personality (alike in child and adult), as by over-indulging it. The Dionysus of *The Bacchae* remains, for me, still the vividest symbol of all Romanticisms—their passionate beauty, their primitivism, their ecstasy, but also their potential cruelty, decadence, and bestiality.

Here too psychological knowledge can throw some light on certain details of the play that at first sight may strain belief. The infectious spread of this Bacchic frenzy through Thebes finds plenty of parallels in the records of revivalism. Repeatedly crowds have developed mass-hysteria, often characterized by an infantile sadism that recalls the havoc of the Bacchanals and their rending of animals limb from limb. The mob becomes like a great, savage child. Voltaire has described an outbreak in the Swiss Jura where women actually devoured infants. The matter was ascribed to witchcraft and six hundred persons doomed by a single judge. In other cases whole convents are recorded as seized with a collective mania and barking like dogs; or mewing like cats, till soldiers had to be sent to bring the nuns to reason. Even in the nineteenth century a certain Methodist sect in Kentucky and Pennsylvania worked up a convulsive ecstasy in which they ended by running about on all fours, yelping like hounds. Here, indeed, the moral suspicions of King Pentheus seem to have been justified; for three nights of such devotional exercises are said to have produced eighty illegitimate children within a radius of four miles. True, the Maenads do not seem to have imagined themselves animals; but they imagine their victim Pentheus to be a lion. And legend made Dionysus himself sometimes bull, sometimes goat, sometimes lion. The fact that such frenzies can really occur does not perhaps make *The Bacchae* more interesting; but it makes life so.[1]

But Dionysus can perhaps lead us deeper still into the dark thickets of the primitive. In *Totem and Taboo* Freud has suggested that long before the beginning of history men lived, like some apes, in groups led by a single male, the jealous lord of his harem and his young. But already the younger generation could knock imperiously at the door. One day his grown sons would find courage to knock the patriarch on the head and eat him (just as Uranus fell by his son Cronus, Cronus in his turn by Zeus). Yet on that grim communion would follow a sense of guilty awe that was to leave lasting memories in human evolution. From this source, Freud suggests, grew up the totemistic type of ritual under which members of a totem-clan would on sacred occasions gather to kill and eat together the otherwise sacred and untouchable totem-animal from which, with their childish oblivion of the barriers between human and animal, they believed their clan to spring. On this theory the tearing in pieces of Pentheus, Orpheus, Osiris, Dionysus himself would be a shadowy remembrance of the fate of the *Urvater*, or the enactment of a like fate suffered in retribution by the rebellious Son. Reik (*Imago* IV, 1915-16) has found elaborate analogies in the initiation-rites of savage tribes, when the young reach the door of manhood; and suggests that Greek tragedy itself was in essence a presentation of the suffering of Dionysus (and later of other heroes in his place) for the guilt of *Hubris*—the primal rebellion.

These suggestions seem highly ingenious, and no less highly speculative. It is not altogether easy, though not necessarily impossible, to harmonize this stress on a

---

[1] The Maenads' habit of twining serpents round them actually existed in Macedon even after Euripides' day. It was practised by Olympias, mother of Alexander the Great.

rebellion in the '*Urhorde*' with the other aspect of gods like Adonis, Attis, Osiris, or Dionysus, as personifications of the rebirth of natural life each spring and its dying away as autumn comes again. But whatever the truth about their misty origins, Dionysus in the pagan world, as Satan in the Christian, remains the immortal embodiment of those untamed forces in the human soul which we find it so hard to live with, or to live without. To reconcile Apollo with Dionysus, self-mastery with self-abandonment, remains the supreme problem of civilization, even more to-day than three thousand years ago. For the Maenads had no atom-bomb.

VIII

Romanticism in Decay: Poe, Surrealism

Ah! wherefore all this wormy circumstance?
Why linger at the yawning tomb so long?
KEATS.

I understood almost nothing of what I read,
and this in itself filled me with pride and
satisfaction.
SALVADOR DALI.

ROMANTICISM, like many Romantics, died comparatively young. That was natural. Neo-Classicism in decline became a bore—but bores can live long: Romanticism became decadent—and decadents mostly die quickly. Let us turn to a typical figure of that decadence.

Edgar Allan Poe has, for some reason, tended to impress the French more than ourselves; just as continentals still often value Byron and Wilde far more highly than English readers can. Perhaps, with all three writers, it is partly a matter of style, about which a foreigner is naturally less sensitive, even if he reads English. For all three (though Byron seems to me far above Poe) tend to be over-emphatic, histrionic, and yet careless. Indeed Pater preferred to read Poe disguised in French.

At all events not only did Poe deeply impress his translator Baudelaire; he has now been thought worthy of analysis in two vast, but arresting volumes by Princess Marie Bonaparte. He remains, indeed, yet one more example of the neurotic whose soul gets caught in the web of childhood. (Fate, one might say, in early years largely moulds our character; then the resulting character largely moulds our fate.) When his mother, an English actress, died of consumption, the boy was adopted by the wealthy Allans. He grew to love his adoptive mother as deeply as he detested his adoptive father. Then he became devoted also to the mother of a school-friend, Mrs. Stanard, who soon afterwards died mad. The boy of fifteen haunted her grave; and it was she that inspired *To Helen*. Five years later death struck a third time—Mrs. Allan died. His step-father prevented Poe from arriving in time to see her; he could only visit her grave also, in the same graveyard where lay 'Helen'. Now he found a fourth mother in an aunt Mrs. Clemm (whom he called 'Muddy'); and six years later he married her daughter Virginia (whom he called 'Sis'). She was only thirteen, 'white as chalk', and destined in her turn to die of consumption, like his mother and so many of his heroines.

> I could not love except where Death
> Was mingling his with Beauty's breath.

Already he had developed his lifelong tendency to self-frustration (whether with the object of plaguing the detested Allan, or of punishing himself, or both); and his other tendency to take refuge from these intolerable conflicts in alcohol and opium. In 1843, for example, he visited Washington where he was to lecture and be interviewed by the President, thanks to the friendly interest of the President's son. What more natural than that he should wreck the whole plan by staging one of his drunken bouts, which prevented both lecture and interview?

All through his life and work Marie Bonaparte traces a combination of sadism and necrophily. Always he was

[133]

haunted by the maternal figures of the dead women he had loved. Their spectres reappear in such poems as *To Helen, Annabel Lee, The Raven,* and *Ulalume.* In *Ulalume,* for example, the poet, accompanied by Psyche, the ideal, maternal image who forbade him the normal love of happier men, sees rise before him the planet Venus, the star of the passionate Astarte; despite Psyche's reluctance, he responds to its call; but, as he hastens in pursuit, he finds his way barred:

> stopped by the door of a tomb,
> By the door of a legended tomb.

His prose-stories are still more significant, in their obsession with teeth, graves, and maternal images. (I must add that many of them seem to me ghastly trash.) In *Berenice* (which might be a dentist's nightmare), Egaeus pulls out, in a trance, the teeth of his entombed fiancée; and finds, on returning to his senses, that the corpse must have been still alive. For not only are there thirty-two little white objects in a box on his table: there are nail-scratches in his flesh.

In *Morella,* a woman of that name dies (needless to say, of consumption), leaving a daughter. Not till ten years old is her child baptized. 'What name?' asks the priest. The widowed father murmurs 'Morella'. With a fiendish expression the girl replies, 'I am here!' and falls back dying. When she is buried in her mother's tomb, that mother's body is found to have disappeared. She had been reincarnate in her child (as Poe's own mother in his child-wife Virginia).

In *Ligeia* another wife dies. Removing from Germany to England, the widower weds a new bride, Rowena. She too dies (Poe's climate is not healthy). But at midnight the corpse revives. The husband finds, amazed, that its hair has changed from gold to black. The first wife, Ligeia, had fought her way back from the

Kingdom of Death to replace her supplanter (again the motif of Poe's dead mother returning as his wife).

In the *House of Usher* and *The Oval* we have the same monotonous obsession—a dead sister buried alive and breaking from her tomb; or a wife who slowly fades away (yet again) in consumption, as her artist-husband completes her portrait on his canvas (another variation of the *Doppelgänger*). In *The Assignation* mistress and lover find a mystic union by simultaneously poisoning themselves in their respective palazzi at Venice; while the hated Allan reappears as the mistress's odious elderly husband. He is again reincarnated in *Metzengerstein* as the old Count Berlifitzing, who is burnt when his stables are fired by the hero, Baron Metzengerstein (whose mother, of course, had died of consumption). But retribution waits. A giant horse (naturally, with terrible *teeth*) in the tapestries of Metzengerstein comes mysteriously to life. The Baron makes it his favourite mount; but one day Metzengerstein's own castle takes fire and the demon-horse bolts with him into his flaming home (a symbolic reunion of Poe with his mother in death; compare the disappearance of the dead Usher and his sister Madeleine in *their* castle, which is not, indeed, burnt, but engulfed in a lake). The association of love and fire lies deep in the human mind; and criminal incendiarism seems often to take its rise from starved affection.

There is no time, nor need, to multiply instances— the womb and suckling fantasies of *Arthur Gordon Pym*; the reappearances of the hated Allan in *The Man of the Crowd, The Cask of Amontillado, The Tell-tale Heart*, and *Hop-frog*; the womb or castration fantasies of *The Pit and the Pendulum, Never Bet the Devil your Head*, and *The Black Cat*; the *Doppelgänger*-motif in *William Wilson*. 'It is idle to be assiduous in the perusal of inferior poetry.' Those who find these interpretations far-fetched should turn to Marie Bonaparte's own exhaustive volumes. Personally I feel that, though one may remain dubious about details, in general she has made a convincing case.

On one rather important point, however, I cannot agree with her penetrating book—that is when she maintains the 'high cathartic value' of Poe's work to the reader (though doubtless it was a valuable release to Poe himself). 'Catharsis' is a Greek idea; but I doubt if Greek good sense would have much admired Poe. The artists of Hellas did not deal in skulls and cross-bones and the rakings of charnels. And Aristotle, who first brought 'catharsis' into criticism, was so far from taking it to justify the writer's choice of *any* subject, however morbid, that he even objected to certain moderately villainous characters in Attic tragedy as needlessly vile.

Aristotle thought that the normal man's tendencies to an excess of pity or fear might be relieved by moderate indulgence; but that is very different from suggesting that indulgence is a cure for proclivities like sadism and necrophily. Suppose the appetite grows with the eating? Would one show crime-films in Wormwood Scrubs? St. Augustine tells how his friend Alypius had such a horror of bloodshed as to shun all gladiatorial shows. One day some friends dragged him there and he sat with eyes buried in his hands—till, seized by curiosity at a sudden shout from the spectators, for a moment he opened his eyes and looked. From that moment gladiators became his passion. The hidden tiger in him had tasted blood. Mud-baths can benefit the body: it seems less clear that they can be relied on to cure the soul.

To normal people, I suppose, Poe is unlikely to do much harm that life would not do anyway. But for the neurotic? (And how many of us are completely balanced?) Certainly Poe's work is capable of stamping itself deeply on such imaginations. Stekel records a patient who became asthmatic in the presence of cats. Had he read Poe's *Black Cat*?[1] No, never! Yet the very next day he brought two whole pages of excited comment on this very story, from an old diary of his own. For it had deeply appealed to certain homicidal impulses in his Unconscious. Did it aggravate them? Who shall say?

For myself, I find that psychological explanations, while they can even deepen the interest of masterpieces like *Hamlet*, seem on the contrary to destroy whatever perverse power writing like Poe's may exert upon the nerves —just as analysis can destroy neurotic fantasies. It is as if one flashed an electric torch on some seedy medium at a *séance* and found the spectres dissolved into tatters of frayed muslin. The intellect was never deeply involved; now even the flesh ceases to creep.

Some lines of Poe's poetry endure; he did much for the detective-novel (if that be a great service); but his horrors seem to me of small value to the healthy, and perhaps the reverse of valuable to those who are not. Strindberg so admired Poe that he at one time imagined himself a reincarnation of the American (unfortunately for this theory, Poe did not die till October 1849, while Strindberg was born in the previous January); but perhaps both these writers are really more interesting for their tragic lives than for their work.

Judgements of value, however, must wait till later; we are at present concerned with interpretation. I would merely suggest that it is worth asking why so many modern writers and artists have been neurotic or definitely insane. There were no Poes, nor Strindbergs, by the Ilissus. It is only since the earlier eighteenth century that this tendency to derangement has become conspicuous; only since the Romantic Revival that it has

---

[1] The black cat which, walled up with the murdered victim, betrays the murderer is, like the Greek Erinys, an incarnation of evil conscience.

become so common. Those who can regard it without a certain disquiet are optimists.

I have suggested that Romanticisms have as their common element a lifting of controls—the controls exerted on the more primitive and impulsive side of the mind by its sense of reality and its sense of society. It was to be expected (since there are always people who never know where to stop) that this lifting of controls would sooner or later be carried to the extreme limit—to utter anarchy. That point some art of the twentieth century has reached—till it seems hardly possible to go much further.

For a time in the nineteenth century Romantic tendencies slackened. One may even see a sort of semi-Classical revival in writers like Tennyson and Arnold in England, the Parnassians or Anatole France in France. And Realism became more powerful than ever before, in the work of Zola, the Goncourts, Maupassant, George Moore, Arnold Bennett, Wells. Others, like Balzac, Stendhal, Flaubert, Dickens, Ibsen, Hardy, Kipling, Synge, and Proust, were Realist or Romantic by turns. Even Zola had also his Romantic side.

But the twentieth century was to bring, as in politics, so in literature, frenzies unparalleled in the nineteenth. It was as if, with the growth of science and industry, the burden of an ever more artificial and repressed existence provoked new paroxysms in the savage under our skins; as if the narrowing of the cage produced in the human gorilla only more frantic efforts to break loose; as if humanity itself were nearing the verge of nervous collapse.

Already before the First World War came Marinetti with his Futurist Manifesto of 1909, clamouring to destroy 'the museums and libraries which cover Italy with so many cemeteries'. 'To admire an old picture is to pour out our sensitiveness into a funeral urn, instead of casting it forward in violent gushes of action. The admirable past may be balsam for invalids and for prisoners; but we will have none of it, we the young, the strong, the living Futurists. Come then, seize the pick-axes and hammers! Sap the foundations of the venerable cities. We stand upon the extreme promontory of the centuries; why should we look behind us? Would you poison yourselves by a knowledge of history? Do you want to decay? Would you waste your strength by a useless admiration, from which you can but emerge exhausted, reduced, downtrodden?' 'We wish to glorify war—the only health-giver in the world . . . the beauti-ful ideas which kill.'

The Romantics of a century before had sought to flee from the present to the past—to 'old, unhappy, far-off things'. This new Romantic shouted to flee into the future. *Plus ça change.* . . . But the future has one disadvantage as compared with the past—it is quite un-known. Already Signor Marinetti is almost forgotten. Yet it was as if he spoke for some deep human death-wish. His dream was to be grimly realized in two wars more destructive of our past heritage than anything accomplished by Napoleon. What Marinetti dreamed, Hitler did. The voice of Art, even of pseudo-Art, is often strangely prophetic.

During the first of these two World Wars Dadaism was born (1916) and was succeeded by Surrealism (1922) —the effort to create as automatically as a dream 'in the absence of all control by the reason, and outside all aesthetic or moral preoccupations'—in short, without reality-principle or ego-ideal. 'In Surrealism one relives the best of childhood.' 'The best of childhood', however, appears to include the most primitive and tedious obsessions with excrement, cruelty, masochism, fetishism, Narcissism, cannibalism, and necrophily.

The Secret Life of Salvador Dali, by himself, is likely

long to remain—at least, one hopes so—one of the most curious documents of literary history. Here, as in so much Surrealist art, the artist seems vainly struggling to psychoanalyse himself in public. One climax in the book is provided by an American Surrealist ball given in the author's honour, which included society ladies almost naked, with their heads in bird-cages, or with wounds, or mouths, or eyes painted on all parts of their persons—'eyes grew on cheeks, backs, under arms, like horrible tumours'. (Presumably even these advanced ladies were ignorant of what the eyes symbolized.) A gentleman clad in a bloody shirt bore, poised on his head, a bed-table, whence flew suddenly a flock of humming-birds. The author's wife appeared as 'an exquisite corpse', with a doll on her head to represent a child's body being devoured by ants, while its skull was gripped in the claws of a luminous lobster.

Signor Dali, however, affects to be even more astonished than astonishing. 'Take such a simple thing as amusing oneself by derailing trains! . . . And what a negligible percentage of those who have a passion for derailing trains ever put it into practice! . . . I cannot understand why man should be capable of so little fantasy. . . . I do not understand, I cannot understand, why toilet manufacturers do not put concealed bombs in the flushing-compartments of their products, which would burst when certain politicians pulled the chain. . . . I do not understand why, when I ask for a grilled lobster in a restaurant, I am never served a cooked telephone.' Signor Dali at all events has never suffered from such 'flabbergasting normality': to woo his future wife he covered himself, he tells us, with goat's dung boiled in fish-glue. But it is interesting that when it comes to carrying such plans through, there are some limits even for Salvador Dali. He did not, after all, pay his addresses in this attire.

His artistic products were to match—films in which a blind man is ill-treated, a dog run over, a son killed by his father on the spur of the moment, a girl's eye slashed out by her lover with a razor—pictures where dead donkeys putrefy on top of grand pianos or a mannequin's corpse rots in a taxi, crawled over by edible snails. The world, it seems, was getting ready for that more prolific artist, Herr Himmler.

It remains interesting that, unlike many modern painters, Dali *can* draw and, unlike many modern writers, *can*, after a fashion, write. It is as if *their* folly concentrated on absurdity of form; his, on absurdity of content. 'Damn braces, bless relaxes.' Yet one may wonder if even Blake would have been wholly happy in his posterity.

I will not pretend to take very seriously this final *reductio ad absurdum* of what began a century and a half before as the Romantic movement. One is told, indeed, that in the nightmare of the modern world art has no longer any answer but *l'affreux rire de l'idiot*. But why? Europe, even now, must surely be a good deal less uncomfortable than it often was in the Middle Ages. But the Middle Ages did not limit themselves to *l'affreux rire de l'idiot*; they produced, along with much that was mad, the towers of Canterbury, and the *Canterbury Tales*.

Milton saw *his* ideals crash amid the Saturnalia of the Restoration; but he did not indulge in 'the frightful laughter of the idiot'; he wrote *Paradise Lost*. Wordsworth saw *his* ideals crash in the French Revolution— and wrote *Resolution and Independence*. Byron saw *his* crash and wrote, not only *Don Juan*, but the *Isles of Greece*. He did even better than write—he went to Missolonghi.

I do not grasp why, because the first War was grim and the Peace disappointing, there should have been nothing left but 'the frightful laughter of the idiot'. Do

not some of us indulge in too much self-pity? If everyone in Western Europe had taken this feeble view, we
should not be here at all. We should probably be dead
—or worse. If one feels like that about life, instead of
trying to demoralize the rest of mankind, why not hop
over the nearest cliff? 'The frightful laughter of the
idiot' seems best left—to idiots.

Sometimes I wonder if the end of human civilization
might one day come, not from atom-bombs, nor world-
famines, nor anything so spectacular, but simply from a
decay of man's intelligence and self-control under the
strain of a too artificial civilization. I do not say it seems
to me likely; merely possible; especially after reading
or looking at modern art of this type.[1] The Elizabethans
thought visiting Bedlam great fun; to us, their taste
seems odd; but apparently it is less extinct than we
supposed.

Conclusions? They seem to me clear. I have been
accused of 'being hard on Surrealists'. I think it is
Nature that they will find hard. In dealing with
decadence She can be slow; but She is terribly sure.
'*L'affreux rire de l'idiot*'? It is not the idiot that laughs
last. It is the children of the healthier young generations
that Nature has so far always known how to bring from
somewhere, to fill the place of stocks and races that rot.

The literature of the twentieth century has contained
much Romanticism, much Realism; both, very often,
of the most debased type. If I were asked what qualities
I missed most in the work of the last fifty years I should
reply, I think—'Wisdom, and dignity'. Some of you
might do worse than try to contribute a little towards
their return.

---

[1] Cf. Henry Miller, ' Open Letter to Surrealists Everywhere ': ' We
have had traitors to race, country, religion, but we have not yet bred any
real traitors, *traitors to the human race*, which is what we need.' (Italics in
original.) Yet it seems to me that there have been, and are, only too
many such traitors—at least in the world of art.

IX

Surrealism (continued), Wit

One leg across his wide arm-chair,
Sat Singleton, and read Voltaire;
And when (as well he might) he hit
Upon a splendid piece of wit,
He cried: ' I do declare now, this
Upon the whole is not amiss.'
And spent a good half-hour to show
By metaphysics why 'twas so.

LANDOR.

I HAVE had a frank and amusing letter from one of you, pleading against my cruelty to Surrealists. 'You approve of Freud; and yet you disapprove of Salvador Dali; who, in so far as I can understand him, is merely trying to transplant the findings of psychoanalysis into art.'

But I do not think there is any real analogy. The scientist who investigates typhoid bacilli and the 'carrier' who disseminates them are, indeed, both busy with typhoid bacilli; but they do not seem equally valuable. I am not urging that Surrealism should be suppressed by the police. I distrust the police as art critics.[1] I think

---

[1] Compare the antics of the Austrian and Papal censorships in nineteenth-century Italy. When a dumb man in a play expressed by gestures his joy in returning to his ' native land ', the censor commented : ' Gestures of this kind are obviously of a very revolutionary tendency and cannot possibly be allowed. The only gestures that I could think of permitting would be gestures expressive of a dumb man's delight in scenery generally.' In the stage-direction ' native land ' had accordingly to be replaced by ' land-scape '. Another censor insisted that a poet who had written of ' the beautiful Italian sky ' should substitute the proper official expression— ' the beautiful Lombardo-Venetian sky '. Even the twentieth century could scarcely do better. (See Oscar Wilde, *A Critic in Pall Mall*, ' Madame Ristori '.)

the suppression had better be left to Nature, who may prove, in the long run, more ruthless than any police. But if the writer should be free, so should the critic. And here I believe it the critic's duty to speak clearly, without that moral cowardice about discussing the moral implications of literature which makes most modern criticism, at bottom, so frivolous and so futile.

I am not arguing about tastes. If people enjoy poetry like—

> The quarrel between the boiled chicken and the ventriloquist
> had for us the meaning of a cloud of dust
> which passed above the city
> like the blowing of a trumpet . . .

or—

> une fois mort on mettra un dirigeable sur mes yeux
> je partirai par la porte de sud-ouest
> j'entrerai dans le petit café-tabac où l'on vend de si beaux
>   dés à coudre en chair d'enfant nouveau-né
> un repas me sera servi dont je ne mangerai rien . . .
> je boirai seulement la mer
> dans mon lit—

why, then, they enjoy it. But when writers sell their fantasies of coprophily and necrophily, of the sadistic slapping of old women's faces, of chopping out girls' eyes with razors, and all the other neurotic orgies [1] offered by

---

[1] Among the spiritual ancestors claimed by Surrealism — Swift (!), Maturin, Pétrus Borel ' le lycanthrope ', Gérard de Nerval, Baudelaire, Rimbaud—a high place is given to Lautréamont (Isidore Ducasse), ' par excellence the Surrealist '. Here is a specimen (quoted by Dr. Praz in La Carne, La Morte, e Il Diavolo) : ' On doit laisser pousser ses ongles pendant quinze jours. Oh ! comme il est doux d'arracher brutalement de son lit un enfant qui n'a rien encore sur la lèvre supérieure, et, avec les yeux très ouverts, de faire semblant de passer suavement la main sur son front, en inclinant en arrière ses beaux cheveux ! Puis, tout à coup, au moment où il s'y attend le moins, d'enfoncer les ongles longs dans sa poitrine molle. . . . Ensuite on boit le sang. . . . Bande-lui les yeux, pendant que tu déchireras ses chairs palpitantes ; et, après avoir entendu de longues heures ses cris sublimes . . . comme alors le repentir est vrai ! ' (A declaration and love-scene follow.) After Sachsenhausen and Auschwitz,

this movement to a Europe that has shown itself only too
sadistic and neurotic already, *then* it seems to me not
unimportant to point out that such day-dreams can be
dangerous—not widely dangerous, perhaps, for the
masses are hardly likely to be much interested in the
antics of a few 'intellectuals'; but dangerous to many
individuals of unstable balance. There is no lack of
them in the world to-day. One may, of course, shrug
one's shoulders and say 'What do they matter? It is
only Nature's way of weeding out the weak.' But that
seems a little harsh; and rash.

I came recently on a curious case recorded by Dr.
Clara Heppel in the *Zeitschrift für psychoanalytische
Pädagogik* for December 1927. In the previous Sept-
ember, during repairs to the drains of Paris, workmen
suddenly encountered a wild figure who could hardly
speak intelligibly. He was finally identified by the
police as a respectable bookseller, M. François Dublot,
who had vanished some twenty years before, after a
woman he loved betrayed him. Since then he had lived
in the sewers. He had found a passage leading down to
them from the market, and came up each night to feed
on refuse and drink water from a leaky pipe. He knew
nothing of what had happened in the upper world—
nothing even of the World War. And he begged only
to go back to his quiet life as sewer rat. For there in the
womb of earth he had found peace and escape from a
reality grown too cruel.[1] (Some might see in him a

---

it is not so easy to dismiss such literary fantasies as mere imbecility without
consequence.

> Yet bards like these aspired to lasting praise
> And proudly hoped to pimp in future days.

[1] A similar case occurred recently in New York, where one Paul
Makushak, aged thirty-three, was found to have spent the last ten years
in a small sealed cubicle, six feet by three, in his parents' house, because
'he did not like the way the world was going'. His mother, the only
sharer of his secret, fed him through a trap-door, while his father
imagined him in Canada.

symbol of the future for mankind, if it cannot abolish war.)

It is a striking case, psychologically. Here in a crudely literal form is that idea of earth as sheltering mother and of the happiness of the unborn in the womb which has moved so many poets. You remember Homer?

> So she said; but already, in the arms of the nurturing earth
> Both lay, in Lacedaemon, dear land that gave them birth.

And the old man in Chaucer:

> And Deth allas ne wil not have my lif.
> Thus walk I like a resteles caytif,
> And on the ground which is my modres gate,
> I knokke with my staf, erly and late,
> And saye 'Leeve moder, let me in'.

And Housman:

> Men loved unkindness then, but lightless in the quarry
>   I slept and saw not; tears fell down, I did not mourn;
> Sweat ran and blood sprang out and I was never sorry:
>   Then it was well with me, in days ere I was born.

But it is one thing to utter these momentary yearnings for that sheltering darkness to which we shall all one day return; it is quite another to take up one's residence in the sewers of Paris—or of the Preconscious. I think Surrealism unhealthy; and I feel that one should say so.

And yet perhaps, in a way, one should be glad that modern movements like Surrealism go as far as they do. If we are to have drunken Helots, let them be roaring drunk. If there must be follies, let them be carried to lengths of cretinism that sicken even those whom more moderation might have deceived. In this one respect at least there is a family likeness between Surrealists and Kremlinists.

All the same some of you, I may add, to judge by letters I get, seem unduly depressed by the modern world—it is so awful, you complain, and modern litera-

ture is so awful; there is no longer any tradition; no
longer any idiom one can write in. But why? The
English tradition is still there—and the English tongue.
And if modern literature is 'awful'—what an opportunity! If it was full of Wordsworths and Goethes, *then*
you might perhaps despair. But as it is . . . here is your
chance to go and do better!

Let us turn back now for a moment from Romanticism in corruption to a quality valued far more by
neo-Classics than Romantics—wit. For, instead of the
raptures of intoxication, it requires, on the contrary,
human faculties at their keenest and most concentrated.
Yet even here, it turns out, the Unconscious plays an
important part.

The psychology of wit has been exhaustively discussed
by Freud in *Der Witz*, with that gift he had for discerning
the bizarrerie of things to which custom makes most men
blind. One could wish that the specimens of wit he
chooses were sometimes less Teutonic, less elephantine.[1]
At moments the English reader is moved less to laugh
than groan; and is tempted to recall that malicious
French anecdote of the German who thought to show
vivacity by jumping out of the window. But, after all,
humour is a wine that travels particularly ill through
space or time; and the material worth of Freud's book
is not essentially impaired by its awful examples. I trust,
however, that French and English literature may afford
us some rather livelier wit to examine than he has
chosen to give.

Freud deals first with Wit, then with Comedy and
Humour; but I think it will be easier to take the wider
problem of Comedy first.

Why do we laugh? Because, it appears, we acquire a

---

[1] E.g. one Jew meets another Jew and looks at his beard : ' You had
beans for dinner yesterday '—' No, the day before yesterday.' It is hard to
see what place this sort of thing has in a book on ' Wit '.

sudden surplus of psychic energy, which we then release in these curious convulsions. There is a type of rubber pig which on deflation utters a piercing squeal. Laughter seems not unlike. A sudden release of tension finds a noisy outlet.

As an elementary type of the Comic, Freud instances the ludicrously excessive effort spent on some simple physical task by a small child, or a clown. The difference between the immense energy which they employ (and which, by empathy, we dimly imagine ourselves employing) and the modest force we should ourselves use in their place, becomes available for discharge in laughter.

And yet, Freud argues, when we laugh at a schoolboy's howler, we feel, on the contrary, that the delinquent has used far *less* thought than we. The reason why we are tickled by greater *physical* but smaller *mental* effort than we should ourselves exert, is that we have grown in the course of evolution to value mental exertion more, and physical less.

This explanation I find far-fetched. The candidate who writes in a Tripos paper (alas!) that 'the Renaissance was partly due to the fall of Constantinople and the flight of the Schoolmen' (when he meant 'scholars') or that 'the poet is a man who is specially sententious' (when he meant 'sensitive'), has not necessarily expended *less* effort to arrive at his absurdities. When Mrs. Malaprop talks of an 'allegory' on the banks of Nile, she may have cudgelled her brains more, not less, than the ordinary person would in saying 'alligator'. Is it not simpler to suppose that here the surplus energy for laughter arises simply because, where we expected to meet a serious statement, we suddenly find ourselves confronted by mere childishness? The whole situation abruptly collapses on to a lower level. We relax and break into laughter, as a stream that comes to a sudden drop in its course may break into foam. At the same time we have a feeling of superiority. Hence Hobbes's description of laughter as 'a sudden glory'—that is, sense of triumph.

Take a rather more complex example—one of Freud's more amusing instances. A small girl of twelve and her brother of ten were acting before the family a play of their own invention. They represented a poor fisherman and his wife; the husband decided that he must seek his fortune elsewhere; and in Act II he returned, after several years' absence, with a fat purse of earnings. When he had related the success of his labours, his faithful wife modestly replied 'I too have not been idle'; and, opening the hut-door, she revealed asleep a row of twelve doll-children. At this point the young performers were bewildered by a roar of laughter from their audience.

Now this laughter was not in the least hostile or hateful, as some misanthropes have pretended all laughter to be. But the sudden drop from sympathetic interest in the reunion of long-parted lovers, acted with all the seriousness of childhood, to this unconscious absurdity, proved too much. It would have been a very restrained family that controlled its mirth. For not only is there the comic collapse with its sudden release from gravity; there is also a release of sexual inhibitions—a sudden excuse for not being perfectly proper, which we shall find important in some forms of wit also. The energy available for laughter here comes from both sources—from the relaxation of serious attention and from the relaxation of habitual propriety.

It may well be, as Freud suggests, that much of the Comic consists ultimately in suddenly seeing our fellows as childish by comparison with ourselves; as when we smile at Horace Walpole's young lady of St. Helena who thought 'there must be a great solitude in London as often as the China ships came away'.

Or, again, there is the anecdote that tells how after some social function Swinburne was so enraged by failing to find his top-hat in the cloakroom that he flung on the floor all the other top-hats within reach and performed a war-dance on them; after which he suddenly remembered that he had left his own at home.

Or there is Hardy's tale of the Wessex rustic who drank plentifully on his last sixpence at the Oak Inn by the simple device of filching it over and over again from the till, being 'too honest to take any money but his own'. If he really believed this, it would be naïve comedy; if he only pretended to believe it, the comedy would become ironic or *narquois*; and his excuse would acquire an element of wit.

On other occasions the difference in potential, released as laughter, may be due less to the difference of level between ourselves and the object of our mirth, than to the sudden drop in our own attitude of respect towards that object. A child sitting on, or running after, its hat will hardly provoke a smile; but if we substitute an archbishop and his top-hat, perfect gravity may become less easy. It used to be told that Lord Curzon once described some popular festivity as 'what I believe the lower orders call a "béāno"'. The point of the story lies in the patrician pride of Lord Curzon, so grotesquely contrasted with his ignorance. 'From the sublime to the ridiculous is only a step', as Napoleon callously observed when he regained Poland, leaving behind him the roads of Russia black with the frozen corpses of his Grande Armée.

This sudden deflation or collapse, which appears to be the essence of comedy, shows itself again in the story of Burke, at the climax of a tirade on the French Revolution, flinging a dagger like a carving-knife on the floor of the Commons—only to have his high tragedy turned to farce by the ironic voice of Sheridan inquiring through

the hush, 'Where's the fork?' Or there is the climax
of the curse in Mr. James Stephens's poem:

> May she marry a ghost and bear him a kitten, and may
> The High King of Glory permit her to get the mange.

Thus the deep seriousness of feature and manner
cultivated by some comedians or jesters explains itself by
their desire to increase the height from which the collapse
takes place.

Needless to say, this laughing release of tension can be
checked by the presence of serious emotion—pity, fear,
hatred, or moral repulsion. If the clown's red nose were
genuine and revealed scirrhosis of the liver, or if the
archbishop hurt himself sitting on his top-hat, only
sadists would laugh. 'The laughable', said Aristotle, 'is
some defect or deformity *neither painful nor hurtful*—
like the distortion of the comic mask.'

Often indeed, if we look deeper, the comedy disappears.
'This world', said Horace Walpole very truly, 'is a
comedy to those that think, a tragedy to those that feel.'
And Hardy was of the same mind:

> Tragedy is true guise,
> Comedy lies.

It would not be hard, for example, to write round
Falstaff a tale of grim tragedy, if only we followed
further and deeper the fates of his fellow-revellers,
doomed at last to perish without mercy in hospital or on
the gallows; of his dupes, his victims, his cannon-fodder
recruits, left maimed or lifeless on Shrewsbury field. Of
that potential tragedy Shakespeare sketched only Falstaff's
final disappointment and his death. The rest is laughter.
The dramatist is ruthless enough with his puppets; but
he keeps his audience on the surface, where mirth is not
marred by deeper sympathy. In Richmond Roy,
Meredith took a not dissimilar figure, but created a story
distinctly more tragic in tone than Falstaff's.

Or, again, comic laughter may be inhibited by a sense of personal dignity, as in Chesterfield or Fontenelle with their refusal to do more than smile ('je ne dis jamais Ah-ah-ah'). Or comedy may be crushed by a too critical intellect—so that men will laugh, when alcohol or herd-hysteria has partly numbed their judgement, at what in soberer states they would greet with a yawn or a smile of pity.

Mimicry can be comic partly because it selects and collects crude or clumsy traits that are less striking in isolation, partly because a human trait seems cheapened by the mere act of reproduction. For the dignity of the individual is lessened when another can exactly reproduce him. We may recall Bergson's identification of the comic with an apparent mechanization of life; but this seems too narrow an explanation for comedy in general.

Even so, mimicry generally prefers to increase its emphasis by exaggeration, as in caricature, parody, or travesty. When Butler writes in *Hudibras*:

> And like a lobster boil'd the Morn
> From black to red began to turn,

the essential comic collapse from serious respect to derision is produced by substituting for the idea of Dawn as a beautiful and majestic thing—Homer's 'rosy-fingered Eos'—this abject image from the fish-market.

A poet may indeed unintentionally seem to parody himself, as Wordsworth in his adaptation of *Helen of Kirkonnel*:

> Proud Gordon cannot bear the thoughts
> That through his brain are travelling,
> And, starting up, to Bruce's heart
> He launched a deadly javelin.

The reader who expects serious poetry on a tragic theme and is confronted, instead, by such prose, crowned by an atrocious rhyme, feels a comic collapse which he cannot understand Wordsworth's failure to see for himself.

[150]

In fine, the comic collapse seems to occur when, in comparing the performance of another with our own, we gain a sudden sense of his inferiority, or when the contrast is not between another and ourselves, but between our initial respect for a situation and its sudden drop to triviality. This effect is much increased if we simultaneously find the situation an excuse for relaxing the energy we normally expend in inhibiting our own aggressive or sexual tendencies—as if a policeman at a gate were suddenly swept away by a merry mob. Indeed a great deal of our laughter draws on this release of human aggressiveness; as can be seen from the aggressive tinge implied in several terms for by-forms of humour—satire, irony, sarcasm, the sardonic.

Darwin derived our friendly smile on meeting acquaintances, which brings into play the same muscles as a dog snarls or grins with, from an original baring of the teeth for an encounter. ('Je revois', wrote Jules Renard, 'dans tous les sourires, des dents de cannibales.') Freud, on the other hand, associates man's smile with the satisfied grimace of the baby on its mother's breast. I suppose laughter may similarly go back ultimately to something like the convulsive chatter of an angry ape, or of a cat at the bird beyond its reach. But it remains clear enough that it would be as rash to call all laughter malicious, as all smiles.

Humour has been neatly defined as a sense for incongruities, in contrast to Wit as a sense for resemblances. But it may be suspected that this is more epigrammatic than true. By humour we seem generally to mean no more than a gift for seeing the comic in situations or persons, even when it is not obvious, or masked by inhibiting causes; particularly in those situations where it is hardest to see comedy, because they concern, perhaps painfully, the person a man tends to take most seriously of all—himself.

Here is perhaps something analogous to the healing value of artistic creation. As the artist lives out his conflicts in creation, while the criminal turns them against society and the neurotic against himself; so the mind with a sense of humour can create from its own troubles a comic situation, with the momentary distance and detachment of a mere onlooker, and with the consoling satisfaction of a semi-artistic activity.

This gift has been not least among the military qualities of the British soldier, who prefers to *Marseillaises* or *Hymns of Hate* wry remarks about 'the seven first years of a war' being always the worst or old soldiers never dying. Similarly war-stricken Berlin under Hitler could still devise its imaginary dialogue between Optimist and Pessimist:

OPT.: We shall lose the war.
PESS.: But when ?
OPT.: And then we shall all have to go and beg.
PESS.: But from whom ?

And, again, not even Secret Police can prevent the oppressed masses of Russia from enjoying at moments a like comic relief—'There is going to be a centenary monument to Lermontov.' 'What will it be?' 'A colossal statue of Stalin with a volume of Lermontov in one hand.'

But here we have reached the problem of Wit.

Freud, who was perhaps a little inclined to take everything back to the infantile, suggests at the close of *Der Witz* that Comedy, Humour, and Wit may be three ways back towards the light-heartedness of childhood. Wit, in particular, he explains as follows. When we are small we enjoy mere nonsense and playing about with words. As we grow up, our critical reason gradually forbids this childish pleasure. Yet we still find a way back to these verbal enjoyments of the nursery, while placating the critical adult within us, by taking some idea that rises in our Preconscious to the brink of utterance, plunging it for a moment into the Unconscious[1] where it plays childishly with words or with nonsense in such a way as yet *also* to make sense, and producing the resulting compromise as wit. Thus the child in us plays with the nonsense; the adult in us is placated by the sense; and the energy employed to inhibit the irrational within us can then release itself in laughter. It is as if some suspiciously grotesque character got past a customs-officer by presenting an impeccable passport; the lynx-eyed official relaxes his vigilance; and life surges gaily forward.

As an example of this childish play with words, Freud quotes the father who summarized the professions of his four sons, two surgeons and two singers, by the curt 'Zwei heilen und zwei heulen'—'Two heal and two howl.' Other instances he gives are 'tête-à-bête' (for enjoyment of the sole company of some imbecile), or 'a young man with a great future behind him'. One might add Wilde's description of a week-end in a country-house as 'ordeal by tattle', or Mrs. Carlyle's reference to a young couple as heading for 'a lawful catastrophe'.

Of apparent *nonsense* as the basis of wit, I know no better examples than Horace Walpole's comment on some social upstart: 'I thought he had not had a grand-father since the Creation, that was not born within these twenty years' (compare the still bitterer 'Nobody's son has married everybody's daughter'); or Donne's

> For the first twenty years, since yesterday,
> I scarce believed thou couldst be gone away;

or Swift's 'nine days every week I dine at home'.

---

[1] Indeed the Unconscious can sometimes be witty by itself, in dreams (as when Verrall dreamt he looked out of a train and saw a large notice, 'Epic Cycle Works') or in misprints (as in Freud's story of the newspaper that, describing a distinguished gathering, referred to some military dignitary as 'the battle-scared general'; when this roused indignation, the next issue apologetically explained that of course the phrase should have read, 'the bottle-scarred general'). A little thought will quite often

In Freud's own words, to produce wit the senseless conjunction of words or the nonsensical combination of ideas must, all the same, make sense. 'The whole technique of wit-making is devoted to finding such words or such constellations of ideas as will allow this condition to be fulfilled.'

Now it is quite true that adults do still enjoy word-play and nonsense. To none should that be clearer than to the English, whose greatest poet seems to have derived a quite sickening amount of enjoyment from the feeblest puns. Indeed in England word-play and nonsense often do not need to justify themselves by turning out also to make sense. When Lamb asks a friend 'Is that your own hare or a wig?', when Edward Lear celebrates toeless Pobbles, or when Lewis Carroll opens his dream-world of Mad Hatters and Jabberwocks, rationalization of Freud's kind is gaily dispensed with. Nonsense they remain; though the hidden meanings in *Alice* can turn that nonsense into wit.

But though nonsense thus rationalized plays its part in wit, I still doubt if Freud is right in making it the root of wit. For wit seems possible without either the childish word-play or the nonsense on which Freud insists as vital. Take Rochester's

> Here lies our sovereign lord the king,
> Whose word no man relies on;
> He never said a foolish thing
> Nor ever did a wise one.

This portrait of Charles II involves neither play of words nor nonsense; unless it be the nonsense of exaggeration. But if this exaggeration be nonsense, nonsense it remains; it is not, as Freud's theory demands, converted into sense.

Again, when Mrs. Siddons called on Johnson, old and ill in bed, there was no chair in the room—'Madam,'

detect the hidden impulse underlying clerical errors or misprints (I hope there are not too many in this book).

said he, 'you who so often occasion a want of seats to
other people will the more easily excuse the want of one
yourself.' Discussions are always hampered by the incorrigible vagaries in meaning of the words we use; but
this remark seems to me 'witty', though it involves
neither play on words nor nonsense.

Nor is there even a moment's nonsense in Prior's reply,
after he had been shown all Lebrun's pompous glorifica-
tions of Louis XIV on the walls of Versailles—'The
monuments of *my* master's actions are to be seen everywhere but in his own house.'

Turn, again, to Chamfort's summary of love and
ambition—'Amour, folie aimable; ambition, sottise
sérieuse'; or to his definition of society love—'l'échange
de deux fantaisies et le contact de deux épidermes'; or
his brilliant contrast between French and English
character—'l'Anglais respecte la loi et méprise l'autorité;
le Français, au contraire, respecte l'autorité et méprise
la loi.' I find here abundant wit, but no word-play and
no preliminary nonsense (such as there *is*, for example,
in the *mot* of the Abbé Galiani—'Que de gens auraient
peur s'ils osaient!'). When Montesquieu says 'Il faut
avoir beaucoup étudié, pour savoir peu', the apparent
absurdity of paradox is there; but I cannot find it in his
remark to Mme du Châtelet, 'vous vous empêchez de
dormir pour apprendre la philosophie; il faudrait, au
contraire, étudier la philosophie pour apprendre à
dormir'.

Again, when the youthful Curzon in an after-dinner
speech observed that he had always tried to associate with
his intellectual superiors and Monckton Milnes, Lord
Houghton, snorted, 'My God, that would not be difficult!', though the wit may be of a modest order, still it
seems to dispense with that nonsense at first sight on
which Freud insists.

What, then, *is* the essential quality of wit? Often,

indeed, it seems to depend on more causes than one. If we take Freud's distinction between 'harmless' and 'tendentious' wit, it becomes clear that the second kind is the commoner. Wit *is* frequently aggressive (as with the 'bottle-scarred general')—a weapon of attack on persons or laws or institutions; improper wit, again, is a veiled substitute for aggression in another form. Rochester is *attacking* the King, Chamfort the 'love' of elegant society, Montesquieu the pedantry of Mme du Châtelet, Lord Houghton the mock-modesty of Curzon. And the epigram of Rochester provides a good example of how the wit, the grace, the neatness of phrasing, can to some extent palliate the aggression—as a velvet sheath may cover a rapier.

But if we take 'harmless' wit in its simplest form, like Johnson's compliment to Mrs. Siddons, I can see here no essential quality beyond a neat compression of thought and language which presents, for an instant, something like a *riddle* to our understanding. It proves a very simple riddle; we burst through it as easily as through a paper door; in consequence, the energy we had mobilized to meet its challenge turns out largely superfluous. We are left with a surplus for laughter, or at least for a kind of triumphant satisfaction. The opponent we confronted has turned out a mere pigmy. And 'brevity is the soul of wit', because this relaxation of tension must be *sudden* in order to be clearly felt; just as a dam collapsing suddenly may produce a burst of foam, when its gradual breaking or crumbling would not. A joke that is not seen at once, because it is too wordy or too obscure, can rouse no laughter. Nor yet a joke that is *too* obvious.

Secondly, we enjoy also the *aesthetic* pleasure of seeing a thought packed with maximum neatness into minimum space. When Philip of Macedon threatened the Spartans that if he reached Lacedaemon he would leave not one stone on another, with typical laconism they sent him a reply in one word 'EI'—('If').

In other words, it seems to me that we may apply the term 'wit' to expressions that present the challenge of an easy riddle, the neatness of a terse epigram. A witticism is a miniature piece of art. Its production resembles inspiration, in that it generally leaps, like a Jack-in-the-box, straight out of the Unconscious. Conscious thought will seldom produce wit, though it may improve and polish a piece of wit when produced. In fact there are analogies between wit, artistic creation, and dreaming. The pleasure wit gives may be, in the producer, largely the pleasure of minor artistic creation; in the hearer, the double pleasure of solving an easy problem and of appreciating a piece of artistic economy.

It is, I believe, this riddling element that accounts for the prominence in wit of ambiguities and symbols, metaphors and similes. For example, Swift, whose prose is in general so sparing of simile or metaphor, yet employs them brilliantly for purposes of wit: 'The Reason why so few Marriages are Happy, is because Young Ladies spend their time in making Nets, not in making Cages.' 'Old Men and Comets have been reverenced for the same Reason; their long Beards and Pretences to foretell Events.'

The effect here does not seem to me to depend, as Freud says, on some childish delight in nonsense, justified by finding sense there after all; it seems rather a combination of the pleasure of solving a very simple momentary puzzle and the pleasure of seeing so much said, so picturesquely, in so economical and vivid a form. The comparison of old men to comets provides also a *comic* collapse, by which these venerable wiseacres are reduced from patriarchal dignity to sudden grotesqueness.

This element of riddle is particularly clear in that by-form of wit called 'irony'. Originally, with Socrates, irony took the form of pretending to be the simplest, while he was really the shrewdest, of disputants; thence follows our more general use of 'irony' to describe words or actions that turn out to mean the opposite of what they seem to mean. It is in this sense that we speak of the 'irony of fate'. Destiny has smiled—but only to stab.

Ironic wit is particularly fond of the comic collapse; as so often in Pope, whether he is attacking aristocratic patrons:

> But still the great has kindness in reserve;
> He helped to bury whom he helped to starve—

or sentimental wives:

> Not louder shrieks to pitying heaven are cast
> When husbands, or when lapdogs, breathe their last—

or literary enemies:

> To please a mistress one aspersed his life;
> He lashed him not, but let her be his wife.

Wit need not involve laughter at all. It is more likely to bring laughter from the hearer than from the utterer, because the utterer has the labour of producing the witticism; and because he often feels some anxiety about its success; whereas the hearer has neither. But, in cases where both laugh, one might compare the laugh of the wit to the creative cackle of the hen that has successfully laid an egg, the laugh of his hearer to the crow of the cock that feels exhilarated by suddenly seeing the light.

On the other hand, there seems no such cause to question Freud's analysis of 'tendentious' wit—the wit that brings the additional pleasure of releasing inhibitions (just as the medieval jester's frankness was licensed by his power to amuse). Take for example, Talleyrand's comment to the too masculine Mme de Staël, who had put him, in a feminine rôle, into a novel: 'I hear, Madame, that we are both in your last romance, disguised as women.' The adroitness of the phrasing may not have reconciled Mme de Staël to its sneering contempt; but it must have enchanted the hearers. Talleyrand had got the laughers on his side; and, when laughter enters, critical fairness, even codes of politeness, may be swept away. The pleasure of wit can release inhibitions; the release of inhibitions can redouble the pleasure of wit.

Similarly with Wilde's still more brutal retort to Sir Lewis Morris's complaint that his work was subjected to 'a conspiracy of silence'—'Join it!' [1] Here, it seems to me, we have (1) the fraction of a second's puzzlement, followed by the resolution into laughter of the surplus of the energy called up to solve it; (2) the aesthetic pleasure at the brevity; (3) the comic collapse of the injured bard into a mere laughing-stock.

So too with wit that is not verbal at all, like the snuffbox the misanthropic Schopenhauer once planned to have made for his own use. It was to have two chestnuts on its lid, but a leaf to show that they were merely *horse*-chestnuts (for it was this pessimist's complaint that at a distance men seemed human, but at closer quarters turned out little better than apes). A less laborious instance of non-verbal wit is Peer Gynt's peeling of the onion, in symbolic search for the essential reality under his many personalities; only to find, when he has stripped layer after layer, that there remains—nothing! 'Nature', he reflects, 'is witty.' Here too we have the momentary riddle—the aesthetic aptness—the comic collapse. And in both cases there is also the veiled aggressive criticism—of humanity at large, or of Norwegian humanity.

[1] See Hesketh Pearson, *The Life of Oscar Wilde* (4th ed., 1949) p. 98.

A Victorian lady, again, might have found a touch of improper aggression in Belloc's epigram:

ON A ROSE FOR HER BOSOM.

Go, lovely rose, and tell the lovelier fair
That he who loved her most was never there.

But she would have been prim indeed if her inhibitions were not at least temporarily disarmed by the wit (which here again, be it noted, involves neither word-play nor nonsense, merely a momentary riddle). And even prudes might smile at the ingenuity of the Chinese adage corresponding to our 'penny-wise pound-foolish'—'It is useless to go to bed to save the light, if the result is twins.'

A little further help may perhaps be given by the history of the word 'wit' in English. Originally meaning 'mind, reason, sense' ('common wit' meant 'common sense'), it acquired by an easy transition the force of 'wisdom', 'intelligence' (as used by Polonius in that quotation which we now misapply to 'wit' in its modern sense—'brevity is the soul of wit'). Thence, by an easy transition, wit came to be used, a little more narrowly, for 'brilliant intelligence', 'cleverness'. (Compare the evolution of *esprit* in French.) For the early seventeenth century an elephant, a serpent, a judge, or Copernicus himself could all be described as 'witty'. Our limited modern meaning does not seem clearly established before the eighteenth century, though we now tend (anachronistically) to read it into earlier passages. Yet there seems no sign in all this of that infantile quality essential to Freud's theory.

In actual practice, indeed, Elizabethan wit was often only too infantile—a childish playing with words, as when the dying Mercutio sees himself becoming 'a grave man'. But with Donne and the 'Metaphysicals' attention turned more to playing with ideas, or with literal and metaphorical senses of the same word (Addison's 'mixed

wit'). Indeed, like English sport, this play often grew
so over-serious that it ceased to be play at all. When
Cowley compared his mistress's eyes to burning-glasses
of ice, or Donne called a friend taking orders 'a blest
Hermaphrodite', the object was not to amuse the reader,
but to stupefy him with admiration. A Sanhedrin of
owls could not be more solemn. And yet was it really
worth devoting all this mental energy to finding resemblances between hearts and hand-grenades, good men
and telescopes? It showed, no doubt, thought and
patience: but so does the training of performing fleas.
Yet there remained a certain frivolity of mind in thus
confusing genius with the ingenious.

On the whole 'Metaphysical' poetry was, I feel, a
pestilent fashion. Writers like Donne, Herbert, Vaughan
are admirable poets in spite of, not because of, their
'Metaphysical' affectations: by their passion, not by
their conceits. Herbert, indeed, came himself to see the
coxcombry of treating poetry as a trapeze for mental
frisks.

> When first my lines of heavenly joys made mention,
>   Such was their lustre, they did so excel,
> That I sought out quaint words and trim invention,
>   My thoughts began to burnish, sprout, and swell,
> Curling with metaphors a plain intention,
>   Decking the sense as if it were to sell . . .
> As flames do work and wind, when they ascend,
>   So did I weave myself into the sense.
> But while I bustled, I might hear a friend
>   Whisper, 'How wide is all this long pretence!
> There is in love a sweetness ready penned;
>   Copy out only that, and save expense.'

In Marvell and Fuller we can watch laughter beginning
to break in. Marvell's *Coy Mistress* is one of the most
effective of 'Metaphysical' poems just because it has, at
last, acquired a sense of humour. Elsewhere, indeed,
Marvell could owlishly compare distant cattle at pasture

to pimples on a face and expect to be admired for it.
But here, with the vast and 'vegetable' loves of his lady
and himself, or that macabre irony of the grave as 'a fine
and private place', 'Metaphysical' writing has begun,
however grimly, to smile. With Fuller, reproached by
his severer fellow-clergy as a buffoon, the smile becomes
almost a laugh—as when he remarks of tall men, 'oft-
times such who are built four stories high, are observed
to have little in their cockloft'; or again, 'some
serious books that dare flie abroad, are hooted at by a
flock of Pamphlets'.

With the growth of the neo-Classic ideal of a gentleman, it was realized at last that the quality of wit, like
the quality of beauty, 'is *not* strained'. The essence of
wit was now seen to lie in presenting not a difficult
riddle, but an easy one—a pointed rapier, not a monkey-
puzzle. The Metaphysicals had been well pleased to
make their hearers sweat; but now it was for the writer,
or the wit, to take the trouble himself, instead of inflicting
it. The perfect image, or the perfect witticism, should
be like Columbus's trick with the egg, something easy to
understand, though far from easy to think of.

This new attitude brought a vast improvement in wit
after 1660. The eighteenth century, in both France and
England, was probably wit's golden age. From Pope to
Walpole and Johnson, from Fontenelle to Voltaire and
Talleyrand, this period's gift for grace and point remains
unrivalled still.[1]

That this golden age of wit was not also a golden age
for poetry, need hardly surprise. Wit involves not only
the Unconscious, to provide its rough diamonds, but a
trained conscious judgement to polish them. The same

[1] Even on their death-beds eighteenth-century men and women showeu
this superiority in wit over the ages before and after them. See the last
words collected in *The Art of Dying*, by Francis Birrell and F. L. Lucas.
Most charming of them all is the young Vicomtesse d'Houdetot : 'Je me
regrette.'

is broadly true, indeed, of poetry; but with poetry the share of the Unconscious seems far larger; and the state of mind it appeals to is far dreamier, less critically awake. The Romantics restored poetry; but, with a few exceptions, their wit has dimmed. Landor, Byron, or Musset are exceptions; but they are still partly eighteenth-century and anti-Romantic. It is not for witticisms that one would go to Wordsworth or Coleridge,[1] Keats or Shelley, Hugo, Vigny, or Lamartine.

In short, in English up to the close of the seventeenth century 'wit' is applied to clever sayings, whether serious or playful (when Dryden found the essence of poetry in Wit, he simply meant 'brilliance of ideas'); but since then wit has become restricted to clever sayings that have at least a tinge of comedy, even when bitter. 'A clever saying, with a playful tinge'—that is as close as I can come to wit's definition. It tends to have a riddling element, because it is a mental shortcut, an abbreviated thought.

To conclude, one may agree with Freud that witticisms, like literary or artistic inspirations, seem born rather than made—that is, they are conceived at unconscious levels. But I do *not* believe that the process can be analysed into this sort of series: (1) idea in the Preconscious awaiting expression; (2) childish desire to play with words or nonsense; (3) inhibition of this desire by adult censorship; (4) mysterious juggling in the Unconscious which turns nonsense into sense after all; (5) emergence as witticism; (6) laughter from release of the energy previously employed to inhibit childishness. Wit seems to me, on the contrary, a kind of extempore artistry, employing many devices—epigrammatic brevity, symbolism, allusiveness, ambiguity, comparison; and all

---

[1] E.g. Coleridge : ' there are *wrongers* of subjects as well as *writers* on them ' ; ' why is a murderer like an unborn Jack-ass ? '—' Ass-ass-in '. Examples could be multiplied ; but it would be cruelty to readers.

this with a nuance of comedy. The result is something that suddenly challenges the hearer's intelligence by its compression and pleases him by its artistic economy, its simplification, its juxtaposition of unexpected ideas. The challenge is easily met if it is a good witticism—for good wit is neither muddy nor cloudy; the mental energy the hearer has summoned up, but finds he does not need, may then be resolved into laughter; especially if there is a marked comic collapse, or if inhibited aggressive or sexual impulses are simultaneously released. But there need not always be laughter: wit can be mordant or melancholy. The hearer is more likely to laugh than the utterer; the utterer may laugh also, but his essential pleasure remains that of a minor form of artistic creation.

To illustrate wit at its best, at the point where it is passing from jest to real art, yet still, I think, remains witty, let me close with some examples from that brilliant, unappreciated writer Jules Renard, who suffered from being born too late.

La théière fume sa cigarette.

Le chat endormi, bien boutonné dans sa peau.

Dans la grande chambre une mouche cause toute seule.

C'est l'eau qui, la dernière, ferme ses yeux pâles.

Dieu nous jette aux yeux de la poudre d'étoiles. Qu'y a-t-il derrière elles? Rien.

X

Creation and Criticism

*Die Künstler kommen mir oft vor wie Väter
und Mütter, welche recht hübsche Kinder zeugen,
ohne zu wissen, wie es zugeht.*

GOETHE.

A WORD may now be said of the actual processes of creation and of criticism. In creation, our new knowledge of unconscious and preconscious mental activity may provide a less vague approach than rhapsodies about 'inspiration'; which merely means that we get ideas without knowing why, how, or whence. It was picturesque to suppose that these were whispered in the poet's ear by a lady with flowing hair and Greek drapery, called a Muse.[1] But Muses do not abide our question.

Alike in art and science fruitful new combinations of ideas seem to form at levels below our consciousness, by a process not unlike our dreams. We may recall the 'Brownies' who worked in the brain of the dreaming Stevenson. Dickens was asked whence he got Mr. Pickwick; he simply did not know—he just 'thought of Mr. Pickwick'. Writer after writer has borne witness to the inscrutable way in which their conceptions came to them—Blake, Goethe, Coleridge, Byron, Keats, Dickens, Thackeray, Charlotte Brontë, George Eliot, Wagner, Yeats. So Pallas Athene sprang full-armed from the head of Zeus.

On the other hand, though good writers may often

[1] Etymologically *Mousa* (Muse) seems connected with *mania* (madness) and *mantis* (prophet, seer).

feel 'inspiration', 'inspiration' does not necessarily make good writers. E. F. Benson has amusingly recorded how Alfred Austin would dilate on the visits of what he mysteriously called 'It'. But 'It', alas, was capable of dictating:

> They rode across the veldt
> As fast as they could pelt.

Wordsworth again, when good, is so totally different from Wordsworth when bad, that if inspiration did not exist, it would almost be necessary to invent it—for how else could the same man be now so fine, now so abysmal? Yet Wordsworth himself remained, apparently, quite unable to distinguish his false Muse from his true, his Puck from his Ariel.

The gift of invention in art, like the gift of invention in science and manufacture, remains a baffling quality. 'The more this special faculty is examined,' says Professor Hatfield of invention,[1] 'the more elusive and mysterious it appears. So far from its being simply the outcome of the highest degree of normal intelligence, it appears to be possessed by persons whose general intelligence is not of a high order. The "master-mind" equipped with an intimate knowledge of the best practice in art, science, or technology . . . in short, those minds upon whom the continued existence and stability of civilized life depend, are not usually inventive or creative. The inventor is frequently a person of distinctly low general intelligence, with a limited mind and outlook, and an incapacity for practical grasp and decisive, effective action.' Though this is written of inventors in science and industry, it can be applied to many creators in art and literature. Perhaps the ordinary man tends to excessive reverence for these creative gifts, which seem to him sheer wizardry. It does not follow that those who possess them are either wise or good.

[1] *The Inventor and his World*, (1933), p. 7.

A sick oyster may be better at producing pearls than Abraham Lincoln; but that does not put Abraham Lincoln below the oyster. Writers and artists are not invariably the salt of the earth, though they often think so.

The creative process appears such a mystery because much of it goes on and emerges from unconscious levels, with their amazing powers of association. Hence the importance in creative work of some general principle for helping, or at least not hindering, this unconscious or preconscious activity. Thus the French mathematician, Henri Poincaré, found his mental activity fall into three stages—conscious work on a problem; then unconscious work; then conscious work again. The first conscious effort stirred up the ideas; in the next, latent phase, like hooked atoms, they formed new combinations; finally, these emerged into consciousness, to be sifted and criticized.

A similar process in artistic creation is already described by Dryden in his dedication of *The Rival Ladies*: 'This worthless present was designed you, long before it was a play, when it was only a confused mass of Thoughts, tumbling over one another in the dark; when the Fancy was yet in its first work, moving the sleeping images of things towards the light, there to be distinguished, and then either chosen or rejected by the Judgement.'

A still clearer passage has been quoted by Freud from Schiller. In reply to a friend complaining of lack of creative power, the poet wrote: 'The reason of your complaint lies, it seems to me, in the constraint your intellect imposes on your imagination. . . . Apparently it is not good—indeed it hinders the creative work of the mind—if the intellect examines too closely the ideas already pouring in, as it were, at the gates. . . . You worthy critics are ashamed or afraid of the momentary and passing madness that is found in all creators.' Hence

[167]

the weakness of neo-Classicism. And hence that anguished cry of Amiel: 'La critique de soi-même est le corrosif de toute spontanéité oratoire ou littéraire. . . . Par l'analyse je me suis annulé.' It was not really so simple. Amiel's mistake lay, not in criticizing himself, but in being unable to stop criticizing himself. Like too many critics in dealing with the work of others, so he in dealing with his own could not wait—could not surrender himself first, then judge afterwards. But it remains true that the orator who listens too closely to what he is saying, while he says it, is probably lost. 'Il faut brutaliser son sujet.' One must learn to let go.

> They that in play can do the thing they would,
> Having an instinct throned in reason's place—
> And every perfect action hath the grace
> Of indolence or thoughtless hardihood—
> These are the best.[1]

Clearly it becomes vital for thinkers and writers to take practical account of this unaccountable factor of 'inspiration'. There are various ways. The first is to leave time for incubation, like Henri Poincaré; just as we 'sleep on a problem'. 'I have put my characters out to grass', writes Ibsen. 'I hope they will fatten.' Brahms, after beginning a song, might shut his book, go for a walk, and think no more of the matter for half a year. Hence poets, in particular, have often led lives that by ordinary standards of working-hours seemed lazy (like Wordsworth); and poets who had to live too busily, have sometimes ceased to be poets (like Arnold). There are minds that seem to need to lie quiet, like milk, before the cream will rise. Yet perhaps the modern world has been too ready to believe this a necessity. The Ancients, the Renaissance, Goethe—these were surely wiser in their belief that it was better for a man of letters to live also, as a man; not an owl, or a mole, or a butterfly.

[1] Robert Bridges.

Einen Blick ins Buch hinein
Und zwei ins Leben,
Das muß die rechte Form
Dem Geiste geben.

A second principle of importance is to write quickly, easily, without strain. Here, I think, Johnson was wiser in suggesting that one should learn to write well by writing fast, than Quintilian in urging, on the contrary, that one should learn to write fast by writing well. Thus Virgil scribbled a number of lines at the beginning of each day, then spent the rest of it reducing them to a few perfect verses—'like a she-bear licking her whelps into shape'. Similarly Addison wrote fluently, but (except in his *Spectators*) corrected long—indeed, Pope thought, perhaps too long.

Alfieri, again, wrote his verse in three stages, so as to gain speed and freedom. First, he would sketch his general ideas; then, write his text in prose 'without hesitation'; and, finally, versify. We hear of Virgil, Jonson, Goldsmith, Coleridge, and Browning similarly drafting poetry first in prose. There is an example of the process in Rossetti's work—a complete prose version of *The Orchard Pit*, together with a few finished stanzas of its verse-form. Different methods, doubtless, suit different temperaments; but one may wonder if Flaubert, for instance, would not have done better to adopt this way of writing at first fast and freely, however badly, and then revising; instead of laboriously composing eight lines a week under the paralysing stare of his relentless conscience. His practice was based on definite theory— 'Il faut écrire froidement. Tout doit se faire à froid, posément. Quand Louvel a voulu tuer le duc de Berri, il a pris un carafe d'orgeat, et n'a pas manqué son coup.' All the same, it seems possible that Flaubert overrated this value of cold-bloodedness—it belongs to the phase of revision, rather than of creation; and that a certain amount of journalism, written in heat and hurry, might have eased his writer's cramp. As the Chinese painter put it—'Thinkee long, work chop-chop.' Ruskin was emphatic about this (as about most things), that the best work was done easily, however painful the apprenticeship. Similarly Stevenson held that an author should alternately strain and play, strain and play—his playful output would be his best.

I can never read without a glow of liking and admiration for the man who wrote it, that passage which Montesquieu once meant to insert before the second volume of *L'Esprit des Lois*:

Vierges du mont Piérie, entendez-vous le nom que je vous donne? Inspirez-moi. Je cours une longue carrière; je suis accablé de tristesse et d'ennui. Mettez dans mon esprit ce charme et cette douceur que je sentais autrefois, et qui fuit loin de moi. Vous n'êtes jamais si divines que quand vous menez à la sagesse et à la vérité par le plaisir.

Mais si vous ne voulez point adoucir le rigueur de mes travaux, cachez le travail même; faites qu'on soit instruit et que je n'enseigne pas; que je réfléchisse et que je paraisse sentir; et lorsque j'annoncerai des choses nouvelles, faites qu'on croie que je ne savais rien, et que vous m'avez tout dit.

This, indeed, is one of the advantages of gaiety in a writer. It saves him from that self-frustrating passion to write better than he really can, that fanatical word-worship, which is so liable to produce over-artificial work, lacking all grace and lightness of touch.

A third way of releasing the unconscious sources has been found in drink or drugs. Report credited Aeschylus with supplementing his midnight oil by midnight wine; Ben Jonson described how, before working on *Catiline*, he had drunk well and 'had brave notions'; Addison, said a Holland House tradition, used to compose walking up and down a long gallery with a bottle of wine at each end, which he would finish during the operation; and Housman in our own day has told how his lyrics were apt to come to him on afternoon-walks after a pint of beer at lunch. (It will be remembered that alcohol does not stimulate the brain, it merely stupefies the critical censorship.) Others, like Coleridge and de Quincey, Crabbe and Francis Thompson, have turned to opium. But it remains dubious whether it is wise in the long run to dope Pegasus; though, of course if a writer can inspire himself, like Schiller, on the smell of rotten apples, there seems no great objection.

But a sounder way, surely, of gaining ease and avoiding these self-conscious inhibitions is to be found in mastering one's craft so completely that it becomes second nature.

> True ease in writing comes from art, not chance,
> As those move easiest who have learned to dance.

Dryden in old age attained the final fluent grace of his *Fables* from having written rhymed couplets by the ten thousand all his life. 'Ce La Fontaine', says Paul Valéry, 'qui a su faire, un peu plus tard, de si admirables vers variés, ne les saura faire qu'au bout de vingt ans qu'il aura dédiés aux vers symétriques, exercices d'entre lesquels *Adonis* est le plus beau.' And Professor Livingstone Lowes has traced in the *Road to Xanadu* how Coleridge produced the vivid imagery of *The Ancient Mariner* by steeping himself in countless voyagers' tales, till memories and images by the score had accumulated and coalesced and bred freely in his mind.

It is important also, even for vigorous creators, to employ an artistic economy of effort, where that is possible. Genius may sometimes be the art of taking pains; but it may also show itself in avoiding them. By stealing the plots of his plays Shakespeare could keep all his mental energy for perfecting them. He was too original to fuss about originality; that can be left to those who have none.

On the other hand, the free flow of ideas from uncon-

scious levels can be seriously weakened by overwork
(Malherbe maintained that after a hundred lines of verse
one should rest ten *years*!) and stimulated by change.
Hence the importance for creative writers, if they cannot
rest, of at least varying their activity. Scott flatly denied,
from his own experience, the supposed advantage of
concentrating on one thing at a time—on principle he
always kept several irons in the fire. It is probably not
uncommon to find that one's best ideas on a subject are
apt to come while one is reading about something totally
alien. It was by the Second Cataract in Egypt that
Flaubert cried, 'Eureka, eureka! Je l'appellerai Emma
Bovary!' And Tennyson composed

> Break, break, break
> On thy cold grey stones, O Sea,

not on the seashore, but in a Lincolnshire lane.

Lastly, inspirations from this mysterious source are apt
to vanish as mysteriously as they came, unless they are
noted at once. Hence Pope's merciless dragging of his
amanuensis out of bed on freezing winter-nights, and
Coleridge's loss of the end of *Kubla Khan*, and Samuel
Butler's insistence on the need of a notebook to 'put salt
on the tails' of ideas.

But the Unconscious, like other indispensable servants,
can grow as insufferable as a spoilt child, if not kept in its
place. It may have been true for poets like Ronsard,
Gray, or Shelley that their power to compose depended
on moods wholly out of their control. But this notion
roused the honest scorn of Johnson ('a man can always
write if he sets himself doggedly to it') and of Trollope.
True, it is easier to make oneself write prose than poetry.
And yet if Shelley's passive waiting on inspiration were
really necessary for all poets, how would an epic ever get
written? How could the Attic dramatists, or Shakespeare,
or Ibsen have turned out their steady tale of plays? I

believe, despite Shelley's hectic protests, that a man—
or at least some men—*can* say 'I *will* compose poetry
to-day'. No doubt it requires an iron will; no doubt
a large proportion of the work thus produced *invita
Minerva* may have to be burnt; but it is a feeble
foppery to pretend it can never be done.

> Tasks in hours of insight willed
> Can be through hours of gloom fulfilled.

Housman might take a year to write the fourth stanza of
a poem, of which the first three stanzas had come in one
afternoon. Yet he wrote it. And in the end that fourth
stanza was indistinguishable from the others. It is in
the nature of Muses to be coquettish; but the best way
with coquettes is not always to humour them.

To scorn Dionysus is dangerous; to idolize him may
be worse. Theories of writing merely by free association,
like many other forms of idiocy, are not new. In 1823,
for example, one Ludwig Börne wrote a treatise on the
art of becoming an original writer in three days, which
was published in 1862 and given to Freud as a boy.
'Take some sheets of paper and write down for three
days on end, without falsification or dishonesty, everything that comes into your heads. Write what you think
of yourselves, your wives, the Turkish War . . . the Day
of Judgement, your superiors—and after three days you
will be astounded at the new thoughts you have produced.' This does not appear to have much increased
the number of original writers. In general, however,
there has been a recurrent tendency since Blake and the
Romantics, culminating in the Surrealists, to give the
Unconscious too much its head; whereas the neo-
Classics of the eighteenth century, on the contrary, kept
their Unconscious too much in a cage. 'He actually *saw*
these things', said Rothenstein to Rodin, showing him
some of Blake's drawings; 'he should have seen them',

replied Rodin, 'three or four times'. Pope's friend, Walsh, suggested that to write love-poems, one should be in love; and out of love again to correct them. That, doubtless, is a counsel of perfection. But the more one studies the methods of first-rate writers, the more one is struck by the infinite pains and patience that many of them took, consciously, to correct what the Unconscious had given them. 'Quand un ouvrage sent la lime,' wrote Joubert, 'c'est qu'il n'est pas assez poli; s'il sent l'huile, c'est qu'on a trop peu veillé.'

After Plato's death the first sentence of *The Republic* was found written seven different ways.[1] Everyone knows Horace's precept of nine years' revision. Ariosto tried fifty-six variants of the opening verse of his *Orlando*. Shelley wondered if it were really worth all that trouble; perhaps not; yet there are plenty of stanzas in Shelley that could have gained by a little more labour. Pascal rewrote some of *Les Provinciales* thirteen times; La Fontaine rewrote some of his simplest *Fables* eight or ten times; La Bruyère took ten years to write his *Caractères*, ten more to revise. Buffon's *Époques de la Nature* was rewritten eighteen times; Xavier de Maistre's *Lépreux* seventeen times; some pages of Chateaubriand ten times. Anatole France required up to eight proofs, Balzac up to twenty-seven (part of his constant indebtedness was due to the fantastic expense of his corrections). Tolstoy rewrote the twelve hundred pages of *War and Peace* seven times and would send a telegram to alter a word; just as Leonardo would walk the length of Milan to add a brush-stroke to his *Last Supper*. Genius clearly does not consist simply in taking pains; but the ordinary public has little con-

---

[1] 'Plato's having had seventy (*sic*) shies at one sentence', writes Samuel Butler in his *Notebooks*, ' is quite enough to explain to me why I dislike him. . . . I cannot conceive how any man can take thought for his style without loss to himself and his readers.' But then Butler, in his own words, was ' the *enfant terrible* of literature '.

ception of the pains that genius often takes. The work of the Unconscious is vital; but it is often only the preliminary to the conscious work. I get the impression that many of those who go in for writing little guess what drudgery it usually costs to write well. They think they can do it with one-tenth of the effort often expended by the immortals.

It is true that there have been writers like Scott or George Sand who could toss their first drafts to the printer's devil without even re-reading. And yet how much the style of both might have gained by shortening and concentration! Byron, too, could not revise; if he missed his spring, the tiger withdrew growling. And yet how many lines of Byron would well bear revision! Trollope wrote his 250 words every quarter of an hour; he would have done better, I think, to spend at least an hour, later on, in revising them. Even of Shakespeare one must surely admit with Ben Jonson that, if he never blotted a line, there are a good many he might have blotted with advantage.

But if a Shakespeare can take liberties, many writers only less great have won their place by conscious labour as much as by inspirations from the Unconscious— Demosthenes, Virgil, Horace, Racine, Pope, Tennyson, Flaubert. In the last century Elizabeth Browning was often thought better than Christina Rossetti; but to-day —the careful style tells.

Complete agreement on this point is doubtless impossible. Human temperaments are too diverse; we can never agree how drunk we like our art to be. Perhaps more aesthetic controversies centre round this one point than any other. Personally I would rather one *Ancient Mariner* than fifty opium-dreams like *Kubla Khan*. But at least it seems wise for authors to respect the conscious as well as the unconscious. Too often 'inspiration' is a cover-name for laziness, an excuse for the writer to shift the labour from himself to the reader. To quote Valéry once more—'la véritable condition d'un véritable poète est ce qu'il y a de plus distinct de l'état de rêve. . . . Celui même qui veut écrire son rêve se doit d'être infiniment éveillé. . . . Qui dit exactitude et style, invoque le contraire du songe.'

And criticism? Here, too, there seem certain lessons to be learnt from psychology. First, the quite inconceivable bizarrerie of human tastes. Stekel, for example, had a patient whose one passion was for men with swollen faces. The mere sight of one produced a frenzy of excitement in which he would break off a conversation, jettison an appointment, or tear out of a restaurant, in pursuit of this grotesque Adonis. He would haunt the doors of hospitals or dentists in the hope of some incarnation of his ideal. The causes of his mania are no matter here; they were complex—an adored governess in childhood, who was addicted to toothache; a younger brother of whom he had been jealous, lying dead with his jaw bound; and so forth. My point is the utterly fantastic capriciousness of aesthetic preferences. Fortunately this victim could not—anyway, did not—paint; but he might have. We have acquired a tendency nowadays, when all standards have toppled into chaos, to murmur bashfully in front of the latest artistic abortion—'Well, I suppose there must be something in it, or people would not like it.' No doubt there *is* 'something in it'; but it may be something deadly sick. Tolerance is excellent; one should respect, if possible, the tastes of others; but a goitre is not a thing to be respected. It is a thing to be cured. The world is perhaps more mentally ill to-day than it has been for three centuries. Our art and literature are full of mental maladies. Many simple souls are hypnotized into admiring them; many more are too timid to protest. But such timidity may not be much less dangerous to society than intolerance. Charles II remarked of a popular preacher, 'I suppose his nonsense suits their nonsense': of many artists of our time one can only echo, 'I suppose his neurosis suits their neuroses'.

But if this is an argument for more critical courage, psychology can also provide warnings enough against critical recklessness. Men's power of seeing the non-existent is equalled by their power of not seeing the existent. There is a wise moral for critics in the affecting case of a husband who saved himself from a romantic elopement by going literally blind on the very morning appointed (his wife, it may be added, was ugly, but had a beautiful voice). Or there is the ludicrous example of an American who developed an actual squint in his conflict between a conscience that forbade him to look at attractive women in the street, and the fiend at his elbow murmuring 'Look!' Another patient of Stekel's dreamt that he snatched away the analyst's spectacles—exactly like the Brahmin who smashed a microscope which revealed to his horrified eyes that even a water-drop was full of animalcules busy devouring one another.

Hatfield, again, mentions a grotesque case of a man so irritated by the noise of his neighbour's dog that he bought it, meaning murder. Such, however, is the magic of property that, after having the creature a few days in his house, he ceased to notice its vocal gifts. It was now the neighbour that complained. In criticism we can blind ourselves far more easily than we might imagine, by far less drastic measures than Oedipus—and without even knowing it. To a great extent we see what we want to see and only what we want to see.

Finally, in an amusing essay on the 'God-complex' (based on a study of that type of extreme Narcissist who believes himself the Almighty) Dr. Ernest Jones has given a list of traits, many of which are comically reminiscent of some modern critics of the lordlier type.

This sort of neurotic, says Dr. Jones, lays stress on the omniscience and omnipotence of his divine position, rather than on his own creative powers; though his secret self-importance *may* compensate itself by a parade of humility. He harps on accuracy in the use of language; yet his own use of it is liable to be turgid, circuitous, and obscure. For, the more important the topic under discussion, the more miserly he may feel about unlocking the treasures of his own wisdom.[1] Hence he may develop a habit of constantly promising fuller revelations on some future occasion. Foreign tongues he may despise—for they are not *his*; and he often shows impatience of new knowledge, which he will belittle as not really new (and then perhaps tacitly appropriate it afterwards). Such a person will veer between extreme intolerance and extreme tolerance (according as his own interests are endangered, or merely the interests of other people). His patronage is kept for the docile young. He tends to be interested in mysticism, religion, and social reform—though when it comes to doing anything, he often proves a bad citizen, who may not even bother to vote. His watch is always right (for he controls time); his memory is always right (for the same reason); and his predictions are always right, be they about the weather or more important matters (for these, too, he secretly controls—as did Nietzsche, for instance, after his mind failed). A typical daydream of his magnificent isolation indulged in by one of these unfortunates consisted in seeing himself drive up to a mountain castle of his own, with a terrific blast from his motor-horn, which made the hills re-echo, while all his servants hid underground. Most of us do not go quite as far as this. And

---

[1] A similar motive may underlie some of the obscurity of modern poets—though even they cannot quite rival the lady recorded by Stekel who wrote *her* poetry with the tip of her tongue on the inside of her mouth, in shorthand.

yet, when reading some modern criticism (especially of the kind written between the Wars), is one not sometimes reminded of Sainte-Beuve on the now forgotten Leroux?—'Il est devenu dieu et je suis devenu bibliothécaire. Nous avons pris des carrières différentes.'[1]

---

[1] Cf. Henry Miller, *The Cosmological Eye*, p. 8 : ' In this life I am God, and like God I am indifferent to my own fate. . . . Yes, the times are bad, permanently bad—unless one becomes immune, *becomes God*. Since I have become God, I go the whole hog always.' One may be reminded of the Zurich patient quoted by Brill (*Psychoanalytic Psychiatry*, p. 214) who always insisted on being addressed as ' Mr. God.' Ten years later the doctor chanced to see him again and inquired the health of ' Mr. God '— only to receive the haughty answer : ' It is *not* " Mr. God ". It is " *General God* " '.

PART TWO

The Judgement of Literature

XI

The Relativity of Taste

*Si les triangles faisaient un dieu, ils
lui donneraient trois côtés.*
                              MONTESQUIEU.

*It is only an auctioneer who can equally and
impartially admire all schools of art.*
                              WILDE.

WHAT is the point, the value, the justification of
literature?

Do we overrate its importance?

Can it, does it, should it, must it affect what we call
'real life'?   Or was Flaubert, for example, right in
passionately asserting the artist's aloofness from the
active world?

Is there any way of judging the worth of books and
authors; or is it all a matter of personal taste, about
which only fools argue?

What does it mean to say 'This work is good'? Is it
merely an emotional noise, meaning 'This tickles me
divinely'—or can it mean something more?

These are questions disputed for over twenty-five
centuries—and disputed still. Many ignore them and
go to literature as a butterfly goes to flowers—for the
honey. They may plead that butterflies both get and
give more pleasure than botanists.

And yet it seems important to ask such questions. To
persist in asking them was one of the master-qualities of
the Greeks and one of the bases of their freedom; it is
one of the habits that tyrants most dislike; over a large

fraction of the globe to-day it is forbidden to ask questions —intelligence is nationalized and the answer to everything is official. That is a good reason why we should ask as many as possible; and to spend years of one's life on literature without facing these vital problems about it is hardly rational.

First, what do we really mean by saying 'This is a good book'? The answer is, I think, that it would be better not to say it.

People have, indeed, said it for thousands of years; no doubt they will continue to say it for thousands more —in all the tongues of Babel. But Babel results. The phrase is too ambiguous.

Poetry may sometimes gain by an ambiguity that treads on 'the brink of meaning'; but in practical prose it becomes a curse. Darkness may enhance a church; a laboratory needs light. It is a strange thing that amid the scientific skill and precision of the twentieth century we still show such bungling incompetence with the first instrument we learn from the lips of mothers and nurses—language; so that after the great of the earth had agreed at Potsdam, they could spend years violently disagreeing as to exactly what they agreed; and that after the terms of coal nationalization seemed settled, new conflicts had to be fought about precisely what the settlement was.

Soon it will be your turn. You are supposed to be learning to write prose. I hope you may be better than your elders usually seem to be, at writing clear prose— so clear that, though others may disagree with what you think, no one, except morons, can disagree what you mean. Anatole France has listed the three prime qualities of French prose—'la clarté, la clarté, et encore la clarté'. It seems to me true of all prose—except that type of emotional prose which verges on poetry.

What can be thought clearly, can be said clearly. And

even if your mind is clouded with doubt, it is still possible to put your doubts clearly.

And if you feel this is obvious, I can only reply 'I wish it were'. The first step towards attaining clarity is to realize that it is more difficult in practice than anyone at first sight could conceive. Ultimately this too is a question of psychology. Quite apart from mere incompetence and wobble-mindedness, our unconscious motives distort our expression of what we think we mean and our impression of what we think others mean.

The phrase 'This is a good book' means in most mouths simply 'I like it'. But that is hardly what it says. I suppose it should mean 'This book conforms to the laws of Absolute Beauty—and, perhaps, of Absolute Goodness'. In other words, it is a book you ought to like; and if you do not, you are wrong.

When Crabb Robinson owned to Wordsworth that he found it embarrassing to read aloud in company those justly famous lines:

> I've measured it from side to side,
> 'Tis three feet long and two feet wide,

Wordsworth curtly replied, 'They *ought* to be liked'. We smile. The reply is clearly ridiculous. But I believe that all such remarks about works of art are always ridiculous; that one can *never* rationally say (as people persistently do, with that familiar air of mingled sorrow and superiority), 'But you *ought* to like it'.

The absolute view of Beauty is to-day less common than it was (though Professor Joad, for example, still holds it). But, while many people have ceased to believe it in theory, you have only to listen to a few literary conversations, or to read a few reviews, to see what a grip it still keeps in practice on men's minds and, still more, on their emotions. And what muddle results! Most persons still feel that you are in duty bound to like what they like; that if you love Donne or Shelley less than they love them, there is something the matter with you—that you must be somehow inferior—perhaps downright wicked. You may be; but it does not in the least follow; and it is often impossible for any human mind to know. Dame Ethel Smyth in her autobiography recorded the sad case of an English and a Swedish boy who were devoted friends till one discovered that the other preferred waxy potatoes to mealy ones, or mealy to waxy, I forget which. That intolerable lack of taste estranged their young hearts for ever. A good many critical controversies seem to me still conducted on much the same level.

It is to Plato above all, I take it, that the world owes its persistent faith in an Absolute Beauty throned above the earth like a sort of Alabaster Lady on a cloud. Though even Plato is far more a symptom than a cause of the incorrigible human drive to dogmatize about all mental values. Such Platonic dogmatism provides idealists with a refuge from the disheartening harshness, cruelty, and ignominy of the world around them; it provides also that blessed sense of certainty craved by so many hearts, homesick for the days of childhood when parents seemed omniscient and infallible.

What confidence, for example, Ruskin enjoyed, when he could write to Rossetti!—'You are a conceited monkey, thinking your pictures right when I positively tell you they are wrong.' No wonder that, as Ruskin candidly records elsewhere, 'I was more and more persuaded every day that everybody was always wrong'. Even some modern critics could hardly go much further. But with Ruskin it was a pity; for he was, I feel, at his best (not at his most purple) a master of splendid prose. Yet at least he was not afraid to speak frankly, when some readers murmured that he was a little dictatorial: 'There are, however, laws of truth and right in painting, just as fixed as those of harmony in music, or of affinity in chemistry. These laws are perfectly ascertainable by labour, and ascertainable no otherwise . . . it is as ridiculous for a person to speak hesitatingly about laws of painting who has conscientiously given his time to their ascertainment, as it would be for Mr. Faraday to announce in a dubious manner that iron had an affinity for oxygen, and to put the question to the vote of his audience whether it had or no.'

Admirable clarity!—at least of language. I could hardly find a better statement of what I do *not* believe. Ruskin's analogy between criticism and chemistry leaves his view crystal-clear; but though analogies are excellent as illustrations to make one's meaning plain, they can never provide proof and often fail to add one grain of probability.

Ruskin ignored—as his modern counterparts ignore— the fate of the neo-Classic critics before him, who did not doubt that a work of art was right or wrong as a sum in arithmetic is right or wrong. In geometry there was Euclid; in poetry there were Aristotle and 'the Rules'. In vain for La Place to suggest that the English theatre might be different because the English temperament was different; 'have not the English', retorted Desfontaines, 'a share of reason like other nations?'

'Oh,' you say, 'typical eighteenth-century dogmatism.' But this next example comes from the twentieth: 'Now the desire for "comic relief" on the part of the audience is, I believe, a permanent craving of human nature; but that does not mean it ought to be gratified. It springs from a lack of the capacity for concentration.' Exeunt, covered with confusion, Hamlet's Grave-diggers, Macbeth's Porter, and the long train of their fellows. The theatre is to become a 'concentration' camp. For, we are told, 'the doctrine of *Unity of Sentiment* happens to be right'.

[187]

So persistent, so incorrigible, is the human desire for certainties and absolutes: so prickly, to most heads, Montaigne's Pillow of Doubt. 'Moses has said'; 'the Church has said'; 'Stalin has said'; and with a sigh of reassurance the faithful murmur 'Q.E.D.'.

But is there an Absolute Beauty? Or has that Alabaster Lady tumbled off her cloud, littering the earth with shining pieces of her anatomy as stumbling-blocks for future generations?

Plato is generally felt to have an excellent style; but I have always had heretical doubts whether he had much good sense. He seems to me, in contrast to the great Ionians before him, one of those cheating philosophers who first decide what they consider to be Goodness and Beauty, then twist and pinch and pummel Truth to fit. Conscience warped his thought. The moralist in him bribed the thinker. And so he arrived at a totalitarian Utopia.

But is there an Absolute Good or an Absolute Beauty?

The Greeks fortunately were a seafaring race. They travelled. As they broadened their geography, they broadened their quick minds. Already one of their greatest travellers, Herodotus, a man fifty years older than Plato, had taken what seems to me a broader and wiser view. He tells how Darius King of Persia asked certain Greeks for what price they would eat their dead parents. 'Not for the world!' was the disgusted answer. Then the Great King called in certain Indians, who always dutifully ate their dead parents, and asked what they would take to burn them, like the Greeks. They answered with equal abhorrence. 'So powerful', comments Herodotus, 'is custom.' Relativity has appeared in the world.

Were the Indians wicked? Who can doubt that, when their grisly banquet was ended, with the pleasures of digestion they combined all the satisfactions of a virtuous conscience?

So Kipling saw two thousand years later:

> The crimes of Clapham chaste in Khatmandu.

Even earlier than Herodotus, another wanderer, the philosopher Xenophanes, had pointed out how we erect our private preferences into absolutes:

> If horses, lions, or cattle were gifted too with hands
> And power to draw such pictures as human fingers trace,
> And they too tried to feature the Gods in form and face,
> *Then* in their own image they would fashion the divine—
> Horses' Gods like horses, like cows the Gods of kine.

Or in Montesquieu's still briefer summary, 'Si les triangles faisaient un Dieu, ils lui donneraient trois côtés.'

Is there, then, nothing to choose between burning the dead and eating them? The state of mind of the mourners might be equally affectionate and dutiful in either case. But it can hardly be supposed that eating the dead was very healthy. There lies the vital difference.

Most of us (though medieval Christianity judged otherwise) prefer health to sickness. The adherents of both customs may be equally virtuous: but the consequences do not seem equally desirable. About the value of states of mind in themselves, it seems hard to argue; but about their consequences it seems not only possible, but vital to argue, as scientifically as possible. How else can we foresee? This, I think, applies both to Ethics and to Aesthetics.

I do not know which offers the greater mass of contradictions—men's ideas of goodness or their tastes in beauty. But I propose, since we are concerned with criticism, to give a large number of examples of this divergency in taste. Partly because I think this divergency is, even now, underestimated; people hate to face

it; it disquiets them. Partly because most writers on
general subjects seem to me far too sparing with their
examples—philosophers in particular can be maddening
in this respect; sometimes, one suspects, because no real
evidence exists, or because they are afraid of being too
clear, lest they be seen through. (This lack of adequate
specimens, for example, is one of the fatal weaknesses of
that too famous controversy between Wordsworth and
Coleridge on Poetic Diction.) A third reason for being
lavish with instances is that though many are merely
reminders of the familiar, some may be of use or interest
in themselves, even if all my conclusions from them are
nonsense.

What is Beautiful in Nature?

The modern who climbs the marble shoulder of
Pentelicus or the long snow-ridge below the smoking
cone of Etna feels he is doing something perfectly natural
and, indeed, valuable; but an ancient Athenian or
Syracusan would have thought it the height of eccen-
tricity. The only ancient I can recall climbing Etna is
the megalomaniac Empedocles; even he is supposed to
have done it, not for the view, but with the highly
practical intention of hopping down the crater.

> Great Empedocles, that ardent soul,
> Leapt into Etna, and was roasted whole.

And the story is a fable anyway.

Similarly in the Middle Ages. When Petrarch was so
original as to climb *le mont Ventoux*, 'we found an old
shepherd in a hollow of the mountain, who strove with
many words to draw us back from the ascent, saying that
he himself fifty years before, in the same impulse of
youthful ardour, had climbed to the very top, and had
brought back nothing thence save sorrow and labour,
and body and clothes torn by the stones and briars; nor
ever, either before that time or after, had men heard of

anyone doing the like.' Yet the Ventoux is a very mild mountain, with a modern carriage-road to the very top.

For the eighteenth century the Alps were still 'huge and hideous'.[1] Switzerland, said Voltaire, was half like Heaven, half like Hell. It is the Hell that is now full of hotels; and it was precisely Burne-Jones's objection to the prettiness of Surrey that it was too like a sort of 'silly Heaven'—he wanted, now and then, 'to see Hell in a landscape'. But it was only as recently as 1857 that the Alpine Club was born.

Yet some moderns react in turn against the supposed beauty of Swiss Nature. Pater found the lakes 'horrid pots of blue paint'. Modern intellectuals sometimes use bitter phrases about 'picture-postcard scenery'. I once drove to Wordsworth's Lakes with a friend who saw nothing in all Westmorland to equal the view of Doncaster's factory-chimneys from the Great North Road.

Who is 'right'?

Similarly with human beauty. Aphrodite and the Graces change their shapes like Proteus, their colour like chameleons, from age to age and land to land—now frail as in Botticelli, now plump as in Rubens; now rosy as Burns's love, now pale and consumptive like the heroines of French Romanticism; now ballooning in crinolines, now tripping in hobble-skirts. Nineteenth-century travellers found African fathers standing with whips over daughters painfully gulping milk by pailfuls, to give them the beauty of the spheres; twentieth-century English ladies were known to starve themselves ill in the effort to be slim young birch-trees—a type of heroism now less often necessary.

'As I entered the room', writes a Victorian young lady,

[1] Similarly for an eighteenth-century eye the purple heather on Northumbrian moorlands could make the landscape 'indescribably hideous'. (G. M. Trevelyan, *Autobiography*, p. 96.)

'I was faced by a row of curly brown beards—a really beautiful sight.' We smile; yet if we took a vote of all the generations since Homer it would show an over-whelming majority in favour of a taste that we now find unusual.

Who is 'right'?

There is no need to multiply examples in the visual arts—Gibbon's disgust in Venice at 'stinking ditches dignified with the pompous denomination of canals, a fine bridge spoilt by two Rows of houses upon it, and a large square decorated with the worst Architecture I ever yet saw'; Smollett judging York Minster as poor as we judge the Albert Memorial—'displeasing to the eye of every man who has any idea of propriety and pro-portion'; Winckelmann's raptures over Graeco-Roman sculpture we can hardly bear to look at; or the Pre-Raphaelite painters thinking Raphael and Reynolds as hopeless as most modern critics think the Pre-Raphaelite painters.

'If all the Princes in Europe like Louis XIV and Charles I were to Patronize such Blockheads,' writes Blake of Titian, Rubens, Correggio, and Rembrandt, 'I, William Blake, a mental Prince, should decollate and Hang their Souls as guilty of Mental High Treason.'

Shelley, again, considered Michael Angelo lacking, of all things, in 'moral dignity'; and felt the paintings in the Sistine Chapel 'deficient in majesty'. One gasps. But if Shelley felt so, for him it *was* true. We can vote him down: we cannot confute his feelings—for he quite certainly had them. We cannot know that some future age may not breed a majority of men like Shelley—though it seems unlikely; and in that case our view in its turn would be voted down.

But here we are mainly concerned with literature. No fame seems firmer than Homer's; even though certain periods have put him as much below Virgil as

most of us would put him above. Yet even Homer
was derided in antiquity by Zoïlus—and Dionysius of
Halicarnassus speaks of Zoïlus, as a critic, with respect.
Landor told Crabb Robinson that most of Homer was
trash. Bentham thought it was worse. And in our day,
after translating the *Odyssey*, Lawrence of Arabia decided
that it was a poor poem after all—'Bother the *New
Statesman*, and the *Odyssey*, and all manufactured
writing! Only the necessary, the inevitable, the high-
pressure stuff is worth having.' 'The *Odyssey* is a
creeping work.' One cannot say of Lawrence, as one
might of Bentham, that he had no feeling for literature,
or no experience of adventure, or no proper acquaintance
with the poem. The brute fact remains: Homer had
ceased to suit the emotional needs of Lawrence. It is
perfectly conceivable that in a few centuries Homer
might cease to appeal to most readers. Then his reputation would tumble. Nothing, indeed, can undo the past.
A poet who has lived a hundred generations must have
had great powers. Nothing can take that away. But the
same applies in a lesser degree to Petrarch now. He, too,
once filled Europe with his name. But to-day how many
can read his verse without feeling him a bore? We
admit that he must have had power. But in our hearts
most of us feel there was an illusion somewhere. From
Petrarch's fate no writer can be quite sure of escaping in
the unimaginable world of the centuries to come. We
can only be certain that posterity in its turn will feel
about some of our most cherished admirations that there
was an illusion somewhere. Yet we continue to dogmatize about our preferences as if we were holding the
Last Judgement. Why? All beauty is only relative.

One of the earliest and liveliest of European critics is
Aristophanes. For him Euripides, however clever, was
a degenerate successor of Aeschylus. Many of his contemporaries agreed. So in part may we—there *are* in

Euripides certain traits that seem decadent and unhealthy. But later Antiquity reversed the decision—
Euripides came to overshadow both his great rivals. He
was, in fact, better suited to a more cosmopolitan world.
With the Revival of Learning he still kept his general
pre-eminence; until the Romantics came. From then
on Aeschylus tended to outsoar his old rival once more
and the view of Aristophanes reasserted itself. Euripides
found himself accused by A. W. Schlegel as lewd,
ludicrous, and vulgar, and likened by Swinburne to
'a mutilated monkey'. Swinburne is thought by some
a good critic. Brilliant moments his criticism certainly
has; but is it possible to be a good critic without at least
some common sense? And surely criticism which is still
at the stage of 'mutilated monkeys' has a long and weary
evolution to go through before it can be called intelligent?
For Swinburne himself, Euripides *was* useless; but how
could a 'mutilated monkey' have inspired cultivated men
for century after century?

Take Virgil again. For Roman Empire and Middle
Ages he was *the* poet. F. W. H. Myers has recorded in
an admirable essay the influence he has had—how men
have uttered in quotations from him their own deepest
feelings at crises of their lives or in the face of death.
Yet for one of his critics his exquisite style is merely
'the pickle that has preserved his mummy'. Shelley in
a letter puts him below Lucan, whom most modern
readers find a clever, but flashy rhetorician, trying to
make an epic out of epigrams. Macaulay, while admiring
Virgil on his own Italian ground, finds parts of him 'as
extravagant as Ariosto and as dull as Wilkes's *Epigoniad*'.
Samuel Butler is more trenchant still. We may dismiss
as mere naughtiness the remark that Virgil was no good,
'because Tennyson ran him'. But Butler was quite
serious—'How then did Raffaele get his reputation? It
may be answered, How did Virgil get his? or Dante?

or Bacon? or Plato? or Mendelssohn? or a score of others who not only get the public ear but keep it sometimes for centuries? How did Guido, Guercino and Domenichino get their reputations? A hundred years ago these men were held as hardly inferior to Raffaele himself. They had a couple of hundred years or so of triumph—why so much? And if so much, why not more? . . . *Populus vult decipi* is the only answer.'

Is it the 'only' answer? Even if Guido, Guercino, and Domenichino *have* lost in repute, it seems a curious answer for an evolutionist like Butler to make. If at a certain period tigers, mammoths, and hippopotami strolled about the site of London, where they certainly stroll no longer, the answer is not that they were illusions and chimeras, but, in part, that the climate has changed. The psychological climate has changed since men went into ecstasies over Guido. But what right has Butler to talk of 'deception'? If men thought they got pleasure from Guido, though some of them may indeed have been aesthetic snobs and only pretending, many of them certainly did get pleasure. What Butler means is perhaps that if they had been wiser and better men, they would have had tastes more like Butler's own. But is not this a little bold? It might be true. But, if so, here is a sudden intrusion of ethics into an aesthetic problem. Unlike many critics, I do not believe that ethics and aesthetics can in fact be kept apart. I think a book is better if it appeals to readers who seem to me persons of a finer type. But if ethics are to come into the business, let them come in openly through the front-door, not up the back-stairs.

For the Renaissance, just as Virgil was *the* epic poet, *the* tragedian was Seneca. For Heywood, he was 'the flower of all writers'; for Scaliger, 'inferior in majesty to none of the Greeks, in culture and polish even greater than Euripides'. To-day Seneca's letters still have a certain charm; but only the learned read his plays. And most of those who read them feel that he was a detestable dramatist, with a detestable influence; and his tragedies an emetic mixture of blood and pepper, rant and epigram. Yet he was clever; one cannot be sure he will never return; one can only hope not.

Dante has already occurred among the aversions of Samuel Butler. To-day his glory is such that few dare blaspheme. But the Devil's Advocates are there. We may discount the contempt he excited in Goldsmith and Voltaire, or Horace Walpole's phrase about 'a Methodist parson in Bedlam', as eighteenth-century prejudice—meaning, in fact, that we disagree with the eighteenth century. And the eighteenth century, being safely dead, cannot smile in return at 'twentieth-century prejudice'. But then there is Landor, who thought that perhaps one-seventieth part of Dante was good; but that the *Inferno* was 'the most impious and immoral work that ever was written'. I have not read all the impious and immoral works ever written; so I cannot judge. But if cruelty and the fear of Hell are evil—as to me they are—I cannot deny that a work which describes with such apparent satisfaction the torments of the damned, does contain, along with its marvellous style, much that *is* evil. I have not read any modern critic who dared to say this. I take the opportunity of saying it now.

Then there is Goethe who is reported to have told a young Italian that he thought 'the *Inferno* abominable, the *Purgatorio* dubious, and the *Paradiso* tiresome'. And Nietzsche with his still terser summary—'Dante or the Hyena that writes poetry on tombs'. While Tolstoy, disliking Nietzsche, at least shared his dislike of Dante.

What are we to conclude? That Landor, Goethe, Nietzsche, and Tolstoy were all four in some way mentally deficient? That would surely be rash. We can only say that here were four gifted temperaments to whom Dante was repugnant. It happens that among cultured people such temperaments are, at present, in a minority. Why, we do not know. How long it will remain so, we do not know. Whether it is best that it should be so, we do not know. But at least do not let us try, with Dante's intolerance, to damn those who disagree with our tastes. Their views are not 'wrong'; they are just different.

Among the poets of France few are better loved than Ronsard. But few poets of any race illustrate better the fallibility of critical judgements, the futility of critical absolutism. For the House of Fame is a Tower of Babel.

Living, Ronsard was recognized as the first poet of his time. Elizabeth of England sent him a diamond; Mary of Scotland, her portrait. When he died, L'Estoile wrote that 'the first and last of French poets' had passed away. 'Then came Malherbe'—who regarded Ronsard's style as not even French and, having struck through most of the verses in his copy of Ronsard's poems, for the sake of completeness drew his pen through the rest as well. Centuries passed. Chapelain pronounced that Ronsard lacked art; La Fontaine, that he was harsh and without taste; Arnauld, that his poetry was pitiable; Voltaire, that he ruined the French language; La Harpe, that he was unreadable; Marmontel, that the Graces took to their heels at the sight of him. Even the Romantic Michelet called him a deaf maniac. From 1629 to 1857, except for an anthology by Sainte-Beuve in 1828, his works were not reprinted. But after two hundred years of neglect suddenly he began to regain his ancient glory. 'I hammer on the book', writes Alfred de Vigny to Sainte-Beuve, 'and shout with pleasure till anyone might think I was mad.' And Flaubert, 'You cannot imagine what a poet Ronsard is. What a poet! What a poet! What wings!' It is a story to make critics cautious—if anything could.

[197]

It may be urged that there is at least something like unanimity about Shakespeare, in spite of Rymer, or Cobbett's scorn for 'the punning and smutty Shakespeare', or the downright detestation felt by Tolstoy. But on a closer view a good many rifts appear in this apparent consensus of opinion. For Johnson, Coleridge, Bradley, he is a compendium of wisdom. But for Bernard Shaw he has no ideas worth twopence—merely verbal magic. Lawrence of Arabia felt the same—the most marvellous language, but a 'second-rate' mind. 'How many critical brains', echoes a character in Aldous Huxley, 'have been deceived by the quickness of his tongue! Because he can say "Shoughs, water-rugs and demi-wolves" and "defunctive music" and "the expense of spirit in a waste of shame" and all the rest of it, we credit him with philosophy, a moral purpose, and the most penetrating psychology. Whereas his thoughts are incredibly confused, his only purpose is to entertain, and he has created only three characters. One, Cleopatra, is an excellent copy from the life, like a character out of a good realistic novel, say one of Tolstoy's. The other two —Macbeth and Falstaff—are fabulous imaginary figures, consistent in themselves, but not real in the sense that Cleopatra is real.'

Here of course there is much that is debatable. When I say 'It is idle to argue about the direct emotions one gets from literature', that cannot of course always apply to the *reasons* adduced to explain these emotions. Whether Shakespeare's psychology is 'penetrating' or not remains a matter for scientific discussion. My point is that here are several minds above the average, by no means feeling as most people do about Shakespeare. They concentrate their praise only on Shakespeare's style; but it was precisely Shakespeare's style that disquieted Dryden, Shakespeare-lover as he was. He found it, often, full of 'solecisms', 'meanly written', 'pestered with figurative expressions', 'obscure', 'affected'; but, 'if Shakespeare were stripped of all the bombasts in his passions . . . we should find the beauties of his *thoughts* remaining'.

Or consider again the attitude of Wells's William Clissold (which is surely Wells's own): 'I liked and admired Shakespeare, though I did not find anything fundamental in him. I regarded—and I still regard— most of the popular fuss about him exactly as I regard the popular fuss about the smile of the Prince of Wales.' Now suppose the dictator of a future world-state were an admirer of Mr. Wells and decided to mass-produce, by eugenic and mind-conditioning methods, a Wellsian type of humanity—which, after all, is quite imaginable— then a far less exalted view of Shakespeare would be everywhere accepted and his nineteenth-century glory prove in its turn 'such stuff As dreames are made on'. You may say it would be a disgusting world; but then you have again slipped into ethics; and you will still not find your view easy to prove. And, anyway, you would by then be dead. *Les morts ont tort.* Over single plays there is sometimes still more emphatic disagreement. I suppose a general vote would choose *Hamlet* as the greatest of all. But we have read in our time that it is 'most certainly an artistic failure'. Others have claimed pre-eminence for *Lear*. But Goethe disliked it; Faguet found it a mere menagerie of wild beasts; and Tolstoy (whose own end, by an irony of fate, was to be so like Lear's) could see in it nothing but absurdity and 'cold, pompous, artificial ravings', far inferior to the old Elizabethan play of *Leire and his Three Daughters* (a work that there are few to read and *very* few to love).

There is no need to repeat the process in detail with Milton. Johnson got into trouble over him long ago. Samuel Butler, as so often, was even naughtier. You may remember the character in *The Way of All Flesh* who retorts to the reminder that Milton only got five pounds for his great epic, 'I would have given him twice as much myself not to have written it at all'. Some time ago we were told that Milton's reputation had been exploded by Mr. Eliot; now, it appears, Mr. Eliot has relented and Milton stands reprieved. But for years a wordy battle has raged between combatants who seemed to assume that there was one *right* answer which could be established by their polemics—that Milton could be proved 'good' or 'not good', without asking 'good for whom?' That he *was* a great poet, was proved already, not by argument, but by his sales for three centuries and by his influence; but that everyone *ought* to feel his poetry great is not susceptible of proof at all. Such obligations do not exist.

I would only add that I do not see how anybody's reputation in creative literature can be 'exploded' by anybody. If he keeps a long enough hold on intelligent readers, his power is proved by the only proof there ever can be.

It would be easy to add other names on which the Fortune of literature has exerted her caprices—Donne, for two centuries eclipsed (so that in 1870 Buchanan could still insult Rossetti by comparing him with the 'justly forgotten' Beddoes, Carew 'the idol of courts', and Donne 'the beloved of schoolmen'). Then there is Herrick, whose grace and gaiety were so unaccountably ignored from the Restoration to the Romantic Revival and still shocked Southey even then; Waller, of whom Dryden wrote that he alone in English, and Virgil alone in Latin, had surpassed the harmony of Spenser—yet now Waller is remembered only for a few pretty lines; Traherne, on the contrary, not famous till two and a quarter centuries after his death, and only then by a stroke of luck; Cowley, one of Milton's three favourite poets—and yet already Pope could ask 'who now reads Cowley?'; Pope himself, the master-poet of one century,

denied by many in the century after to be a poet at all;
Wordsworth, long ridiculed, then long revered, but
to-day perhaps tending to lose ground again a little,
with many readers that find him, for all his talk of the
Universe, a trifle parochial.

It might be said that literary fashions were here at
work rather than differences of temperament in readers;
that it was a matter of herd-instinct rather than genuine
judgement. But consider Shelley. It is just over a
century since his reputation was established. During
that century he has been extolled as the greatest lyric
poet in modern England, perhaps in modern Europe.
Yet all the while there has remained a persistent minority
that felt him tedious, hysterical, or worse. Matthew
Arnold got himself into hot water with his 'ineffectual
angel'. But it was no unique peculiarity of Arnold's.
Lamb had found Shelley's voice 'the most obnoxious
squeak I was ever tormented with'. Hazlitt denied that
anyone was better or wiser for reading him. Tennyson,
while admiring his imagery, thought him tenuous and
lacking in common sense. Carlyle would have had him
hanged. Patmore and Morris I have already quoted.
And Mr. Max Beerbohm has summed him up in the neat
phrase 'a crystal crank'. How often I remember having
arguments on the subject—for in those days I still
believed in arguments on such subjects—with Golds-
worthy Lowes Dickinson, who was a saint and idealist
himself and loved Shelley as if the poet had been an
idealistic undergraduate!

I am not urging that people should cease enjoying
Shelley; or that he is not a considerable poet. That is
proved by the only thing that ever could prove it—
statistics. But I have just re-read most of him—and
vowed that I never will again. The gulf of temperament
is too great. And there are enough irritations in life
without looking for them.

Another instance of irreconcilable differences in readers' temperaments is provided by Jane Austen. Here, too, period or fashion can have little to do with it. First let us hear the faithful:

Macaulay: 'There are in the world no compositions which approach nearer to perfection.' A 'prose Shakespeare'.

Tennyson at Lyme Regis: 'Don't talk to me of Monmouth—show me the exact spot where Louisa Musgrave fell.'

G. H. Lewes: 'Surpassing all the male novelists that ever lived.' (Note the tactful 'male'.)

George Eliot: 'The greatest artist that has ever written; the most truthful, charming, humorous, pureminded, quick-witted, and unexaggerated of writers.'

Kipling—

> Jane went to Paradise;
>   That was only fair.
> Good Sir Walter followed her
>   And armed her up the stair.
> Henry and Tobias
>   And Miguel of Spain
> Stood with Shakespeare at the top
>   To welcome Jane.

The verse may not be remarkable; but is it not astounding, this fascination exerted on the poet of blood and iron and Empire by a provincial spinster who wrote (in the years of the Retreat from Moscow) as if it were a catastrophe to have to drive home in a carriage through half an inch of snow?

Now a few voices on the other side.

Elizabeth Barrett Browning: 'Miss Austen whose people struck me as wanting souls, even more than is necessary for men and women of the world. The novels are perfect as far as they go—that's certain. Only they don't go far, I think.'

Charlotte Brontë: 'A complete and most sensible lady; but a very incomplete and rather insensible (not senseless) woman.' (And again, of *Pride and Prejudice*): 'An accurate daguerreotyped portrait of a commonplace face; a carefully fenced, highly cultivated garden, with neat borders and delicate flowers; but no glance of a bright, vivid physiognomy, no open country, no blue hill, no bonny beck.' For, whereas George Sand 'is sagacious and profound, Miss Austen is only shrewd and observant.'

Alice Meynell: 'The essential meanness of Jane Austen's art.'

Herbert Read: 'Atmosphere of a marionettes' opera . . . mere quaintness.' (It seems hard to believe that 'mere quaintness' could appeal to Macaulay or Kipling.)

Oliver Elton: 'She abides; we acknowledge her, we do not quite like her, and we quit her—perhaps run away from her, not without relief, bidding to such cold voices a somewhat long farewell.'

Professor Garrod: 'Not good writing: frequently not even grammatical writing . . . land flowing with milk and water.'

My own feelings agree closely with Elton's; but clearly many good judges do not.

Here, to conclude, is a miscellany of judgements by nineteenth-century writers, who cannot after all be just dismissed as negligible noodles. Wordsworth thought Goethe an immoral and 'artificial' writer; Coleridge agreed and held him far inferior to Schiller; de Quincey foretold the decline of his reputation to its just level; Landor put him below Mme de Genlis! Wordsworth said Byron's poetry was 'not English'; Byron, that Wordsworth was 'the blind monarch of the one-eyed'. De Quincey, again, accused Keats of trampling on the English tongue 'with the hoofs of a buffalo'. Arnold always felt Tennyson to be provincial and second-rate; and could only call Patmore, whom Francis Thompson believed the greatest genius of the century, 'that worthy, but mildish author'. FitzGerald could never find in Browning anything but the 'Cockney energy' of a 'Gargoyle School'. Browning in his turn loathed what he called the 'effeminacy' of Rossetti and his group. Ruskin was 'grieved to know' that no publisher could possibly take Christina Rossetti's *Goblin Market*. Bridges could see nothing in the poetry of Hardy; and Lionel Johnson accused Francis Thompson of doing 'more to defile the English language than the worst American newspapers'. One could fill pages with the scorn heaped by Carlyle alone on now established English writers from Wordsworth to Swinburne. And Tolstoy, with grim consistency, anathematized Greek tragedy, Aristophanes, Michael Angelo, Raphael, Tasso, Milton, Goethe, Baudelaire, Verlaine, Wagner, and Ibsen.

In a word, though critics strive century after century to grade the artistic merits of authors as precisely as medieval theology determined the precedence of angels, they are trying to map a rainbow that shifts with every different observer. In taste there can be no Acts of Uniformity.

It is, in part, a mere ambiguity of language that makes the violence of critical disagreements seem surprising— if it does seem surprising. When we talk about a 'book' or a 'work' or a 'novel' or a 'poem' we may mean (1) a material object—a number of sheets of white paper with black marks on them; or (2) we may be thinking of the mental events which occur in the reader who interprets those black marks to himself. In this second sense what we call a 'poem' is the result of a collaboration between poet and reader. They are partners. And the reader is no mere sleeping partner—or if he is, the poem is not being very successful. Let us call the printed poem 'P', and the readers 'R1', 'R2', and so on. When R1 and R2 imagine they are differing about the same

object—'P', they are really differing about 'P+R1' and
'P+R2'. Which are clearly two different things. The
wonder is not that our artistic judgements disagree so
much; the wonder is that they agree as much as they do.

Ruskin talked of the laws of art being as rigid as those
of chemistry. But I think chemistry can provide a less
misleading illustration.

The relations of readers to writers may be compared
with the relations, say, of metals to oxygen. And
readers' disagreements are as futile as if calcium and
iron and silver were to wrangle with each other:
'Oxygen makes me white and burning'; 'No, it makes
me red'; 'No, brown.' But why disagree? Calcium
oxide *is* white, iron oxide *is* red, silver oxide *is* brown.
The effect of a book is a *compound* of author's mind and
reader's.

I have never forgotten the comment made years ago
by a young and brilliant philosopher of my college,
Frank Ramsey, who died in the first spring of his promise.
In the sceptical, smiling simplicity of his general
character I imagine he must have been very like David
Hume. And I suspect that he listened to our aesthetic
controversies with the calm, detached, indulgent amusement of an anthropologist watching the war-dances of
Bushmen. Anyway, his comment once was: 'It seems
to me like one person saying "I walked to Grantchester
this afternoon" and another shouting "No, I did *not*!"'
What we confusingly call a 'poem' is, in its most
important sense, like a child begotten on the reader's
mind by the mind of the poet. If two women had by
the same father two children, one dark and one fair, it
would not seem very intelligent if they quarrelled
whether 'the child' was dark or fair.

In fact no two persons can experience the same work
of art; indeed (to adapt what Heraclitus said of rivers)
no reader can experience the same work of art twice.

[205]

For he will himself have changed slightly in the interval. What wonder that we sometimes wonder how on earth we could admire so passionately works that now leave us frozen? It was a different 'we', now dead. We generally assume that our latest view is the last word; as old gentlemen say to young ones—'Ah, so I thought at *your* age.' We love to think we grow wiser and wiser every day. In matters of fact that may be true—or a merciful illusion. But when it comes to *feelings* (I shall speak later of *consequences*), Titania's ecstasies over an ass's head may be as genuine, while they last, as Romeo's over Juliet.

You may reply—especially if you are English: 'No doubt all this is very logical—but I distrust logic. Your arguments are too like Zeno's proof of the absurdity of motion—that Achilles could not catch the slowest tortoise. But that does not prevent us from doing a thousand miles an hour; and you will not prevent me from believing that, say, Goethe's view of Dante was just—wrong!'

I fully share this distrust of logic. That was why I first gave what seemed to me adequate—perhaps superfluous—evidence of the actual existence of this subjectivity and relativity of taste. But once a fact is established, then it seems reasonable to look for a logical explanation.

I might even add that the real diversity of taste may well be even greater than quotations show.

'Sensible men', as Disraeli put it, 'never tell.' That prudent precept is often followed in matters of critical, as well as religious, orthodoxy. There are, indeed, persons of irritable temperament who find a fierce pleasure in iconoclasm—in trying to destroy the reputation, say, of Milton or Tennyson or Arnold or Meredith. (Sometimes these people are really searching among authors for hated father-substitutes.) But many think it safer, and saner, to hold their peace, where they can do so without insincerity. Hate-criticism is not very attractive except to the sadistic; and why try to destroy other men's pleasures, when they seem harmless enough? Why go about pouring cold water into other people's soup? (Except when you seriously believe that the soup is going to poison them.) Accordingly, many reputations of established authors are silently accepted by thousands whose silence is very far from assent.

Further, among the majority of readers suggestion plays an enormous part in making them think they like certain works. But, you may say, if they think they like them, they do like them? What is the difference? The difference lies hidden, I think, in another ambiguity of language. One may say 'I like that'. But one may have several 'I's. One may persuade oneself that one likes a writer, when one's real motive is a desire to be liked, or not to be despised. And so one may imagine one loves what unconsciously one even detests.[1]

This power of suggestion may be exerted by critics and connoisseurs—until simpler people become, in Blake's phrase, 'connoisseured out of their senses'. Or it may be exerted by fashion. Or it may be exerted by tradition:

> Then fame was cheap, and the first-comers sped;
> And they have kept it since by being dead.

Dead authors may preserve their fame, because no one reads them any more—except perhaps scholars; or because their prestige awes the living. Few critics say openly 'Tell me who it is by and I will tell you how good it is'; but it remains a far-reaching principle in practice. Indeed if in some cataclysm the world lost its literature and then rediscovered parts of it without knowing the authors' names, it is hard to doubt that there would be some extraordinary changes in valuation.

[1] Cf. pp. 112-13, 278.

Try confronting even the most cultivated persons with a
few passages by writers now accepted as classics, mixed
with others by writers generally thought inferior; if the
writers' names are suppressed and the passages not
recognized, the judgements passed will often prove
shattering.

Again, apart from differences of individual temperament, it is not always realized what different aspects of
literature different psychological types of reader look for.

There are those we may call the literary epicures, who
concentrate on particular beauties—here a perfect phrase,
there a graceful touch.

Quite different from these gourmets of style is the
Dionysiac type of reader who seeks, above all, intensity,
intoxication, passion—to be taken out of himself and the
world of every day into some enraptured dream.

Then there are those who talk unceasingly of 'form',
'structure', 'organization', 'pattern', 'integration'. To
the epicures of literature they are apt to seem tiresome;
to the drunkards of ecstasy, pedantic.

Then again, there are those who cannot read a book
without keeping their other eye on real life—is the
writer being true or false, fine or ignoble, sane or
decadent?

Epicure, drunkard, organizer, moralist—there are
doubtless other types as well. Nor are these four
mutually exclusive. I seem to myself to sympathize
most with the first class and last. Often I care far more
for my favourite passages—a line here, a cadence there—
than for a book as a whole; and I cannot help thinking
all the time whether the author's values seem to me to
bear the test of life. So that often I find myself feeling
for writers long dead a personal fondness, or loathing, of
an intensity that I do not easily feel for people of flesh
and blood. On the other hand, I find the literary
dipsomaniacs often tiresome; and the 'integrators', with

their passion for that equally hideous word 'organic', leave me cold and weary. The fault may be mine. Possibly it would be ideal to combine all four types of taste. But once again, the conclusion seems: What wonder if men cannot agree about literary values? What remedy except to face this fact and try to be tolerant?'

That may sound easy. Experience shows it is terribly difficult. Let us turn for a moment from books to real life. There is none too much affection in the world; and one of the saddest things is the way so much of that affection is killed in the end by slow estrangement. Often, no doubt, it is inevitable. But sometimes the estrangement starts or is aggravated by miserable trivialities like disagreements on mere matters of taste. I have heard of a wife telling her husband she could no longer care for him so much because he did not admire modern poetry. What a *casus belli*! And I remember a clever woman telling me how she had got engaged, but in her absence it was necessary for her unfortunate lover to furnish and decorate the house. The result was (in her opinion) so lacking in taste that she broke off the engagement; though they were both serious people, no longer young. It had been terribly sad, she said; but there it was. She spoke of it as if she had had no choice —as if the man had been convicted of murder, or found to have two wives already. It is true that her instinct may have been sound—that this difference in taste was possibly a symptom of incompatible differences in character. But since she did not take this line, I own that I was dismayed by so dogmatic a damnation of a well-meaning lover. People are not content to differ about taste. They *will* assume that their own taste is superior. Not even that contents them. They must make the other person feel it. Everyone has this impulse: a few overcome it.

Anyone who allows himself even to imply that
another's taste is bad, is in effect saying 'I am better than
you'. Yet it is constantly done by persons whose
manners are not otherwise gross. The effect on human
relations is hardly happy. Coleridge (whom some consider a good psychologist) wrote to his wife: 'Permit me,
my dear Sara, without offence to you, as Heaven knows!
it is without any feeling of pride in myself, to say, that
in six acquirements, and in the quantity and quality of
natural endowments, whether of feeling or of intellect,
you are the inferior . . .' Alas! The matrimonial results
of that candour were not encouraging.

Maeldune and his comrades, in Tennyson's poem,
came to an island with two towers, one of carved stone
and one plain, and suffered a similar conflict of opinion.
Primitive folk as they were, on this occasion they behaved only too like the cultured.

> The passion of battle was on us, and all took sides with the
>   Towers,
> There were some for the clean-cut stone, there were more for
>   the carven flowers,
> And the wrathful thunder of God peal'd over us all the day,
> For the one half slew the other, and after we sail'd away.

Or there is the sad case of the two Renaissance gallants
who, it is said, defied each other to a duel over the merits
of Tasso and Ariosto. One fell mortally wounded—and
then confessed that he had not even read the poet he
was dying for. Would he have been any less imbecile if
he had? You may recall that pleasant evening at Lamb's
house, when Lamb's brother and Hazlitt got involved in
a slight difference of opinion about the colouring of
Holbein and Vandyke, upset a card-table, and grappled
each other by the throat. But when Talfourd offered aid
to Hazlitt, who had by now acquired a black eye, he
received the calm answer: 'You need not trouble yourself, sir; nothing affects me but an abstract idea.' (An

astonishing statement for the author of the *Liber Amoris*.)

The Lady Murasaki, writing her tale of Genji in far-off Japan in the days of Ethelred Evil-counsel, had already more sense. People wrangled, even then, whether spring or autumn were more beautiful. But 'it is useless', she answers, 'to argue on such subjects, as has often been done. It is a matter of temperament.' I repeat, 'a matter of temperament'.

No, tolerance in taste is not easy. When Mr. A calls Mr. B's favourite novelist 'sentimental and vulgar', he is in effect calling Mr. B personally 'sentimental and vulgar'. Men have done murder for less. Hence that acrimony in critical controversies which astonishes the simple, who marvel by what mystery books written merely to give pleasure should inspire men with such a rage to inflict pain.

Above all, tolerance is difficult for professional critics and connoisseurs. They have spent years, perhaps a lifetime, on their subject; how should they not know better? Doubtless they know more; but not necessarily about judgements of value. A man may lose his taste in libraries, as well as find it. Sappho or Shakespeare did not write for professors; it is far from certain that professors are the most competent judges of Sappho or Shakespeare. I have already quoted Blake on being 'connoisseured out of one's senses'. Experts are admirable servants, but often bad masters. In first-century Judea there were certain experts in ethics and religion; but they are not treated with much respect in the Gospels. Art, too, has its Pharisees.

How often, as I turn the pages of literary periodicals, I am reminded of dear, human Goldsmith and his two snobs bullying that poor widow at Vauxhall!—'She perceived now that she had no pretensions in the world to taste; her very senses were vulgar, since she had praised detestable custard, and smacked at wretched wine; she was, therefore, content to yield the victory, and for the rest of the night to listen and improve. It is true, she would now and then forget herself, and confess she was pleased, but they soon brought her back again to miserable refinement. . . .' 'Miserable refinement'— admirable phrase!

If what I have said is true, what do the conclusions amount to? Briefly, I think, to this:

(1) Every work of art is different for every percipient, since the percipient's own faculties and associations must collaborate with the artist's work to produce the artistic impression.

(2) Therefore every percipient, cultivated and intelligent enough to give a work a fair trial, is his own—and only—judge how far it is artistically satisfying to him. It is idle to tell him he is 'wrong', or 'ought' to like something different. If he has given the matter due consideration, it merely amounts to saying he should be a different person. Which is seldom very practical; never very polite. (The important question of the psychological *after*-effects of art will be dealt with later.)

(3) The rank of writers can only be assigned on the basis of their power to go on pleasing intelligent readers in general. I see little point in pontifical orders of merit of the type: 'Crashaw is a greater poet than Keats and Shelley, but Keats and Shelley, had they lived, would probably have been greater poets than Crashaw.' This amounts to saying: 'The intelligent public doubtless prefers Keats and Shelley to Crashaw. But I am more intelligent than the intelligent public; and I tell the intelligent public that it would do well if it could be born again in my image and prefer Crashaw.' This seems neither very modest nor very useful. It is hard to see much purpose, anyway, in such class-lists of private preferences. Their interest, such as it is, seems

autobiographical rather than critical. If asked to produce an order of merit of the fifty foremost writers in Christendom, the wisest critics would wildly disagree, not only about the order, but even who the fifty were.

What, then, is the task of critics? Merely, as Anatole France and Rémy de Gourmont suggest, to relate their adventures among books and confess themselves in public? This view seems to me far preferable to absolute judgements like Brunetière's. But I should prefer to answer: 'Yes, but also, and above all, to interpret.' It is a better service to others to enable them to form their own judgement, than to try to form it for them. The critic is usually more useful pleading cases than pronouncing verdicts. He is only the advocate; the reader is the judge.

To do his duty, the critic must indeed often describe and explain his own reactions, say what he likes and why; and his task is often far wider—to explain, not only why he likes, say, Chaucer, but why Chaucer was like that; his background, his time, his ideas, his language, his text. All these many branches of criticism are covered by the word 'Interpretation'. In the hands of masters like Johnson or Sainte-Beuve criticism becomes itself an art—an art of interpretation—like portraiture. But once the interpretation is complete, the reader must still decide for himself.

It follows that appreciation is more likely to be of use than depreciation. If love is often blind, hate is often blinder. If you like a work, it proves that the work has power to please. If you dislike it, that proves only that the work lacks the power to please *you*—which need not be of vast significance. It is very negative evidence. Critics would generally be well advised to write about authors that appeal to them, rather than with intent to murder. I find it a little strange, and saddening, that nine out of ten examination candidates, when asked to write 'an appreciation' of a poem, seem to assume that what is wanted, to show their mettle, is a depreciation.

It is, indeed, possible to debate and question the *means* used by writers to get their effects. A critic can bring arguments to show that the characters, say, of a poet are false to any known human psychology, his ideas illogical, his plot inconsistent, his time-scheme impossible, his diction ungrammatical, his verses unscannable. Such points are matters of fact and can be demonstrated. Yet they may still fail to disenchant the enraptured reader. Are the characters false? He may answer, like a pragmatist, that, for him, truth is what works. Is the grammar bad? Like the Emperor Sigismund, he may be above grammar. Is the verse unmetrical? Like many a modern poet, he may neither know nor care what metre is.

The time-scheme of Othello may be impossible; who cares? Bohemia may have no sea-coast; who cares? The absurdities in the plot of *Lear* do not prevent audiences from being enthralled. Malory's *Morte d'Arthur*, when it was thought to be a single book, seemed full of careless inconsistencies; but it remained one of the great books of English literature. John Buchan has pointed out that in Scott's *Antiquary* the sun sets in the east and there are two Tuesdays in one week; what of it?

This may seem extraordinary. Critics still try to forget it. But experience shows that it can be true. The eighteenth-century French sculptor of Peter the Great's monument at St. Petersburg, after comparing its horse with that of Marcus Aurelius at Rome and pointing out the many faults and falsities in the ancient work, concluded: 'And yet this wretched beast is alive—and mine is dead.' He was wiser than most.

I repeat, the critic's first task is to interpret. Let him speak his own preferences and values, his own likes and

dislikes, freely and fearlessly. That is part of the business
of interpretation. But let him speak only for himself;
and make it clear all the time that he is speaking for
himself. In the Republic of Letters would-be dictators
are as odious as in politics; and tolerance, of all except
intolerance and corruption, as vitally necessary. I would
have all critics learn by heart the lines of Suckling:

> There's no such thing as that we beauty call.
>   It is mere cozenage all;
> For though some long ago
> Liked certain colours mingled so and so,
>   That doth not tie me now from choosing new;
> If I a fancy take
>   To black and blue,
> That fancy doth it beauty make.

> 'Tis not the meat, but 'tis the appetite
>   Makes eating a delight,
> And if I like one dish
> More than another, that a pleasant is:
>   What in our watches, that in us is found;
> So to the height and nick
>   We up be wound,
> No matter by what hand or trick.

Admirable verses in their vigour and clarity (though
I wish, myself, that the poet had less tortured the natural
order of his words).

But though I believe what Suckling says to be true,
I do not think it the whole truth. Though I believe that
the critic's main duty is to interpret and that every
intelligent reader must be his own judge of literary
values, since they depend on his own temperament, I
think the subjectivism of Anatole France is, all the same,
not enough.

Why? Because art is not merely a matter of pleasur-
able or ecstatic moments. There are also the moments
after. Every man, as Suckling says, is his own judge of
the food he likes; but what about the effects of that

food? These are no longer a matter of personal taste; they are a matter for reason, knowledge, science. I do not believe that the beauty of anything is absolute; but I believe the truth of facts is; and that we can sometimes find out approximately what it is. Pleasure is a matter of individual temperament and in the main outside our control; but health and disease, of body and mind, are *not* matters of subjective taste—they can be scientifically studied, argued about, modified by human action. Now the power of literature to strengthen or to poison seems to me immense. When Suckling used the analogy of food, he forgot that food not only tickles the palate, but descends the throat—that food and drink are also nourishment or the reverse. And modern criticism, outside the totalitarian states, seems to me to have neglected the after-effects of literature in a way that is frivolous, timorous, and scandalous. Critics argue about the pleasure-value of literature, where argument is futile; about its consequences—its influence-value, which can and should be discussed, they are often, especially to-day, obstinately silent.

Yet it seems to me vital to distinguish between the pleasure-value of literature (its power to give us valued states of mind) and its influence-value (its power to induce future states of mind that are sometimes valuable, sometimes lamentably the reverse).

To take an example—and escape from these hideous abstractions—if you know a person who reads Baudelaire constantly and keeps Joyce's *Ulysses* under his or her pillow, but regards, say, Homer and Chaucer as bores, I doubt if it would be much for your happiness to marry that person. And if it were a question whether my children should study Ovid or Plutarch's *Lives*, it would not take me ten seconds to answer. My main criteria, whether valid or no, are simple. I believe it is usually better to take a true view of things than a false; and better to be sound than sick. Sophocles and Meredith, indeed, have both expressed the view—doubtless in moments of spleen—that it is happier to be an idiot. But they were thinking of a blissfully complete idiocy which is beyond the reach of most of us.

If I prefer books that seem to me true, it is because a false picture of the world seems to me often so dangerous, in the long run. I say, 'in the long run'. In itself, the idea that the sun and moon are divine beings driving their golden chariots in glory across the blue vault of Heaven has marked poetic advantages over the stupendous but infinitely bleak Universe of the modern astronomer, which Blake hated and Patmore did not much like.

> The best that's known
> Of the heavenly bodies does them credit small.
> View'd close the Moon's fair ball
> Is of ill objects worst,
> A corpse in Night's highway, naked, fire-scarr'd, accurst;
> And now they tell
> That the Sun is plainly seen to boil and burst
> Too horribly for hell.[1]

But if you begin believing that the sun is a person, you may end by burning your children to him, as the Semites in honour of Moloch. And similar false beliefs about the moon once nearly ruined Athens, when an eclipse prevented the Spartans from marching to her help before Marathon; and later did ruin her, when another eclipse prevented the pious Nicias from retreating before Syracuse. All may look lovely in the Fool's Paradise; but it has too many trap-doors into Hell.

I labour this apparent platitude only because one much-read modern critic has put forward the view that poetry is totally unconcerned with truth; arguing, in effect, that what one asks of an opium-dream is not

---

[1] Patmore, *The Two Deserts.*

truth, but rapture. Ecstasy, in short, laughs at facts. Unfortunately, after a series of such ecstasies, the facts are apt to grow somewhat grim. Opium-dens seldom prove in the end very satisfying.

Therefore I cannot share the indifference of some critics to the truth of literature, provided only that it intoxicates. The pleasure-value of a work may be great, even though its fundamental ideas are false; but its influence-value may be sinister.

Our age has had some painful experience of the cost of mental sickness. We shall be a good while paying for the mental quirks of Hitler and those he infected. Once in the last two thousand years civilized life has gone down before invading Barbarians. The Barbarians are still there. Not only just across the Elbe, but also in the depths of the human soul. If the world were not going to last beyond next week, it would not matter to anyone but ourselves in what literary diversions we indulged. But if we wish our world to last beyond the next few years—if we hope that it may grow rather more civilized than it is—I think we should do well to think rather more of the after-influence of books than modern critics in the western democracies usually care or dare to do.

This is not in the very least a plea for didactic writing. Usually that is dismal and defeats itself. The precepts of Hesiod or Pope, excellent as they often are, have moulded the human mind far less powerfully than Homer or Shakespeare, who seem only to entertain. Is that surprising? Here at Cambridge you go to lectures and you make friends. The lecturers teach and preach all the time; the friends (unless they are peculiar) do not teach or preach at all. But I suspect that the friends you make and the company you keep are usually a far more important influence than any lectures.

I shall go into more detail later; for the moment I am

concerned to make clear, if I can, this fundamental distinction between pleasure-value and influence-value. To put it another way—for Plato, the pleasure-value of Homer was great, the influence-value worse than nothing. For Plato believed that Homer and other poets, however delightful, made men immoral, cowardly, emotional. For Bentham, the pleasure-value of Homer was, I imagine, nil; the influence-value, less than nil, since Bentham believed that Homer made men bloody. I doubt if any critical interpretation, any description of one's own enjoyment of Homer, could have made Bentham enjoy him—probably the temperamental difference was too great. Certainly no amount of mere argument could have. Yet I think it conceivable that argument might have convinced Bentham, who was a reasonable man, that Homer did not usually make men bloody—on the contrary—and that his view of Homer's influence-value might have been changed. I do not think any arguing would have changed Plato's mind on this matter; but then I do not think Plato was a reasonable man—I think he was a neurotic genius.

XII

Art for Art's Sake

Why, she is worse than ugly, she is good.
Lord Henry in WILDE'S *Picture of Dorian Gray*.

What is art that it should have a sake?
SAMUEL BUTLER.

I HAVE suggested that critical judgements of value, if we are to avoid hopeless muddle, must be sharply divided into judgements of pleasure-value, which every competent individual must assess for himself, without useless wrangling about tastes; and judgements of influence-value, which are necessarily uncertain, yet must at least be considered, unless criticism is to abandon all social responsibility.

In the light of this let us go back, for example, to the conflict over Jane Austen. We may now perhaps lay a little of its dust.

It is clear from her admirers that her pleasure-value is extremely high. There are, indeed, intelligent readers who enjoy her less because her style is sometimes rather slipshod; her field narrow—to some, oppressively so; and her mind hardly poetic. But her partisans do not mind these things; they are too fascinated by her understanding, her balance, her irony, her delicacy of touch. Ultimately, each reader after hearing both sides must, and can, only judge for himself. He can taste with no tongue but his own.

But after pleasure-value comes influence-value. And, here, to praise Jane Austen with vehement phrases like 'a prose Shakespeare', is surely rather unbalanced. It is not simply that her slice of life remains so narrow, however finely cut. It is not just the smallness of this little world of handsome soldiers or sailors, dignified squires and demure parsons, comfortable mansions and neat lawns, where the main question is always 'Will she catch him?' After all, the tiniest, most frivolous head we pass in King's Parade contains a whole Universe. But, by leaving out so much of the heights and depths even in the restricted range of characters she chooses, Jane Austen does inevitably exaggerate the importance of what she retains in her picture. If mankind learnt from her, they might well, one feels, be far more sensible, far happier; but also smaller. The provincial circle in which Flaubert's Madame Bovary moves is narrower still; the theme is the same—the eternal danger of sensibility, of false romance; yet how much vaster the treatment! It is like passing from a neat parlour in Lyme Regis to Rouen Cathedral. This is not blaming Jane Austen; few writers, probably, have used their own genius with such admirable precision, to get the utmost out of it. But to call this perfect miniaturist 'Shakespearean', or 'the greatest of literary artists', is surely to distort life, by over-emphasizing certain sides of it and showing a certain lack of intellectual energy and curiosity about the rest. It suggests a lack of proportion. And that can always become dangerous. For proportion is one of the most difficult and most vital secrets of the art of life.

In a word, Jane Austen's admirers feel the excellence of what she did; her critics—the reasonable ones—see the importance of what she left undone. Her miniatures are exquisite: but those who pore over them too much may grow a trifle near-sighted.

To conclude, a work that gives little pleasure can hardly do much good or harm; a work that gives a great deal, may still have little visible effect, good or bad, on men's lives; on the other hand, its influence can sometimes be splendid—or poisonous. These after-effects seem most marked in literature and, perhaps, music; but none of the arts can be wholly without them. If you move men at all, you move them in some direction.

A critic, especially a literary critic, who does not face all these issues seems to me one-sided. He may say 'Very well, I shall have to be one-sided. I accept my limitations. I specialize on what I feel able to do.' That is reasonable. But if too many critics limit themselves to pleasure-values or erudition, criticism itself becomes one-sided. The results of that may be bad. In our own century I think they *have* been bad. And the paradox is that it is precisely our own century which has a chance, thanks to psychology, of judging the influence-value of literature rather better than ever before. On this problem I doubt if we shall find the philosophers, from Plato on, very helpful: but I believe that the psychologists can, on the contrary, bring a good deal of new understanding.

I have spoken of 'influence-value'. Yet some deny that it even exists. Their objections must first be faced. What exactly *are* the effects of literature? What is the point of it? Its justification?

Pure amusement, some say. It is merely an intoxicant —or an anaesthetic. The opium of the intellectual.

You are spending some of the best years of your lives studying it. Some of you intend to devote the rest of your lives to it. Yet our country is passing through one of the most dangerous crises it has ever faced. We wonder if we can feed our population: yet we are short of man-power. We who sit studying literature through it all are costing more than miners get for sweating all day in filth. What do we show for it? 'Amusement'? A rather expensive amusement. Why are we not all

turned out, lecturers and undergraduates, to dig potatoes
at Coton? What shall we reply? It is not too easy.

On the other hand, if literature is 'amusing' to read,
it can be far from amusing to create. I commend to the
attention of those who think of writing as a career
the most vivid picture I know of its darker side—a
passage from Zola's *L'Œuvre*. It is far from the whole
truth. Nothing could be less like the picture Trollope
gives of his own happy craftsmanship. But Zola's description remains true enough of many a writer's life;
and I quote it as another part of that cost of producing
literature which literature must somehow justify—
unless, as Plato thought, most of it should be stopped
by the police.

This passage is put by Zola into the mouth of the
writer Sandoz; but one can hear that Zola is speaking
for himself. 'Listen, my work has robbed me of my
life. Little by little it has deprived me of my mother,
of my wife, of all I love. It is a microbe. . . . The
moment I jump out of bed in the morning, my work
seizes hold of me and nails me to my desk, without
allowing me a mouthful of fresh air. It follows me to
lunch; dumbly I masticate my phrases with my bread.
It follows me when I go out; comes home with me to
dine off the same plate; lies down again in the evening
on my pillow—so pitiless that I have no power to stop
the book I am composing—even in my sleep it continues
its vegetable growth. No one exists any more outside
myself. I go up in the morning to greet my mother, so
absent-mindedly that ten minutes later I have to ask
myself whether I have really said good-morning to her
at all. My wretched wife is a widow; I am no longer there
beside her, not even when our fingers touch. Sometimes I grow acutely conscious of the sadness I cast over
all their lives and I am full of remorse, for the whole
happiness of a home is built on kindness, frankness,

[223]

gaiety. But how am I to escape from the claws of the monster! . . . Never a walk in the morning sun, never a stolen visit to a friend, never an idle folly. . . . I have shut the gate of life behind me and tossed the key out of the window. Nothing is left, nothing is left now to inhabit the hole I live in, except my work and I. It will devour me; and then there will be an end to it, an end.'

The whole novel (powerful, but not, to me, a good novel—I am not recommending you to read it) is devoted with Zolaesque, blue-book thoroughness to depicting the lives of artists and writers in the Paris of his day. It is not gay. The artist-hero sacrifices the woman he loves to the art he loves still more. He sacrifices to the same Moloch his unhappy, neglected child, which dies. Finally he hangs himself before his abortive masterpiece—a naked woman standing in mid-Paris beside the Seine.

And around this central figure dance the other lost souls of this Inferno—the quacks of art, the snobs, the intriguers, the Iscariots; the *arrivistes* who slide smoothly and swiftly downhill into pot-boiling or the *lâchetés* of art-journalism.

An ironic contrast, surely, to Shelley's extraordinary definition of poetry as 'the record of the best and happiest moments of the happiest and best minds'.

Yet this is part of the actual price of art and literature; how do we justify it? Of course novelists like strong colours. Zola has inked his pages with his deepest black. But it is really no blacker than many a reality in the lives of 'mighty poets in their misery dead'. It is worth reading the journal of Keats's friend, Haydon the painter, who killed himself in the end like Zola's hero. For, whether or no he could paint, Haydon could write. Listen—'Thank God with all my soul and all my nature, my children have witnessed the harassing agonies under which I have ever painted; and the very name of painting—the very name of High Art—the very thought of a picture, gives them a hideous and disgusting taste in their mouths. Thank God not one of my boys, nor my girl, can draw a straight line, even with a ruler, much less without one. And I pray God, on my knees, with my forehead bent to the earth, and my lips to the dust, that He will, in His mercy, afflict them with every other passion, appetite, or misery, with wretchedness, disease, insanity, or gabbling idiotism, rather than a longing for painting—that scorned, miserable art—that greater imposture than the human race it imitates.'

Read Mrs. Carlyle's letters with their picture of Carlyle toiling like a dyspeptic, frenzied galley-slave; or the career of Balzac, his brain pulped like an orange by the time he was fifty; or the correspondence of Flaubert, contemplating the remaining years of life as a Sahara of white paper to be blacked—a martyr who has forgone happiness as austerely as his own St. Anthony, yet with no such saving faith. Is not writing, he asks, just like scratching an ulcer, or turning out serviette-rings, or playing skittles? 'Skittles' Malherbe and Boileau had already called their art. Newton considered poetry a sort of 'ingenious nonsense'; and sculpture, 'stone dolls'. Pascal thought poetry less important than hunting; Bentham, than push-pin.

'Prejudice apart,' writes Bentham, 'the game of push-pin is of equal value with the arts and sciences of music and poetry. If the game of push-pin furnish more pleasure, it is more valuable than either. Everybody can play at push-pin; poetry and music are relished only by a few. The game of push-pin is always innocent: it were well could the same always be asserted of poetry.'

Elsewhere the great Utilitarian (who, after all, was a very remarkable man) comments on the fondness for *solitaire* of Potemkin, the minister of Catherine the Great—'How much better was the minister occupied than if, with the *Iliad* in his hand, he had stirred up

within his heart the seeds of those ferocious passions
which can only be gratified with tears and blood!'

You may dismiss Bentham as a tedious Philistine. But
you can hardly say that of Congreve, who shocked
Voltaire by valuing himself on being a gentleman, not
on being a writer (just as Heredia loftily remarked,
'Écrire, c'est une de mes élégances'). Yet there were
times when Voltaire himself could feel how trivial was
literature in comparison with life—'Il y a un plaisir bien
préférable à tout cela; c'est celui de voir verdir de vastes
prairies, et croître de belles moissons; c'est la véritable
vie de l'homme, tout le reste est illusion.'

'A pack o' lies, that fule craitures writ for diversion',
such was Carlyle's summary of poetry; or, more briefly,
'jingling'.

Harsher still than the voices treating art and literature
as largely futile, are those that have denounced them as
often fatal—philosophers, priests, puritans, from Plato
to Tolstoy. It is worth reading, in *What is Art?*
Tolstoy's vivid description of an opera rehearsal—the
ridiculous, unreal scene, with its inane procession of
impossible Indians chanting their fatuous refrain, amid
the howling and cursing of the three directors of music,
orchestra, and stage. 'Art, for the sake of which the
labour of millions, the lives of men, and, above all, love
between man and man, are being sacrificed—this very
art is itself becoming a thing more and more vague and
uncertain.' Not a very different picture from Zola's
L'Œuvre.

What is the answer? For surely one is needed.

Various views are possible. For example:

(1) That the writer can—some would say, inevitably
does—influence the lives and characters of his readers;
and therefore should try to be a good influence. This is
the view of puritans. For them art is food—or poison.
The stress is on the influence-value.

(2) That, on the contrary, he cannot influence his readers; or, alternatively, that he can, but must never try. This is the view of aesthetes. For them art is wine. Only its pleasure-value matters.

Let us consider first this second attitude, which in the nineteenth century became a conscious creed and a noisy one, with its war-cry of 'Art for Art's sake'. What people think about it to-day in the surviving free countries is not clear; sometimes one might infer that most of them had ceased to think about it at all. They have grown tired of the problem; they have not solved it, but shelved it. Yet can we shelve it? There is a certain danger that if the literary refuse to consider what they are really doing, the unliterary, in these hard days, may consider it for them. We live in an age when those who cannot justify their existence may cease to exist.

The phrase 'l'art pour l'art' has been attributed to Victor Cousin (1792-1867)[1]; on the other hand, Victor Hugo apparently claimed to have launched the idea in discussion about 1829—violently though he disclaims it in *William Shakespeare* (1864), 'C'est le contraire de ce mot qui est écrit dans tout notre œuvre et, insistons-y, dans notre vie entière'. But, as we shall see, its first important champion was Gautier.

Such catchwords may seem a rather dreary mixture of banality and untruth. But the fortune of slogans is mysterious. This one succeeded. For 'l'art pour l'art' filled a need of the time—the time of Louis-Philippe, who owed his throne to a banker, held it as 'le roi-citoyen', and was to flee from it under the appropriate pseudonym of 'Mr. Smith'. The Revolution of 1830 had displaced the old aristocracy; like the reign of Victoria, the reign of Louis-Philippe became a golden

---

[1] Cf. his words in the *Revue des Deux Mondes* (1845) : 'Il faut comprendre et aimer la morale pour la morale, la religion pour la religion, l'art pour l'art.' For Cousin, 'le seul objet de l'art est le beau'. (To which one may murmur, 'But Iago ? Caliban ? ')

age of business-men and bourgeoisie—the world of Balzac. Even the anti-bourgeois grew utilitarian. The Socialist Proudhon had no more use for Homer than Plato or Bentham had—a cobbler, he observed, was more useful. Similarly the Saint-Simonist 'Père Enfantin' pronounced that the loveliest poem the desert could inspire was not worth one canal.

The artistic part of France was not unnaturally provoked. They were less useful, were they, than Egyptian fellaheen shovelling sand for a canal? But instead of setting out, like Sidney or Shelley, to prove the invaluable benefits of art, some of them defiantly accepted this very charge of uselessness, and gloried in it.

It seems worth tracing, very briefly, the fortunes of 'Art for Art's sake', on both sides of the Channel[1]; for modern criticism, though unavowedly, seems largely influenced by it still.

In 1835 appeared Théophile Gautier's *Mademoiselle de Maupin*, with a famous preface, which still repays reading, as a curiosity. 'Il n'y a de vraiment beau que ce qui ne peut servir à rien. . . . Tout ce qui est utile est laid.' It is easy to reply: 'What about a Greek vase? What about a Chippendale chair?' Surely William Morris was right in most cultivated people's eyes, when he contrasted the quiet charm of many a cottage kitchen, just because everything there does serve its purpose, with the horror of its uselessly ornamented parlour. And then architecture? Can only useless buildings be beautiful? When he visited Athens, Gautier was swept off his feet by the Parthenon—even Gothic could not compare; even Venice paled. But the Athenians who raised the Parthenon to the goddess of their city would have been a good deal astonished to hear their temple was quite purposeless. Or take the Fellows' Building at King's (unless you take the view that Fellows also are quite useless).

[1] Interestingly recorded in A. Cassagne, *L'Art pour l'Art*, 1906.

Of the drama, again, Gautier has written in the same amusingly insolent style: 'L'homme m'est parfaitement égal. Dans les drames, quand le père frotte sa fille retrouvée contre les boutons de son gilet, ça m'est absolument indifférent; je ne vois que les plis de la robe de sa fille.'

He must have missed a good deal. When Homer brings Penelope to her husband's arms.at last, he has little to say of the folds of her robe; when Posthumus cries to the Imogen he has found again:

> Hang there like fruite, my soule,
> Till the Tree dye,

Shakespeare gives no sign of being much concerned with her costume. And when Cleopatra, following her lover to death, does exclaim:

> Go fetch
> My best Attyres; I am againe for *Cydnus*,
> To meet *Marke Anthony*,

how baldly are the 'best Attyres' dismissed! It was earlier in the play, in the unheroic atmosphere of Lepidus' house, that Shakespeare let Enobarbus dwell on Cleopatra's toilet. When Michael Angelo condemned one of the Popes as a poor creature, because he criticized some detail of dress in a painting instead of feeling the greatness of the whole, he was taking exactly the opposite view to Gautier's laboured amoralism. One suspects, indeed, that Gautier was more concerned to pull his readers' noses than to broaden their minds. All the same, men took seriously Gautier and his *Mademoiselle de Maupin*, 'this golden book of spirit and sense'.

We have, too, to remember that Gautier began as a painter; even when he became a writer, his pen was still liable to turn back into a brush and paint in words. Now in painting, whatever be the case in literature, Gautier's view of 'Art for Art's sake' prevails to-day.

We have swung to the opposite extreme from Ruskin. With his fantastic consistency Ruskin could write of 'the utter inutility of all that has been hitherto accomplished by the painters of landscape . . . no moral end answered, no permanent good effected'. Landscape 'never taught us one deep or holy lesson'. And in those days Frith dared not paint a girl smoking a cigarette, and was reprimanded because his 'Ramsgate Beach' contained no devoted mother tending her convalescent child.

In the twentieth century, on the contrary, for many critics of painting, subject is of no importance whatever —only pattern, form, pure art-value. The body of Christ in a Crucifixion becomes merely 'this important mass'—in itself, a ferret nailed to a barn-door would do as well. I cannot help wondering if Leonardo was not wiser than either type of extremist, when he wrote: 'A good painter has two chief things to paint—man and the intention of his soul. The former is easy, the latter hard.' But painting is not our concern. Let us return to literature.

In one other way Gautier is typical of the advocates of Art for Art's sake. His thesis is simply that Art is amoral: but, vehement anti-bourgeois as he is, he cannot rest there. He becomes not merely amoral, but anti-moral. 'A town interests me merely for its buildings. . . . Let the inhabitants be utterly vile and the town a haunt of crime, what does that signify to me, so long as I am not assassinated while looking at the buildings?'

Similarly the Goncourts. 'Demander à une œuvre d'art qu'elle serve à quelquechose c'est avoir à peu près les idées de cet homme qui avait fait du *Naufrage de la Méduse* un tableau à horloge et mis l'heure dans la voile.' (It is a great part of the art of controversy to choose analogies that are amusingly grotesque—the reader may be too much amused to see that these analogies are also false.) Again, 'Le Beau est ce qui

paraît abominable aux yeux sans éducation.' (Exactly
the opposite extreme to Tolstoy.) 'Le Beau est ce que
votre maîtresse et votre servante trouvent d'instinct
affreux.' It is a little curious to note in what sort of
circles the Goncourts assumed that their readers sought
romance; by an odd paradox the housemaid becomes the
arbitress of elegance. But it grows clear, I think, that
such utterances were moulded less by thought than by
exasperation. The Goncourts' journal is a fascinating
book: but here they seem not very intelligent.

Even Renan, however, was influenced by the same
almost mystical desire to separate art from any rough
contact with practical life. Hence that extraordinary
contrast he draws between Jesus, the exquisite artist of
Christianity, and Paul, the man of action—'l'homme
d'action est toujours un faible artiste, car il n'a pas pour
but unique de refléter la splendeur de l'univers.' What,
indeed, are we to make of such 'enfeebled' artists as
Aeschylus, Thucydides, Dante, Chaucer, Camoens,
Leonardo, Michael Angelo, Sidney, Shakespeare, Cervantes, Milton, or Goethe—all of them men of imagination who let themselves be sullied by living active lives?

Then there is the great and tragic Flaubert—perhaps the noblest of all believers in Art for Art's sake
—and yet, as we shall see, a believer with strange
inconsistencies.

One could find, indeed, no better example of Art as a
Religion. 'No great poet', cries Flaubert, 'has ever
drawn conclusions.' 'Il ne faut jamais conclure.' 'What
did Homer—Shakespeare—think?' (But it seems to me
not really very difficult to read between their lines a
great many things that they thought.) 'Paint—paint
without theories.' (And yet however fervently one
eschews theories and judgements, surely the very act of
painting or writing involves selection, and therefore
judgement of values?)

[231]

But this hermit of Croisset lived according to his faith. 'Enough', he wrote to his fuming mistress, 'if one meets once in ten years.' For what mattered in life except art? And the artist should live like a grocer, with his imagination in the empyrean—should mortify his passions, as the Amazons cut off one breast to wield the bow.

And yet, paradoxically enough, though the artist must never draw conclusions, there are, I believe, few tracts with as terrible and penetrating a lesson as *Madame Bovary*. Did not Flaubert call a novel *L'Éducation Sentimentale*? And did he not say above the ruins of the Tuileries that this senseless destruction could not have happened had men but understood his book? And though he maintained that the artist must forgo all personal life, perhaps there are few glimpses of Flaubert so poignant as that moment in his later years which found him on his knees before a small girl, murmuring in tears: 'Voilà ce qu'il m'aurait fallu.' 'J'ai été lâche dans ma jeunesse', says one of his later letters. 'J'ai eu peur de la vie. Tout se paie.'

'Tout se paie.' Those three words are the very essence of what I am trying to say of the consequences of art and literature. 'Careless raptures' are lovely, doubtless: but the reckoning is sometimes heavy. Why make a virtue of shutting one's eyes to this simple, yet inexorable fact?

In a letter of 1879, the year before he died 'weary to the very marrow', Flaubert penned what seems to me very like a recantation of all his Art for Art's sake: 'An esthetico-moral theory—the heart is inseparable from the intelligence. Those who have drawn a line between the two, possessed neither.' How wise—at last!

Then there is Baudelaire, who pronounced: 'Poetry has no end beyond itself. . . . If a poet has followed a moral end, he has diminished his poetic force and the result is most likely to be bad.' And again, of George Sand in particular, 'Elle a toujours été moraliste, aussi elle n'a jamais été artiste.'

Criticism is full of such bravadoes of generalization. For, scientifically, most of our criticism remains pre-Baconian, medieval, on a level with astrology. Baudelaire did not feel it necessary to discuss the loss of force so marked, for example, in Isaiah, or Aeschylus, or Dante, or Donne's *Sermons*, or Bunyan, or Milton, or Johnson, or Dickens, or Tolstoy, or Ibsen.

No doubt he was enraged by extremists in the opposite camp, such as the younger Dumas, who wrote in his preface to *Le Fils Naturel* that all literature *without* moral purpose must be 'rachitique et malsaine'. But such crude didacticism is not the real issue. The actual question is not 'Shall literature preach?'—it does so at its own risk—sometimes a heavy risk; for the sermon is an exceptionally difficult and often repellent form of literature. The real question is: 'Since literature influences, can we wholly forget that influence?'

Clearly the poet of *Les Fleurs du Mal* might have found this question embarrassing. The cry for 'pure art' is nowhere louder than in the mouths of those who realize that by ordinary standards their own art is anything but 'pure'. And yet Baudelaire, though a tortured, self-divided character, could be a sincere one. Like Flaubert, he too seems to recant. There is a frank letter to Ancelle about *Les Fleurs du Mal*: 'In that appalling book I put my whole heart: all my most tender feelings, all my religion (in a disguised form), and all my hatred. Even were I to write to the contrary, and swear by all the gods that it was only a composition of pure art, of artistic jugglery with words . . . I should only be lying like a trooper.'

In Verlaine reappears this common tendency of Art-for-Artists to turn from the amoral to the aggressively anti-moral. 'I love this word "decadence", all shimmering in purple and gold. . . . It is redolent of the rouge of courtesans, the games of the circus, the panting of the gladiators, the spring of the wild beasts, the consuming flames of races exhausted by their capacity for sensation, while sound the trumpets of an invading enemy.' Which means, in effect, 'I wish art to be irresponsible in order that I may indulge without reproach my sadism, my masochism, and my anti-parental neurosis. For like all neurotics I find adult responsibility too harassing and prefer a second childhood.'

Indeed Verlaine had a curious delight (which will mystify no psychoanalyst) in invading enemies. In 1870, when over the peace and plenty of the nineteenth century fell the shadow of the coming desolations of the twentieth, and the Prussian armies moved towards Paris, Verlaine's comment was, 'Now we shall have some good music.'

The remark is amusing: but somewhat less amusing since Belsen and Auschwitz.

But I know no better example of Art for Art's sake put logically and consistently into practice than Huysmans' *À Rebours* (1884). The character of its hero was based on an eccentric of the day, Robert de Montesquiou, whose own autobiographical work, *Les Pas Effacés*, remains a curiosity of demented aestheticism—for example, its picture of M. de Montesquiou's bathroom, where the water flowed in two 'harmonious' jets from the lapis-blue trunk of a great china elephant, which also supported M. de Montesquiou's sponges. His bedroom was more striking still. For its bed was made of fragments of Chinese wood-carving, in the shape of a chimera. 'Il m'avait semblé, car j'obéissais toujours à des suggestions fantaisistes, dans lesquelles entrait quelquechose de sentimental, que s'endormir et s'éveiller dans sa chimère offrait une idée engageante et rassurante, qui devait enchanter l'entrée dans le sommeil et embellir le retour à la lumière.'

But Huysmans' *À Rebours* is far odder. As art, it seems grotesque; as an example of Art for Art's sake, it is sinister; but it has a good deal of interest as psychology. Its hero, des Esseintes, son of a decadent duke, withdraws to conduct a solitary orgy of aestheticism in a house at Fontenay. There he is attended only by an old couple (whom he arranges to keep out of sight and hearing [1]) in 'un rigide silence de moines claustrés'. In case he should glimpse the old woman through a window, she has to dress like a *béguine*—'l'ombre de cette coiffe passant devant lui, dans le crépuscule, lui donnait la sensation d'un cloître'.

Inside his dining-room he built, as its inner shell, a wooden ship's-cabin, with a single porthole looking out, through the waters of an aquarium, towards a window in the original wall. Here he could imagine himself a voyager, as he snuffed tar-vapour blown into the cabin down a pipe and, through his submerged porthole, watched clockwork fishes swimming and entangling themselves in the imitation seaweed of his aquarium. (In fact, little as he or his author realized it, this imbecile, in choosing as his refuge from reality this cell walled by water, had made himself a very passable imitation of a maternal womb.[2]) At other times he would read the steamship-notices hung on the walls, or turn the pages of 'un seul livre, relié en veau marin, les aventures d'Arthur Gordon Pym,[3] spécialement tiré pour lui, sur papier vergé, pur fil, trié à la feuille, avec une mouette en filigrane'. By this method, amongst others, he could live in an artificial hallucination—'et substituer le rêve de la réalité à la réalité même'.[4] 'Nature's day is done; by the disgusting monotony of her skies and landscapes, she has finally exhausted the patience of connoisseurs.'

---

[1] Cf. p. 178.
[2] Cf. p.144.
[3] Of course, Poe's story.
[4] Cf. p. 26.

As with Nature, so with Art; des Esseintes fills his house only with the exotic and the decadent—not with such classics as 'les grâces éléphantines d'Horace', but with the corruption of writers of the Lower Empire, with pictures like the inevitable Salome (by Gustave Moreau), or with drawings that exactly anticipate modern Surrealism—'a horrible spider with, in the middle of its body, a human face' or 'an enormous player's-die, winking a melancholy eyelid'. No less agreeable are the visions of his past life on which the hero loves to dwell, as he smokes in his armchair by the fire; how he once encouraged a friend into marriage, because he saw it would end in disaster and adultery; or how he picked up a boy in the rue de Rivoli, took him to a *maison de passe*, and paid for him to revisit it every fortnight, so that his expensive tastes might finally make him into a murderer. For des Esseintes feels the sadist's hatred for humanity as intensely as Caligula wishing the Roman people had but one neck.

Not surprisingly the book ends with the complete nervous breakdown of its hero; and, not surprisingly, its publication roused a tempest—even in France. But one of its critics was penetrating. In July 1884 Barbey d'Aurevilly wrote: 'Après un tel livre, il ne reste plus à l'auteur qu'à choisir entre la bouche d'un pistolet ou les pieds de la croix.' In 1892 Huysmans chose the Cross.

In art or politics, England seldom moves so fast or so far as France. It was so with Art for Art's sake. (For the English, as the exasperated Marx complained, are 'possessed with a mania for compromise'.) But, even in England, it went quite far enough.

Here the most important figure is Walter Pater. True, he had been preceded by Swinburne (a fervid admirer of Gautier) with his *Poems and Ballads* of 1866. But Swinburne was not a reasoner; he was a musical prodigy, who died at seventy-two still aged seventeen. It was

Pater who could claim to be the major prophet of English Aestheticism.

Yet even Pater remains full of contradictions—a strange blend of Epicurean and ascetic, hedonist and moralist, pagan and High-Church ritualist. He created his own image in Marius the half-Christian Epicurean; but his spiritual son was the not always very spiritual Oscar Wilde.

The key-passage for our purpose is, of course, the famous paragraph from *Studies in the History of the Renaissance* (1873): 'Every moment some form grows perfect in hand or face; some tone on the hills or the sea is choicer than the rest; some mood of passion or insight or intellectual excitement is irresistibly real and attractive for us—for that moment only. Not the fruit of experience, but experience itself, is the end. A counted number of pulses only is given to us of a variegated, dramatic life. How may we see in them all that is to be seen in them by the finest senses?'

Some of this is obvious truth. Many of us do go through life with eyes bedimmed and ears waxed gross.

> The snow has gone from Chung-nan; spring is almost come.
> Lovely in the distance its blue colours, against the brown of the streets.
> A thousand coaches, ten thousand horsemen pass down the Nine Roads;
> Turns his head and looks at the mountains—not one man![1]

So wrote Po-chu-i far off in ninth-century China, a thousand years before Pater was born.

Yet the old Chinese poet remains free from the somewhat sickly unreality of Pater. A 'wise passiveness' may, at times, be admirable; but it is still more important, in my belief, to be also wisely active. It is fine, doubtless, to 'burn with a hard gem-like flame': but it is well at

---

[1] A. Waley, *170 Chinese Poems* (1918), p. 116.

times to use it to forge something—not to be, in Byron's words:

> A flame unfed that runs to waste
> With its own flicker, or a sword laid by
> Which eats into itself, and rusts ingloriously.

One sentence of Pater's paragraph is particularly relevant: 'Not the fruit of experience, but experience itself is the end.' That may be a true definition of aesthetic feeling; but it does not abolish 'the fruit of experience'. We cannot just gather its flowers. Pater might have recalled those wise, sad lines of Christina Rossetti:

> I plucked pink blossoms from mine apple-tree
> And wove them all that evening in my hair:
> Then in due season when I went to see,
> I found no apples there.

The danger of Art for Art's sake is that it thinks too exclusively of blossom—and then its autumn brings bare boughs, or perhaps only Apples of Sodom.

Pater never wrote anything more typical, I think (though he wrote many things that seem to me better criticism and better sense), than his famous purple passage on Leonardo's *Monna Lisa*. As an account of the fat bourgeoise who sits in Leonardo's canvas this seems fantastic, masterly though her one-sided, enigmatic smile may be. It makes a very 'Imaginary Portrait'. Yet this curious mixture of Madonna and 'Belle Dame sans Merci', Christian saint and pagan vampire, which Pater sees in the picture, gives no ill likeness of his own pallid Muse. So true is it that criticism often throws most light on the critic himself.

Four years after Pater's *Studies*, in 1877, appeared W. H. Mallock's *New Republic*, with a prominent caricature of Pater. Yet, for a caricature, it does not seem to me unfair. I shall quote at some length because Mallock's one brilliant book is to-day too little known;

and it would do some of us no harm to realize that the
Victorians could sometimes ridicule their age quite as
cleverly and caustically as we. What Gilbert and
Sullivan did for Aestheticism in *Patience*, Mallock did for
it, among other things, in his *New Republic*.

Three familiar faces, in particular, you will meet
there: Matthew Arnold, as Mr. Luke; Ruskin, as Mr.
Herbert; Pater, as Mr. Rose. And the best of these, I
think, is Mr. Rose.

"'I every now and then," said Mr. Rose, "when I am
in the weary mood for it, attend the services of our
English Ritualists, and I admire their churches very
much indeed. In some places the whole thing is really
managed with surprising skill. The dim religious
twilight, fragrant with the smoke of incense; the
tangled roof that the music seems to cling to; the
tapers, the high altar, and the strange intonation of the
priests, all produce a curious old-world effect, and seem
to unite one with things that have long been dead. . . .'"

"'Yes,'" Mr. Rose went on, "there is a regretful
insincerity about it all, that is very nice, and that at once
appeals to me, *Gleich einer alten halbverklungnen Sage.*
The priests are only half in earnest; the congregations
even. . . .'"

"'Do you seriously, and in sober earnest, mean'",
Allan again broke in, "that you think it a good thing
that all our art and architecture should be borrowed and
insincere, and that our very religion should be nothing
but a dilettante memory?'"

"'The opinion,'" said Mr. Rose, "which by the way
you slightly misrepresent, is not mine only, but that of
all those of our own day who are really devoting themselves to art for its own sake. I will try to explain the
reason of this. In the world's life, just as in the life of a
man, there are certain periods of eager and all-absorbing
action, and these are followed by periods of memory and

reflection. . . . Upon such a reflective period has the world now entered. It has acted and believed already; its task now is to learn to value action and belief—to feel and be thrilled at the beauty of them. And the chief means by which it can learn this is art—the art of a *renaissance*. For by the power of such art, all that was beautiful, strong, heroic, or tender in the past—all the actions, passions, faiths, aspirations of the world, that lie so many fathom deep in the years—float upwards to the tranquil surface of the present, and make our lives like what seems to me one of the loveliest things in nature, the iridescent film on the face of a stagnant water.'''

No wonder that Pater could lament: 'I wish they would not call me a "hedonist". It produces such a bad effect on people who don't know Greek.' Yet if we turn for a moment to Pater himself—exquisite as some of his style is, both in a good sense and in a bad—I do not think we shall feel that Mallock's satire was outrageous. And it is worth trying to understand Pater, for his life and work are very typical of Art for Art's sake. This is what can breed it: this is what it can breed.

He is sensitive, subtle—and yet he seems always enervated by the same bloodless aestheticism, whether he is speaking of art or of learning, of the beauties of this world or the mysteries of the next. As an undergraduate he professed to be tickled by the idea of 'what fun' it would be 'to be ordained and not to believe a single word of what you are saying'. Apparently it was only by the intervention of friends, who informed the Bishop of London, that three years later his actual ordination was stopped—Art for Art's sake in church.

But it is much of a piece with Pater's reported reply to the question whether he was related to the painter Jean-Baptiste Pater: 'I think so; I believe so; I always say so.'

Towards Nature, as towards God or Truth, Pater tends to show the same somewhat sickly unreality. 'Certain flowers', he is said to have said, 'affect my imagination so that I cannot smell them with pleasure. The white jonquil, the gardenia, and the syringa actually give me pain. I am partial to the meadow-sweet, but on an evening like this there is too much of it. It is a fault of nature in England that she runs too much to excess.' A tiger-lily, one feels, might have killed him. Gautier with his red waistcoat, his meat-diet, and the boxer's punch he was so proud of, would have cast a disdainful eye on this degenerate disciple.

But after such glimpses of the man it is easier, I think, to understand the writer who would not read Kipling or Stevenson because their style was 'too strong'; who could only read Poe in French—'he is so rough'; and whose pet words are 'wistful' (for Pater even the Sacristy of San Lorenzo becomes 'wistful'), 'dainty', 'weary', 'strange', 'fantastic', 'exquisite', 'vague'.

No wonder he thought all art 'constantly aspires towards the condition of music'—literature, for example, trying to lose sense in sound. No wonder he could propound the view (which would have infuriated Tolstoy or Dickens) that 'the literary artist is of necessity a scholar. ... His appeal is to the scholar, who has great experience of literature'. No wonder, finally, that there are marked neurotic traces in his work—a sadistic streak in *Denys l'Auxerrois* or *Apollo in Picardy*; and a corresponding masochism in his ascetic leanings, or in that grotesque portrait of Emerald Uthwart, whose submissiveness, we are told, 'had the force of genius.'

There are also traces of that still stranger aberration which finds a physical charm in death—necrophily; particularly in *Emerald Uthwart*, with its grotesque *post-mortem*, which reveals the exquisite formation of the hero's internal organs. When Pater calls the Virgin in Fra Angelico's *Coronation* 'corpse-like in her refinement', he was but too well describing a quality of his own prose, which merits one critic's description of it as 'lying in state'.

Pater was a devoted artist, whose place in English literature abides. I have no desire merely to pelt him with hideous psychological terms of abuse, the very sound of which would have caused him anguish as acute as their meaning. I think it was well for English prose that he existed: but I think it would also be well for humanity that not many of his type should exist. He remains too like a churchyard lily, a slightly inebriated swan, a bat flickering in the aisles of a twilit cathedral— exquisitely sensitive, yet strangely blind.

But it is only fair, before we leave him, to note that like so many other Art-for-Artists, he had moments when he forsook his wax Madonna with her immortelles for a fresher air and a bolder faith. He could write in his *Essay on Style* (1888) of the power of letters for 'increase of sympathy, amelioration of suffering, service of humanity'. And, again, what a return to Nature is here!—'Complex and subtle interests, which the mind spins for itself, may occupy art and poetry or our own spirits for a time; but sooner or later they come back with a sharp rebound to the simple elementary passions —anger, desire, regret, pity, and fear, and what corresponds to them in the sensuous world.'

This indeed was a divided soul.

It was strikingly different with his great contemporary, William Morris. Morris did not wait so long as Pater to regain his true bearings. After all, he at least was no neurotic and his master was Geoffrey Chaucer. He had written one of the loveliest of all confessions of the Art-for-Artist's faith:

> Of Heaven or Hell I have no power to sing,
> I cannot ease the burden of your fears,
> Or make quick-coming death a little thing,
> Or bring again the pleasure of past years,

Nor for my words shall ye forget your tears,
Or hope again for aught that I can say,
The idle singer of an empty day. . . .

Dreamer of dreams, born out of my due time
Why should I strive to set the crooked straight?
Let it suffice me that my murmuring rhyme
Beats with light wing against the ivory gate,
Telling a tale not too importunate
To those who in the sleepy region stay,
Lulled by the singer of an empty day.

But Morris was to find at last in Scandinavia and Ice-
land that 'patience of the North' which breathes through
the epic pages of *Sigurd the Volsung*; he was to force
himself, the 'idle singer', into yearlong toil for a Com-
munism that was at least genuine—not the modern
imposture, whose Sion is a police-state; he was to die,
largely of overwork, after a life happy as few poets' lives
have ever been. And *his* final judgement on Art for Art's
sake was unhesitant and blunt: 'Its foredoomed end
must be that art at last will seem too delicate a thing
even for the hands of the initiated to touch.' We have
seen in our time this recession of art into the jungles of
the incomprehensible. Did not Joyce tell Max Eastman?
—'The demand that I make of my reader is that he
should devote his whole life to reading my works.'

But Pater was not to die without an heir—Oscar Wilde;
though he died just a year before Wilde's tragedy. Wilde
went a good deal further; and went more outspokenly.
'There is no such thing as a moral or immoral book.
Books are well written or badly written; that is all.'
'No artist has ethical sympathies. An ethical sympathy
in an artist is an unpardonable mannerism.' 'All art is
quite useless.'

And yet, like Pater, Wilde could be curiously con-
tradictory. In *Dorian Gray* appears a significant reference to Huysmans' *À Rebours*: 'It was a poisonous book.

The heavy odour of incense seemed to cling about its pages and to trouble the brain.' The whole of *Dorian Gray*, indeed, with its theme of the ugliness of evil revealing itself in ever more sinister lines on the portrait's face, so that we recall *Dr. Jekyll and Mr. Hyde*, becomes in essence as moralizing as a tract. And it is surely strange that Wilde, who was so proud of his paradox about Nature imitating Art (so that night over Battersea Bridge, for example, assumes the shapes and shadows Whistler has taught us to see), should not have drawn the parallel conclusion that *human* nature, for better or worse, can likewise imitate art. What of the suicides that followed *Werther*?

> Wherefore in dreams of Art
> And loftiest culture I would stand apart,
> Neither for God nor for His enemies.

So Wilde wrote, remembering Dante; but he forgot what happens in Dante to the angels who did that.

> Misericordia e giustizia gli sdegna:
> Non ragioniam di lor, ma guarda e passa.

With the close of the 'nineties this cry of Art for Art weakened in England. The ruin of Wilde, the humiliations of the South African War, the rise of Kipling and the new imperialism, the growing menace of Germany, may all have helped. But George Moore, with his French influences, still upheld the rebel cause; and, naturally, in a form more extremist still. If Wilde had denied that any book could be immoral, Moore on the contrary proclaimed that it could; and indeed was all the better for being immoral. 'Novelists have often shown how a love-passion brings misery, despair, death, and ruin upon a life, but I know of no story of the good or evil influence awakened by the chance reading of a book, the chain of consequences so far reaching, so intensely dramatic.[1] Never shall I open these books (Gautier's) again; but were I to live a thousand years, their power in my soul would remain. I am what they made me.' And again: 'The village-maiden goes to her Faust; the children of the nineteenth century go to you, O Baudelaire, and having tasted of your deadly delight, all hope of repentance is in vain.' (Even Moore's grammar seems here to share the general demoralization.)[2]

Further, if Art has involved human misery like the final death in hospital of the girl from whom Ingres painted *La Source*, or if Israelite multitudes perished to build the pyramids (which seems highly dubious history), so much the better. 'Nay more, the knowledge that a wrong was done—that millions of Israelites died in torments, that a girl, or a thousand girls, died in hospital for that one virginal thing, is an added pleasure which I could not afford to spare. Oh . . . to fill the languid hours with the agonies of poisoned slaves! Oh, for excess, for crime!'

One may doubt if the private annals of George Moore contained much of this Neronian ferocity. Anything more violent than feeding his pet python in Paris on live guinea-pigs tied to a Louis XV tabouret seems to have remained for him merely a pious aspiration. (Some will feel that even this was more than enough.) And that rather pathetic old gentleman one saw in Ebury Street, suggesting a blanched but still lively cockatoo, seemed long past pythons and unlikely to have poisoned even a single typist.

[1] Moore overlooks Dante, and Francesca's reading of that story of Lancelot which cost her immortal soul—' Galeotto fu il libro, e chi lo scrisse.'

[2] Compare (and contrast) Goethe's account of the influence exerted on him by *The Vicar of Wakefield* : ' It is not to be described, the effect that Goldsmith's *Vicar* had on me, just at the critical moment of my intellectual development. That lofty and good-humoured irony, that fair and kindly view of all weaknesses and faults, that equanimity amid all changes and chances, and all the other virtues that went with it, proved my best education.'

Yet it is interesting to find how regularly these advocates of Art for Art's sake ran to egotism and sadism. Probably because their whole attitude was itself largely infantile—an angry desire to be left to play with their toys, unvexed by adult responsibilities. Other neurotic traits too recur in Moore's circle; for example, a necrophily recalling Pater's or Poe's. Conversation with Cabaner: 'My dear George Moore, you always write about love, the subject is nauseating.' 'So it is, so it is—but after all Baudelaire wrote about love and lovers: his best poem. . . .' 'C'est vrai; mais il s'agissait d'une charogne et cela relève beaucoup la chose.'

This piece of wisdom recalls an article in the *Cambridge Review* between the wars, whose burden was how much better *In Memoriam* would have been had Tennyson really visualized Hallam being eaten by worms. One should try to keep an open mind. I have duly visualized Hallam being eaten by worms. But I am bound to say I remain doubtful if it would have improved *In Memoriam*. After all, 'Monk' Lewis pursued this simple recipe in the resurrection of his Alonzo the Brave to claim the Imogine:

> The worms they crept in and the worms they crept out
> And sported his eyes and his temples about,
> While the spectre address'd Imogine.

But such worms catch only gudgeons. I doubt if John Wolcot, 'Peter Pindar', was a much better poet than 'Monk' Lewis; yet at least he wrote better sense:

> Envy not such as have in dirt surpassed ye;
> 'Tis easy, very easy, to be nasty.

Or, again, there is the view of art attributed to Degas: 'Est-ce que c'est fait pour être vu, la peinture?' One should paint, he said, for two or three living friends—and for some who were dead. 'Art is a vice. One does not wed it—one rapes it. Art is dishonest and cruel.'

What would Chaucer have answered? I suppose he would have smiled—and there might have appeared another pilgrim on the Canterbury road.

But no doubt, just as Arnold found that Chaucer had too little 'high seriousness', Moore would have felt that even Chaucer had too much. Certainly he felt this of Shakespeare. 'Could he be freed from his ideas, what a poet we should have! Therefore let those that have taken firsts at Oxford devote their intolerable leisure to preparing an edition from which everything resembling an idea shall be excluded. We might then shut up our Marlowes and our Beaumonts, and resume our reading of the bard.' I am not aware that the 'intolerable leisure' of Oxford has ever responded to this appeal; however, Shakespeare seems still to contrive to be read, ideas and all.

There remains, outside England, another important and unexpected—though very temporary adherent of nineteenth-century aestheticism—Ibsen.

In 1865, the year of *Brand*, Ibsen wrote to Björnson: 'If I were asked . . . the chief result of my stay abroad, I should say it consisted in having rid myself of the aestheticism that had a great power over me. . . . Aestheticism of this kind seems to me now as great a curse to poetry as theology to religion. . . . You have never gone about looking at things through your hollowed hand.'

This 'hollowed hand' is an allusion to Ibsen's poem *On the Fells* (1859). Its hero affects to care for nothing but the aesthetic aspect of things. On Christmas Eve he sees a fire destroy his home and aged mother—his Mephistopheles, the Strange Hunter, comments:

> What a contrast rare
> The moonlight made with the fire's red glare!
> 'Twas a wonderful effect.

The attitude, in fact, of Nero towards Agrippina and

burning Rome. Next midsummer the hero's bride (one cannot blame her) leaves him to marry another. He watches her ride to her wedding:

> I held to my eye my hollowed hand
> To get the perspective right. . . .
> Her dress—what a fine effect
> Seen red through the white birch-trees!

It is a curious episode for a writer who was to be, though one of the greatest artists in the history of the stage, at the same time one of its profoundest moralists.

The twentieth century has indulged less in theories of Art for Art. Even Surrealists pretend to serve a purpose. 'There is,' claims M. Georges Hugnet, 'in addition to its poesy, its complete adhesion to the principles of dialectical materialism, its revolutionary position, and its struggle against patriotism and the bourgeoisie, . . . unremitting defeatism, demoralization, and aggressiveness.' Actually, with characteristic wisdom, Surrealists are here trying to saw off the very branch they sit on; for they are themselves a typical product of bourgeois decadence; and it is highly dubious if they would be tolerated six weeks in the world of the Kremlin. The masses prefer follies less exotic.

But a word must be said of one great twentieth-century work which also embodies a kind of mystical aestheticism. In some ways Proust's *À la Recherche du Temps Perdu* recalls Flaubert; it is, in a sense, a vaster *Éducation Sentimentale*. Proust with his asthma was to become a hermit even lonelier than Flaubert with his epilepsy. Nothing could be more aptly symbolic than the picture of this sick genius driving in his closed carriage among the orchards in bloom, whose beauty he so loved, but whose perfume on the May air he dared not breathe.

Both writers, too, were sick in mind as well as in body. In both one may read the symptoms of the tragedy that

follows when a child becomes too tied in soul to his
mother and can never wholly win free to the independence of normal manhood.

The creed of Proust is desolately and desperately clear.
We are all prisoners—inside ourselves. We are all
'irremediably alone'. All the Paradises whose gates real
life seems to throw wide before the feet of youth are
merely dreams; the only real Paradises are the Paradises
we have lost, the Paradises of memory. For we can
never see imaginatively anything we already possess.
(This seems to me not true.)

Friendship is an illusion. A man might as well
imagine the furniture was alive and could talk to him.
(This did not prevent Proust from writing a dedication
to Léon Daudet as 'l'incomparable ami'.) Love is an
even more painful illusion—its only use is to make us
unhappy; for unhappiness stings us to open our eyes on
the bleak truth. Love is always just a ghostly quadrille
danced by the real A and the real B (who can never
meet), together with A's fantasy of B and B's fantasy of A.
The pain of jealousy, the pain of passionate regret—
these are its only realities. 'Nous sommes irrémédiable-
ment seuls.'

What remains, then, in this abomination of desolation
called life? Only the mystic power of the imagination.
This comes, above all, from memory (hence '*La
Recherche du Temps Perdu*')—not from deliberate recollection, but from those spontaneous visions of the past
that rise, glorious in their ineffable remoteness, from
some sudden association—'real without being ideal, ideal
without being abstract'.

Thus for Proust, as for the Greeks, the Muse is the
daughter of Memory. For him, as for the Greeks, Beauty
springs from the deeps; not of the Aegean, but of the
Unconscious, with its store of mysterious associations by
which the rolling years once more give up their dead;

[249]

as when, for example, a peculiar inequality of the Paris pavement under the feet of Proust's hero makes the remembered glory of Venice rise like another Venus from her sea.

> His eyes, fixed on the crystal of his soul,
> Watch the long pageant of the past unroll,
> Painless, most perfect, blest days and unblest,
> In that high vision where the heart at rest
> Beholds itself, at last, possess the unpossest.

It is—at least, it was for me—a remarkable experience to read Proust's book. Not for its philosophy, which seems to me morbid: but for its poetry, for the brilliant flashes of intelligence that illumine its unconscionable length.

Yet its mysticism about Art and the 'duty' of Art seems to me fantastic. It is a poignantly intelligent book, not silly like *À Rebours*; it is a civilized—over-civilized book—not barbarous like Joyce or D. H. Lawrence; but one can already hear the tramp of the barbarians at the gates of Proust's melancholy, decadent, tragic world. Its pleasure-value can be great; but its health-value? I know few better examples of a thoroughly neurotic work which yet has genius.

This may not matter, if the reader is forearmed against it. But the France that produced it was not forearmed. It was sick.

The author is himself a prisoner, shackled to that past which is his Eldorado. He too cannot surmount his childhood. His unhappy homosexuality is only one of the bitter fruits of that. But the basis of mental health is exactly the opposite of Proust's creed. For health of mind depends on accepting reality, on surmounting the past, on growing up, on moving with the years. We have seen, again and again, how the neurotic is like a caterpillar, whose tail is fastened to a point behind him, while Time drags his head forward and forward; till the tension and the strain end in a split.

[250]

And so the reader of Proust can already glimpse in these beautiful, but sombre pages, with their picture of an aristocracy tied likewise to its fading past, the deepening shadow of the Fall of France and the Rise of Vichy —just as the France of Flaubert and Baudelaire was heading for Sedan. Flaubert's final verdict was true: 'Tout se paie.' 'J'ai été lâche; j'ai eu peur de la vie.' Often the France of the last hundred years, with all its brilliance, seems tragically changed from that vital and brilliant land which could produce the gay, confident energy of the *Chanson de Roland,* of Joinville and Froissart, of Ronsard and Molière, of Montesquieu and Voltaire, of Michelet and Victor Hugo and the elder Dumas; an energy, or so it appeared then, that could not be exhausted even by the reckless and ruthless years of the First Empire.

I have dwelt on Proust, because he is a fascinating case —and because such an example can, I think, bring out more clearly than ever the dangers of all literature that turns from life, all literature that loses health of mind. For the Ivory Tower in this world, like Virgil's Ivory Gate in the world below, is, I believe, in the long run, the haunt of dreams that lie and of visions that betray.

XIII

Art with a Purpose. Plato

The Master spoke of the Succession Dance as being perfect beauty and at the same time perfect goodness ; but of the War Dance as being perfect beauty, but not perfect goodness.

CONFUCIUS.

This was the fault of Plato. He knew of nothing but virtues and vices and good and evil.

BLAKE.

THE advocates of Art for Art's sake do not seem to me to have made a very cogent case, either in theory or practice. Yet it would be rash to condemn their cause simply for that. The fault might lie with its advocates. Men of letters often make poor controversialists; they tend to be too temperamental and behave more like bulls than toreadors. Hence the depressing effect of the history of criticism—often it seems a vast cemetery of ideas, many of which had better not been born. Still worse, many of them indulge in pertinacious resurrections.

The times has bene,
That when the Braines were out, the man would dye,
And there an end. But now they rise againe. . . .

The defenders of Art for Art's sake needed only to prove that Art was something quite distinct from Ethics —a sovereign and independent kingdom of its own. But again and again in the heat of conflict they let themselves be irritated into making Art not merely amoral but anti-moral. Their hate of preaching goaded them to

[252]

preach. They developed a righteous indignation against righteousness. No doubt, systems of morality do often cry out to be attacked; often they are stupid; or have become so; but it seems a little childish to write as if society could exist without any principles at all. Mrs. Grundy stood on her head does not grow any more intelligent than Mrs. Grundy on her feet.

The second mistake made by the advocates of Art without purpose, as by so many other critical theorists, was that they persisted in bandying generalities, instead of examining actual instances. If, for example, it is maintained that books with a purpose are, or tend to be, bad, the first step is surely to examine a number of such books, and see. But that was the last thing Gautier or the Goncourts were prepared to do. Here at least their instinct of self-preservation was sound.

The opponents of Art for Art's sake, the moral philosophers and the priests and the puritans, have on the whole been less airy. When Plato, for example, says poets are wicked, he does at least produce from their works actual specimens of their wickedness. If in the process he sometimes gives the impression of being himself not very rational, the fault lies, not in his method, but in his curious notions of human nature. It was indeed only to be expected that moralists who were often professional philosophers should be better at arguing than aesthetes; but they were also, I think, on firmer ground to start with. Even those who exaggerate the influence-value of art find it hard to be quite so blind as those who cannot even see that it exists.

The history of Art with a purpose is less amusing than the history of Art for Art's sake. Butterflies are brighter than owls. But it is also an enormously longer history. It reaches back into prehistory, whereas the *theory* of Art for Art's sake was mainly a maggot of nineteenth-century brains. Art with a purpose is the oldest art we know; and so here, I think, it becomes essential to look briefly at a few of those examples which the Art-for-Artists so carefully ignored.

As is well known, art very early acquired its first purpose—magic. Clearly, even the cave-artist must have learnt to draw and paint before his drawing and painting could be employed to help the hunter. Art must have begun with play. But it seems to have been quickly put to use. Even birds sing with a purpose; even flowers, as H. G. Wells put it, are advertisements for bees. The oldest meaning of words like ᾠδή, ἐπῳδή, *carmen*, *cantus*, *vates*, is magical. The oldest type of music is the Pied Piper's.

Take Egypt, for instance. Here, from its Feudal Age (*c.* 2000 B.C.), is an engaging charm to keep demons from a child.

Avaunt the comer in darkness, entering by stealth, with his nose behind and his face turned backward, on a bootless errand.
Avaunt the comer in darkness, entering by stealth with her nose behind and her face turned backward, on a bootless errand.
Comest thou to kiss this child? I will not let thee kiss him.
Comest thou to soothe him? I will not let thee soothe him.
Comest thou to harm him? I will not let thee harm him.
Comest thou to take him away? I will not let thee take him away.[1]

Slowly magic develops towards religion. Here is a passage from *The Book of the Dead*, still moving in its agonized passion to believe.

I shall not decay, I shall not rot, I shall not putrefy, I shall not turn into worms, I shall not see corruption before the eye of the God Shu. I shall have my being, I shall have my being; I shall live, I shall live; I shall germinate, I shall germinate, I shall germinate; I shall wake up in peace; I shall not putrefy; my intestines shall not perish; I shall not suffer injury; my eye shall not decay; the form of my countenance shall not disappear; mine ear shall not become deaf. . . .

[1] Based on J. H. Breasted, *The Dawn of Conscience* (1934), pp. 247-8.

With Iknaton's *Hymn to Aton* (*c.* 1375 B.C.) religion has fully replaced incantation. And here already is an answer more than three thousand years old, older than Homer or the Bible, to those who cannot reconcile purpose with fine poetry:

> Thy dawning is beautiful in the horizon of heaven,
> O living Aton, Beginning of Life!
> When thou risest in the eastern horizon of heaven,
> Thou fillest every land with thy beauty. . . .
>
> When thou settest in the western horizon of heaven,
> The world is in darkness like the dead.
> Men sleep in their chambers, their heads are wrapped close,
> Every lion cometh forth from his den.
> The serpents, they sting.
> Darkness reigns, the world is in silence:
> He that made them is gone to rest in his horizon.
>
> Thou art he who creates the man-child in woman . . .
> Who gives life to the son in the body of his mother,
> Who soothes him that he may not weep,
> A nurse even in the womb.
>
> When the chick crieth in the egg-shell,
> Thou givest him breath therein to preserve him alive . . .
> He cometh forth from the egg to chirp with all his might,
> He runneth about on his two feet.
>
> How manifold are thy works!
> They are hidden before us.[1]

Already there had also grown up an equally purposeful literature of ethics. Here is Ptah-hotep, a Polonius of the twenty-seventh century B.C., instructing his son on the delicate ordeal of eating with a social superior.

'Take what he puts before thee, look not at his portion, look at thine own, and shoot not many glances at him. Turn thy face downward when he addresses thee and speak only when spoken to. Laugh when he

---

[1] Based on A. Weigall, *The Glory of the Pharaohs* (1923), pp. 146-7.

laughs, so shalt thou find favour in his heart and what thou dost will be well-pleasing to his heart. One knows not what is in the heart.' [1]

If that is comic, this, from a dialogue between an intending suicide and his soul, is as grim as *Ecclesiastes*:

'Then my soul opened her mouth to answer me: "What thou sayest of burial, that is but sorrow, but bringing of tears, but giving of grief, but dragging a man from his home and casting him on the western hills. Never wilt thou come forth again to look on the sun. They that builded of granite, that made a hall for themselves within their pyramid, that fashioned fair works— as soon as the lord builders are dead, their tables of offering stand empty and they are no better than the weary wretch that dies on the dyke-side and leaves none to remember him; who has found his end by the flood, and henceforth the noon-sun and the fishes talk with him. . . . But, thou, follow after the day of joy and forget thy cares."' [2]

Egyptian literature did also develop love-songs (which, after all, are primarily art with a very distinct purpose) and stories for entertainment. But these remain of minor importance. In other words, most ancient Egyptian literature is rammed with purpose; yet some of it is fine literature. Surely those nineteenth-century dogmatists who banned purpose in art so confidently, already look a little parochial?

It is the same in early China—only that secular race offers us more ethics and less religion.

First, again, magic. Mo Tzu prescribes the rites for defensive war.

'When an enemy comes from the East, build an altar towards the East, eight feet high, and a hall with eight sides. Let eight men eighty years old preside over the

[1] Based on J. H. Breasted, *The Dawn of Conscience*, p. 131.
[2] Cf. A. Erman, *Die Literatur der Ägypter* (1923), p. 125.

offerings. They hold a blue banner with the Blue God painted upon it, and eight men eight feet tall with eight bows shoot eight arrows, and no more. The general of the troops, dressed in blue, is then to sacrifice a cock.' [1]

War, alas, has grown less simple.

Then ethics. Confucius would have thought little of Art for Art's sake. 'The Master said, A man may be able to recite the three hundred *Songs*; but if, when given a post in the government, he cannot turn his merits to account, or when sent on a mission to far parts he cannot answer particular questions, however extensive his knowledge may be, of what use is it to him?' Aeschylus, Chaucer, Byron might have heartily agreed.

And again: 'The Master spoke of the Succession Dance as being perfect beauty and at the same time perfect goodness; but of the War Dance as being perfect beauty, but not perfect goodness.' [2]

In this one simple sentence there seems to me more sense than in all the tirades ever written on 'Art for Art'.

It is, however, only fair to add that the Taoists disagreed with the Confucians. Here is a Taoist legend of a dispute between Lao Tzu and Confucius on this very point—a dialogue from whose witty wisdom I quoted earlier.

Confucius said to Lao Tzu, 'I have edited the *Songs*, the *Book of History*, the *Rites*, the *Canon of Music*, the *Book of Changes*, the *Chronicle of Springs and Autumns*—six scriptures in all—and I think I may say that I have thoroughly mastered their import.

'Armed with this knowledge I have faced seventy-two rulers, expounding the Way of former kings, the achievements of Chou and Shao; but there was not one ruler who made the slightest use of my teaching. . . .'

'It is a lucky thing', said Lao Tzu, 'that you did not meet with

[1] A. Waley, *Three Ways of Thought in Ancient China* (1939), p. 263.
[2] A. Waley, *The Analects of Confucius* (1938), pp. 172, 101.

a prince anxious to reform the world. Those six scriptures are the dim footprints of ancient kings. They tell us nothing of the force that guided their steps. All your lectures are concerned with things that are no better than footprints in the dust. Footprints are made by shoes; but they are far from being shoes.'[1]

This is very clever. But the Taoists, of course, did not want Art for Art's sake either—they were mystics and wanted Quietism for Quietism's sake. An early Taoist Utopia expressly states that there shall be no books.

But here we already encounter one of the eternal charges brought by philosophers against poets: 'Poetry teaches things that are not true.'

Certainly the statements of literature are often false, or become so. Hesiod's *Works and Days* and Virgil's *Georgics* make poor manuals for the practical farmer. But literature is less concerned with truths of material fact than with truths of finer feeling. Even these are subject to change; even human nature does alter; and yet even in these utterances thousands of years old it is amazing how much living truth can still remain. Surely there is more than mere 'footsteps in the dust' in such a passage as this from Confucius himself:

The Master said, The true gentleman is easy to serve, yet difficult to please. For if you try to please him in any manner inconsistent with the Way, he refuses to be pleased; but in using the services of others he only expects of them what they are capable of performing. Common people are difficult to serve, but easy to please. Even though you try to please them in a manner inconsistent with the Way, they will still be pleased; but in using the services of others, they expect them (irrespective of their capacities) to do any work that comes along.[2]

Or again: 'the true gentleman is conciliatory, but not pliable; common people are pliable, but not conciliatory.'

[1] A. Waley, *Three Ways of Thought in Ancient China*, p. 31.
[2] A. Waley, *The Analects of Confucius*, p. 178.

Might not that well be hung on the wall of every government office in the world to-day?

Such utterances are partly philosophy (ethics); partly science (psychology); but they are also art—one aspect of the art of living brilliantly expressed in the art of words. By their balance and brevity, they rouse in the hearer a ripple of emotion that doubles their effectiveness. They gain even a touch of poetry.

There is no need to dwell on the writings of Israel. No great literature is more concentrated on religion and ethics. None provides a completer refutation in itself of the extraordinary statement that didactic literature cannot be great.

But on Greek literature we must dwell a little. For the Greeks not only produced a great literature in practice, much of it full of purpose; they were also the first to theorize in detail about the place of literature in life.

As Hesiod watched his sheep among the grey boulders of Helicon, between cloud-capped Parnassus and sunlight-loving Athens, he had a vision of the Muses:

> Fair too the song that the Muses once taught to Hesiod,
> Feeding his flock on Helicon, the Mount of God.
> Thus on the mountain-silence the Olympian Muses broke,
> The Aegis-wielder's daughters, and thus to me they spoke:
> ' Ye shepherds of the upland, ill-famed, ye bellies blind,
> Many a falsehood like to truth our tongues can find,
> But many a true word also, when truth is to our mind '.

In these two last lines is already comprised the whole scope of literature—the fictions of free imagination, but also truths that matter. Yet at first this 'truth' of the Muses was too crudely understood. Men did not realize how soon the truths of fact were to be wrested away from the poets by more expert and scientific minds, leaving to creative literature only the truths of human feelings and

values. Thus Aristophanes in the fifth century still puts
in his swinging verses the already outdated view:

> First Orpheus taught you religious rites, and from bloody
> murder to stay your hands;
> Musaeus, healing and oracle lore; and Hesiod, all the culture
> of lands,
> The time to gather, the time to plough. And gat not Homer
> his glory divine
> By singing of valour, and honour, and right, and the sheen of
> the battle-extended line? . . .
> For boys at school a teacher is found, but we, the poets, are
> teachers of men.[1]

But this was claiming dangerously much. Already
Homer's tactics were obsolete; and the philosophers, even
before they ceased to write in verse themselves, had
begun denouncing his theology and his ethics. Thus
Xenophanes (*c.* 525 B.C.) assailed the epic poets in their
own hexameters:

> Homer and Hesiod fathered on the Gods' divinity
> All deeds most blameful and shameful that here on earth
> there be—
> Yea, thieving, and deceiving, and adultery.

Heraclitus said Homer and Archilochus should be
whipped; Solon denounced Thespis for mounting a stage
to tell lies; Pythagoras is said to have declared that he
saw Hesiod tied to a brazen pillar in Hell, Homer hung
on a tree encircled by serpents, for their slanders of
the Gods.

But both sides were already at cross-purposes. Believed literally, Homeric theology would indeed be
sometimes revolting. Here Xenophanes certainly marked
an advance:

> Of the Gods and these other matters none knows the verity—
> No man that lived before us, no man that yet shall be.
> However full-perfected the system he hath made,
> Its maker knoweth nothing. With fancy all's o'erlaid.

---

[1] *Frogs*, 1032-6, 1055 ; transl. Rogers.

But the philosophers, I think, already made two mistakes. They thought they were experts where the poets were mere amateurs. Yet after twenty-five centuries these 'experts' have agreed on nothing and settled nothing. Often they have been less wise than the poets: for, where the poets mostly knew their dreams were only dreams, the philosophers have mostly thought their dreams visions. Yet they too have often been employed merely in remaking the world in their own image. They have projected the desires and conflicts of their own temperaments on the Universe, and called it truth. Even if the psychoanalytic explanations that have been offered of the theories of a Plato or a Schopenhauer may remain unproven, I cannot help suspecting that this is often the real process—that philosophies have been largely like the cooings of a pigeon at its own reflection in a mirror. Often when man thinks himself being most intellectual, he is actually being fooled by that part of him which is least so. To say this is not to disbelieve in reason; it is merely to disbelieve that its use is easy.

Secondly, the philosophers have often tended to underestimate the importance of the non-rational, not only in their own thinking but in all living. Despite Socrates, knowledge alone is *not* virtue. Without emotion, no energy. The driest scientific researcher, who devotes a lifetime to potsherds or to snails, could not do it unless he had also some driving passion—be it curiosity or ambition or the desire to serve mankind. All values are vain, unless we can feel, as well as see, their value. Knowledge without feeling is like an electric motor without current.

We may recall the wise words of Lytton Strachey on Bacon, even if they are touched with exaggeration: 'His intellect swayed him too completely. . . . It is probably always disastrous not to be a poet.' For then we may be blinded by baser emotions that are but half conscious.

The thinker goes to experience for the sake of conclusions; the poet (and his hearers) go to experience for the sake of experience—yet conclusions follow. The writer may state them, like Isaiah or Bunyan; or he may only imply them, like Homer or Shakespeare. But at least imply them he must, whether he will or no; if only by what he selects. And because the effect of these implications on his hearer is partly unconscious, they go all the deeper. Very seldom does Homer pass judgement; yet that final scene of pity and reconciliation between Priam and Achilles which closes the *Iliad* seems to me more effectual than all the moral treatises ever penned. None the less the creator of that noble masterpiece could be banned as immoral by Plato; whose own final ideal for mankind was a regimented state which forbade that very freedom of thought and discussion for which Plato's master Socrates had died. For the trouble with Plato was partly that he never learnt from his teacher that teacher's saving doubt of his own knowledge, and of everyone else's.

Indeed one may question, despite the eloquence of the *Apology*, whether Plato had really much in common with Socrates. It is worth remembering that simple but devastating reply of Aristippus to some bitter comment made by Plato at his expense: 'How unlike our Master!' After all, there could hardly be much likeness between a man whose main claim to knowledge was that he knew he knew nothing and a man who claimed to know what was best for everybody and dreamed of the right to gag by violence all who disagreed. And was not Socrates 'the Master,' also, of such utterly different thinkers as Antisthenes the Cynic and Aristippus the Hedonist?

Yet Plato, with Tolstoy, holds a central position in this long debate. Indeed he marks a turning-point in European thought. When Plato appears in the Greek world, one may feel, despite all the Greek charm of his younger work, 'Here begins the end'. With his coming, there falls already the first cold shadow of the Middle Ages, with their sense of sin, their Inquisitions, and their Infernos.

In all civilized society, the ego must indeed acquire its super-ego, its phantom guardian. But this guardian can become a tyrant, who may win over as his bodyguard much of that accumulated aggressiveness which millions of years of Natural Selection have made a vital necessity for all species that have not solved the problem of survival by becoming prolific as rabbits, impenetrable as tortoises, or elusive as swallows. Then arises the Puritan, torn by a civil war within him, and often spreading civil war outside him as well. 'Power tends to corrupt, and absolute power corrupts absolutely.' That is no less true of the human conscience than of human governments. How far this tyranny of conscience in Plato was embittered by struggles with his own homosexuality[1] (as has been suggested by a writer in *Imago*) we cannot know. It is more than enough that this ascetic tyranny was there, and grew only narrower and more intolerant with the coming of old age. Hence the rage felt against Plato by Blake: 'This was the fault of Plato. He knew of nothing but virtues and vices and good and evil.' This may be extreme. But I believe that Blake is at least the healthier extreme. Better a jungle than a concentration camp.

First, the *Ion*. Here Plato's Socrates plays ironic cat with a mouse-rhapsode, Ion—half reciter, half expounder, of Homer. The conclusions are merciless.

---

[1] It is interesting that the vivid allegory of Plato's *Phaedrus*, where the soul is visualized as driving a chariot with a white horse and a black (the symbols of its higher and lower impulses), finds its counterpart sometimes, without any apparent influence from Plato, in the fantasies of modern patients; their fear of being overmastered by some passion may disguise itself, in waking life or in dream, as a dread that a horse will bolt with them.

(1) Poetry is a form of intoxication. Divine, doubtless; but not knowledge.

'The poet is a light, winged, sacred creature, able to create only when in an inspired ecstasy and out of his sober senses.'

He infects the public with his own frenzy, so that even merrymakers at a carnival will weep. For the poetic experience is a kind of magnetism. (The Greeks knew of natural magnetic stones.) The prime source of this magnetic force is the Muse; next to her in the line of transmission is the poet; next, the rhapsode; the last link in the magnetic chain is the public itself.

But (2) all this fine frenzy still remains remote from true knowledge. For example, Homer writes of navigation and Ion expounds him: but who would trust Ion with a cock-boat? Homer writes of war and Ion expounds him; but would the Athenians dream of making Ion a general?

And so follows the last polite slap in Ion's face:

'Are we to think you a quack or a man inspired?'

'Oh, inspired, Socrates, if you do not mind.'

'Very well. In your praises of Homer, we will suppose, not that you know what you are talking about, but that you are "inspired".'

With that bouquet Ion is sent gratified away. But of course the bouquet contains a serpent.

Yet the irony is so silken that generations of literary men have failed to see any irony at all—just as High-Church Tories were taken in by the irony of Defoe's *Shortest Way with the Dissenters*. Like Ion, these innocents thought it splendid to see themselves as inspired with 'poetic fury'.

But Plato came to bury poetry, not to praise it. For what signifies a drunkard, however 'divine', in the presence of a sage?

There could be no such wishful misunderstanding of

Plato's *Republic*.[1] Its Second Book, from the point of view of education, brings against the poets the now familiar charge of telling immoral stories of the Gods. This complaint was partly justified. There is little to be said for such a story as the castration by Cronus of his father Uranus—a survival of primitive folklore, interesting only as showing how old in human prehistory is the Oedipus-complex.

But there seems less sense in Plato's objection to passages like that in Homer which tells how at the door of Zeus stand two jars, one of good things, one of evil. To some men Zeus gives lives where good and evil are mingled, to some he seems to give evil only: but no human destiny is drawn from the jar of good alone.

One might have thought this a very true, and beautiful, symbol of human fate. No man is wholly happy—so do not expect to be.[2] But Plato will have none of it. God must never be depicted as sending evil to men except as a just punishment. For Providence must be credited with perfect righteousness. Job (like Homer) was less narrow and less naïve. The whole burden of that great book is a passionate protest against this facile notion that virtue is sure of being rewarded with worldly prosperity. Plato's master Socrates, when his wife wailed that he died innocent, is said to have retorted, very cogently: 'Would it be better if I died guilty?' None the less Plato will have the poets preach only 'poetic justice'.

Criticism on this level recalls the indictment brought against *Madame Bovary* by M. Pinard, *avocat impérial* —that Flaubert had reprehensibly allowed Emma

---

[1] ' *Republic* ' seems a bad translation of Plato's title, ' *Politeia* '. ' Republic ' tends to suggest enthusiastic democracy, which Plato hated. Better, perhaps, ' The State ' ?

[2] Compare the noble simplicity of an epitaph by Philetas of Cos (3rd century B.C.)—I mourn you not, best friend. Much good and fair
You knew. Of evil, too, God sent your share.

Bovary to feel happy for a time (brief enough, one would have thought) after her adultery; and to look physically more beautiful. She should, of course, have been gnawed horribly and visibly by lightning remorse.

In the next book of the *Republic* (III) Plato condemns Homer for giving a gloomy picture of the world beyond. This is bad for military morale and should be censored. And yet Alexander the Great, who carried a special copy of Homer with him on his conquest of the world, seems somehow to have survived Homer's insidious attacks on his military morale.

Plato is also offended by the lamentations in Homer for comrades dead, and by the laughter of Homeric Gods. For the Platonic ideal, such emotions show an excess of humanity or of humour. Lord Chesterfield also thought that superior persons should never laugh. The world remains, fortunately, unconverted.

Then Plato repeats his objections to the immorality of certain Homeric episodes like the seduction of Zeus by Hera or of Aphrodite by Ares. Certainly these are not for the young, though they seem to me far less hateful than things like Samuel's butchery of Agag before the Lord; on the other hand, why treat adults also as if they were children? No reader in his senses could suppose that the *Odyssey* condoned adultery. But the tale of Ares and Aphrodite is part of the atmosphere of Phaeacia; and with his Immortals Homer's fancy is far more playful than with his human characters.

Plato's most important discussion of poetry, however, is in *Republic* X. Here we learn that Art is not only a snare, but a delusion. The curious argument is familiar.

The craftsman who first made a wooden bed must have got his idea of a bed by some intuitive perception of an ideal bed, in that realm of ideas which alone contains the true reality. Then comes the painter who puts on canvas a few strokes that merely look like a bed—what is he producing but the shadow of a shadow, twice removed from reality?

I cannot help wondering if Plato was partly influenced towards his theory of ideas by the vastly older Egyptian conception that the shadowy soul in its tomb utilized the *souls* of the material objects interred with it to ease its age-long sojourn in the land of shadows. But wherever Plato got it from, as an objection to art it is a mere oddity. No need to battle with a shadow itself more than twice removed from reality. Aristotle, as we shall see, was very tellingly to retort that poetry is *more* philosophic than history. In other words, Achilles has a more abiding reality than Alexander. And, after all, if we are going to talk of merit in terms of greater or less 'reality' (though why?), of what can we be certain, if not of our own emotions? All may be illusion sooner than those. But Plato came to disapprove of most human emotions.

Finally, the great iconoclast, reverting to his old tactics in the *Ion*, asks ironically what use Homer has been, for all his influence, in the practical world. What constitutions of cities, what inventions, what military knowledge had he brought to men? And why was he so neglected in his lifetime, compared even with such sophists as Protagoras and Prodicus?

That this supposed neglect of Homer in his lifetime is a legend hardly matters. No one knows whether Homer, if a person of that name ever lived, was neglected or not. But Plato might have considered that Homer had hardly been neglected since his death—he was the Bible of Greece. This, indeed, was Plato's real objection—that Homer was *not* neglected.

And if Homer *had* been neglected in his life, what would that have proved? What test is worldly success, except in the eyes of Philistines? Socrates was not simply neglected; he was put to death. But far as Plato might have wandered by now from that master's breadth of mind, he would have been justly indignant had this rather ignoble sneer at worldly failure been brought as an argument against the real worth of Socrates.

When Judge Braxfield (partly Stevenson's original for the old judge in *Weir of Hermiston*) was trying some radical sympathizer with the French Revolution, the prisoner pleaded that Christ Himself was, after all, a reformer. 'Muckle guid that did him', muttered the old judge. 'He was hangit.'

Braxfield's retort is more amusing than Plato's—at least, to us who are not in the dock. But Plato's plea is just as ungenerous. The Chinese have a proverb which is less mean: 'Better to be a crystal and be broken than perfect like a tile upon the roof.'

To invent constitutions or water-wheels is no business of creative writers. Sometimes still they do justify Plato's charge of talking about matters beyond their competence by parading more science than they possess—as when Balzac speaks of himself as a 'docteur en médecine sociale' or Zola poses as a sort of human biologist in *Les Rougon-Macquart* or as a criminal psychologist in *Thérèse Raquin*. A psychoanalytic case-history is far more satisfying than pseudo-science. Indeed the growth of psychology already tends to make the average novel, with its amateurish knowledge of human nature, seem as inadequate and obsolete as versified agriculture or astronomy. But the great writers remain unscathed. Homer or Shakespeare make no such pretensions as Plato; yet, quite apart from their pleasure-value, one may ask if Plato has done one-tenth as much as either of them to make men more merciful, more understanding, or more loyal.

His next charge against the poets is that they encourage emotionalism. Here too, perhaps, Plato is not wholly unfair. From the interminable lamentations of Greek tragedy, or from those howls of Lear which so irritated

Tolstoy, it becomes, for some readers at least, a relief to turn to the passionate reticence of Icelandic saga. Yet if poetry seriously tended to make men over-emotional, surely the English, with their wealth of poets, should be by now a race of inordinate hysterics. The world has found many faults in us; but hardly this.

Jane Austen, indeed, true daughter of the eighteenth century that she was, took a view of poetry in some ways not unlike Plato's. She made it her Anne Elliot's opinion that 'the strong feelings which alone could estimate it truly, were the very feelings that ought to taste it but sparingly'. And yet, reading Jane Austen's own letters, one feels that they would be no worse for a little more poetry and emotion. In any case, Plato's idea of improving mankind by repressing emotion is certainly not the lesson of modern psychology.

Here, then, we have three main objections to imaginative literature—it is unreal, it is unrighteous, it is unrestrained. In short, it remains an intellectual fraud, an emotional debauch. Therefore Plato banishes it from his Republic, with the grudging exception of Hymns to the Gods and praises of good men.

There is no need to dwell on the hierarchy of souls in his *Phaedrus*, where professions are ranged in a curious order of merit—philosopher, ruler, politician or man of business, athletic trainer, soothsayer, poet or artist, artisan or farmer, sophist, tyrant. More important is that grim work of Plato's old age, *The Laws*. Here he offers us a state-board of censors for literature and music; a state-anthology of approved poems ancient and modern, compiled exclusively by gentlemen over fifty; and a limitation of poetic subjects to praises of the Gods (as before) and of virtuous men (but now only after they are dead). Tragedy may be produced if approved by the censors; and even Comedy, provided it is acted only by slaves or hired aliens. We may also be refreshed with state dances representing the soldier of valiant soul in war, the citizen of continent soul in prosperity and temperate pleasure.

By the time Plato has finished with the poets, one is reminded of Sir Guyon's treatment of the Bower of Bliss in the *Faerie Queene*:

> But all those pleasaunt bowres, and Pallace brave,
> Guyon broke downe with rigour pittilessse;
> Ne ought their goodly workmanship might save
> Them from the tempest of his wrathfulnesse,
> But that their blisse he turn'd to balefulnesse.
> Their groves he feld; their gardins did deface;
> Their arbers spoyle; their Cabinets suppresse;
> Their banket houses burne; their buildings race;
> And, of the fayrest late, now made the fowlest place.

The same treatment Spenser's fellow-Puritans were to apply to English churches half a century later.

Spenser, indeed, provides a good example of what Plato (with some reason) distrusted in writers. Idealist and Platonist as the Elizabethan was, yet the sensuous beauty that he loved was too strong for him. He may paint vice only to condemn it; but he paints it with so passionate a sense of physical beauty, that the picture lasts while the moral fades. The Bower that Sir Guyon laid waste, remains, despite Sir Guyon, perhaps the most famous passage in that vast and often tedious poem. But though Spenser helps us to understand Plato's attitude, he hardly justifies it.

'Be not righteous over much; neither make thyself over wise; why shouldest thou destroy thyself?' The writer of *Ecclesiastes* was nearer to Aristotle than to Plato; nearer also, I think, to sanity. In some ways Plato has closer affinities with the Fascist-Nazi ideal, than with the Communist, at least in theory; for in practice both remain only too alike. Still the Communist theory is to produce happy individuals; where Plato and the

Fascist are more concerned to produce the perfect State. Not for them any Marxist millennium where the State is fondly expected 'to wither away'. To that insentient Moloch, Nietzsche's 'coldest of all cold monsters', are sacrificed in effect the unfortunate millions who can and must feel and suffer. Actually the Rule of the Saints remains curiously similar whether in Calvin's Geneva, or Cromwell's England, or Stalin's Russia. These ruling angels soon grow as proud as Lucifer, and as fallen. The end is Gestapolitics and Ogpurity. No body of men, no succession of men, has ever been good enough to remain other men's absolute masters. It is not sexual passion that costs most human misery, nor the passion for money, but the passion for power—alike in the ascetic who kicks himself, and in the official, who is happy even to be kicked provided he too in turn can kick. Democracy is not a good form of government. All governments are at best, only necessary evils. But democracy is the least evil, for civilized men, because it can change its masters before they become monsters. Plato, I believe, taught much evil, largely because his psychology was too simple; one can only plead in extenuation that it is a type of evil which human aggressiveness hardly needs teaching anyway.

But let us not too hastily assume that Plato may not in the end get his way with the poets, though he will have had long to wait for it. There have been moderns who thought that all art would be banished at last, not by the fiat of philosophers, but by the force of progress. Thus Renan foresaw a time when even the great artist would seem a useless relic of the past, while his place was taken by the scientist. Similarly Mr. Clifford Bax has suggested that mankind, like Leonardo, will pass from art to science, as a man leaves the playthings of childhood—'three or four hundred years hence poetry, like rattles and tooth-corals, will be found only in state-homes for incubated infants'. But perhaps I may be allowed to add that I doubt it.

Finally, let us also admit that Plato did recognize the influence-value of literature, even if he thought that influence almost wholly corrupt and corrupting.[1] He did not regard poetry as a sort of ivory skittles in an ivory tower. He expelled the poets from his Republic; but luckily there was one poet he could not expel—himself.

[1] Apologists have, of course, tried to explain away Plato's denunciations of poetry as not really meaning what they say. This was inevitable. Plato has great charm ; he was himself an artist who would recast a sentence half a dozen times ; therefore some of his admirers yearn to vindicate his wisdom also. But if a writer explains himself so incompetently that it takes centuries, or even millennia, to find his true meaning, it seems to me to matter little what he meant. And in this case it is enough to look at the poetic quotations which Plato produces for condemnation. They are unpardonable. I am afraid my views on Plato will outrage the faithful; but they will find a still severer judgement in K. R. Popper, *The Open Society and its Enemies*, 1945.

XIV

Art with a Purpose
(continued)

Aristotle. The Renaissance. Tolstoy. The Totalitarians

> *Avremo una cosidetta rivoluzione economica, grazie alla quale, come ora abbiamo le ferrovie dello Stato, il chinino, i sali, i fiammiferi, i tabacchi dello Stato, così avremo il pane dello Stato, le scarpe, le camicie e le mutande dello Stato, le patate e i piselli freschi dello Stato. Sarà un progresso tecnico? Ammettiamolo. Ma questo progresso tecnico servirà di punto d'appoggio ad una dottrina ufficiale obligatoria, ad una ortodossia totalitaria che si servirà di tutti i mezzi, dal cinema al terrore, per distruggere ogni eresia, e tirannizare il pensiero individuale.*
>
> IGNAZIO SILONE, *Pane e Vino.*

AMONG the pupils of Plato was a far inferior artist, but a better psychologist and a healthier mind— Aristotle. His *Poetics*, without naming his master, makes short, sharp work with several of that master's prejudices. Of Plato's theory of ideas Bertrand Russell has written: 'I do not agree with Plato, but if anything could make me do so, it would be Aristotle's arguments against him.' But it would be hard, I think, to say that of Aristotle's arguments on poetry.

First, as already mentioned, to Plato's scorn for the

'unreality' of poetry, Aristotle replies that it is, on the contrary, more philosophical and more serious than the history of real persons and events. Tartuffe and Pecksniff have become, as it were, immortal embodiments of Hypocrisy. The Cleon of Aristophanes may be a travesty of the Cleon of history; but he remains the eternal Demagogue. We may recall, too, how Balzac after perfunctory inquiries about the welfare of Jules Sandeau's family, could exclaim: 'And now let's get back to *reality* —who is to marry Eugénie Grandet?'[1] Or how, again, at the close of a real love-affair, he could remark regretfully, 'Encore un roman de perdu!'

Next, where Plato had derided the factual ignorance of poets like Homer about tactics or navigation, Aristotle makes the obvious observation that in works of imagination minor lapses in accuracy do not signify; indeed, 'a probable impossibility is better than a possible improbability'. (Caliban, say, than Sir Charles Grandison.)

But far more important is Aristotle's famous doctrine of the *Catharsis*, or purgation (*not* 'purification'), by Tragedy, of emotions like pity and fear. Plato had condemned poetry as encouraging emotion; on the contrary, replies Aristotle, it provides emotion with a healthy outlet.

One may recall Keyserling's account of the Chinese temperament as usually self-controlled, but liable to fits of unprovoked bull-fury—'the Chinese explain this phenomenon through the accumulation of the substance of anger, *Ch'i*'. Similarly the scorpion that Ibsen kept on his desk grew ill unless it was sometimes given a piece of fruit on which to vent its venom. In his extant work Aristotle speaks only of the Catharsis of Tragedy. Presumably he thought that other kinds of poetry like Epic and Lyric had a similar, if milder, effect; while

---

[1] Similarly for Madame de Staël (such was the power of Richardson) the great event of her own youth was, she said, ' l'enlèvement de Clarisse '.

Comedy might release and relieve other emotions such as aggressiveness, malice, or licentiousness. In fact, literature becomes a device for re-establishing that happy mean which Aristotle found the basis of the virtues.

As an answer to Plato, this is ingenious. It is like explaining to some Puritan that one dances for exercise and drinks wine for one's health. It may give a reason why the state should allow drama; but it scarcely gives the reason why the public enjoys it. Did the Greeks go to the theatre to get rid of emotions? Do we? Surely, rather, to feel them. Indeed in our modern industrial civilization there seems less danger of emotional excess than of emotional atrophy. It may be that the English, in particular, tend to be emotionally *too* inhibited.

Besides, the drama is not merely a matter of intoxication, but also of experience. Real life is often drab; it is only natural (in spite of prigs pursing their lips at 'Escapism') to seek wider and richer experience in fantasy. And even if our real life is not drab, it remains brief and limited. What more natural, or more rational, than to wish to travel like Odysseus among other ways of living?

> I am a part of all that I have met;
> Yet all experience is an arch wherethro'
> Gleams that untravell'd world, whose margin fades
> For ever and for ever when I move. . . .
>   Life piled on life
> Were all too little, and of one to me
> Little remains.[1]

So old Ennius, knowing three languages, Latin, Greek, and Oscan, could boast that he had not one heart only, but three. No doubt living in fantasy can become, in excess, a drug. In the modern cinema and novel it often does. But here, too, the fault lies in forgetting Aristotle's happy mean.

[1] Tennyson, *Ulysses.*

In short, Aristotle's purgation, though a good enough answer to Plato, seems an inadequate answer to the wider question: 'What good is imaginative literature?' On the other hand, though this idea of emotional purgation may be far from the whole truth, it remains a real truth, confirmed by modern psychology. Here Aristotle was definitely right; not Plato. Let us turn again to a few case-histories.

A patient of Stekel's had for three years been tormented with insomnia, headaches, and heart-attacks. In consequence, he daily and nightly stuffed himself with drugs. He could not suggest any psychological cause of trouble. True, he had divorced his wife. But that was merely a good riddance, which had cost him no pangs.

She had been pursuing a love-affair with a friend. He found out, because the friend was killed in an accident on a motor-tour with him; and the dead man's pocket-book told all. (So curiously does real life sometimes imitate improbable fiction.)

While relating all this, he suddenly had a heart-attack. The next night he dreamed that he saw his divorced wife, told her she was the only person he could really love, and then, when she scorned him, stabbed her to the heart.

Shortly afterwards he learnt his late wife was engaged. How? He confessed that he still had daily confidential reports on the doings of this woman about whom he 'did not care'.

A few days later he actually tried to shoot her, but missed.

He had been pretending to himself that he was not in love with his wife, and not miserable to lose her. But it was mere pretence. The mental conflict and anguish that he would not face, only re-emerged in a physical disguise. Stoicism is not always so wise as the Stoics too hastily supposed.

Intellectual or emotional dishonesty is a dangerous game. Men cannot be passionless angels. No amount of Platonic theorizing can make them so; but it may make them something a good deal lower. The fox who persuaded himself that the grapes were sour and that he did not want them in the least, was perhaps a philosophic fox; yet it appears that some grapes, even though one fails to eat them, may still set the teeth on edge.

> But play no tricks upon thy soul, O man,
> Let fact be fact and life the thing it can.[1]

This does not mean that the unhappy should brood on their unhappiness. 'Gnaw not the heart' is an excellent maxim. The diet is poisonous. But the right course, I believe, is not repression or make-believe, but distraction; above all, active distraction—'fût-il', as Stendhal puts it, 'de se casser le bras'; though a walking-tour in mountains seems a better remedy than immobilizing oneself with a broken arm and endless hours to think. For one cannot *think* unhappiness away. The essential is to deflect thought from the past to the future; to plan actively, in place of suffering passively: and to keep one's physical health, and with it one's resistance, to a maximum. Cold baths may be considerably more effective than hot tears.

Another case. A fabulously rich American claimed to be a perfectly happy man. Only, at the time when he made this boast he had an electric heater on his stomach; he was suffering from colic and insomnia; and he was taking drugs in order to sleep (really, as so commonly, in order not to dream). He had also an obsessional neurosis, which made him perpetually count things; and a phobia about cancer. However, apart from all this, he pretended his felicity was complete.

His brother had, indeed, eloped with his fiancée. But

[1] Clough.

how fortunate that this had happened before he married her! In short, a most philosophic character.

His dreams, however, revealed that he too was chewing over and over those bitter grapes from the past, although too proud to admit to himself that he suffered. 'No one can escape his allotted measure of pain.' Refusal to feel enough may be as unhealthy as excessive feeling.

So true, up to a point, is Aristotle's catharsis, that literature and drama have even been used in treatment— Cocteau's *Les Enfants Terribles* for a patient tangled in a brother-sister relation, Hauptmann's *Vor Sonnenuntergang* for an ageing woman tortured by rivalry with her own daughter. In this way the sufferer may live out his emotions in the realm of fantasy. He may realize, too, that he need not feel overwhelmed with guilt as if he were some exceptional monster, some Cain marked off from mankind. In the universality of art he gains, as Goethe advised, 'his distance from things'.

There is nothing surprising in this, when we consider how often writers find their work a remedy for themselves. Thus Goethe, it has been said, whenever he found a woman threatening to destroy his peace, simply turned her into a statue; that is, put her in a book, like Lotte Buff in *Werther*, Frau von Stein in *Iphigenie*. Similarly Fra Lippo Lippi, we are told, would gratify his desires, if he could, in reality; but if he could not, would paint them—and paint them away.

K. A. Menninger records a patient who had lost her power to write, yet suddenly in his office dashed off pages and pages, in a different hand and signed by a different name, full of hatred towards persons she thought she loved, and of reasons for that hatred. Only after she had finished did she realize (with a marked drop in blood-pressure) what she had written, and that it was the real truth.[1]

[1] *Man against Himself*, p. 368.

Aristotle's catharsis is, then, no empty fantasy. Indeed, in an early stage of his own work with Breuer, Freud for a time adopted this very term; until he found that release of emotion was not enough—repressions must also be analysed.[1] It should, however, be added that the cathartic effect itself may be more than a simple emotional release. For the artist who expresses his feelings in an imaginary situation may also feel a new and reassuring mastery both of the situation and the emotions; instead of suffering passively he becomes active; just as a child frightened by a dog or a dentist may afterwards find reassurance, and actual pleasure, in turning the experience into a game. This can apply to an audience also. And in some forms of group-therapy, patients are said to gain relief by acting out their feelings on a stage together.

But though Aristotle has thus successfully justified the influence-value of literature against Plato, he would of course have seemed intolerably moralistic to Gautier or Wilde. For his justification of Tragedy is largely medical. He insists, too, that characters in serious drama should be as decent as the plot permits, not gratuitously vile. But it remains, to me at least, an enormous relief to come back from Plato to common sense—even that somewhat prosaic and pachydermatous common sense which may at moments give the reader of Aristotle a vision of a very large and sagacious elephant picking up very small pins. And I think it should be counted to Aristotle's credit that no critic before him, and none for over two thousand years after, brought to the problem an attitude so essentially psychological.

On other ancient views there is no need to dwell. Eratosthenes (3rd century B.C.) pronounced that poetry aimed not at instructing, but at transporting the soul

[1] Cf. S. Ferenczi, *The Principle of Relaxation and Neocatharsis.* (*Internat. Journal of Psychoanalysis*, 1930, p. 428.)

(ψυχαγωγία). This seems true enough, provided we do not entirely forget in what sort of direction the soul is transported.

Philodemus of Gadara (1st century B.C.), fragments of whose work have been excavated at Herculaneum, held that the moral effect of literature was a by-product. This too is a healthy departure from that crude didacticism which only leaves literature to be crushed between puritanical philosophers, who shout that it teaches wrongly, and hedonistic critics who clamour that it should not teach at all.

'Longinus' (1st century A.D.?) summed up the matter better still, when he described *great* literature as 'the echo of a great soul'. The 'echo', note—not the sermon. I believe that from Homer to Hardy this is true.

Plutarch (c. 46-126 A.D.) seems by contrast a little timid with his comparison of poetry, for the young, to a dish of octopus—a nourishing diet, but liable to cause disturbing dreams. And the same timidity recurs in some of the practical criticism of the ancients. Thus Aristarchus, the great Alexandrian (2nd century B.C.), rejected on moral grounds the lines in the *Odyssey* where, with shocking unmaidenliness, Nausicaä wishes she could have a husband like Odysseus.

But let us not be too severe in our turn. Did not Coleridge, whose criticism suffers from a good deal of cant, refuse to conceive that Shakespeare could have written the part of that disgusting porter in Macbeth?

In any case, whatever ancient critics may have wished to do, ancient Greek writers remained considerably freer than most moderns before the twentieth century. They need fear neither Church nor Puritans.

That Republican Rome should long remain austere was inevitable. That people of soldiers, farmers, and administrators did not even allow themselves a permanent

[280]

stone theatre till Pompey's day, when the Republic was already tottering to its fall. Actors were regarded as disreputable; to men of the old school, like Cato, Greek culture exhaled corruption. The race that had produced legends like those of Horatius, Scaevola, Coriolanus, Camillus, or Regulus, must, indeed, have once possessed a poetic imagination of its own—but imagination of a kind that would fortify the spirit of the race. Even Lucretius regards the verse into which he puts his philosophy as jam to sweeten powder. Even Virgil and Horace gave their share to the propaganda of that imperial reformer who, on the other hand, exiled the immoral Ovid to the Black Sea.

Then appears Christianity, which was to build at length in the Medieval Church something in some ways nearer to the hierarchy of Plato's *Republic* than anything the world had yet seen. Unfortunately its attitude to literature was as narrow as Plato's.

Where men think too exclusively of right and wrong, virtue and vice, they develop a sort of colour-blindness that sees all life as white or black, and loses its sense of the rainbow-hues of the real world. Which is not to say that white and black do not also exist.

It even became an article of belief with zealots like Cyril of Alexandria, that Christ Himself had been the ugliest of men. Tertullian gloats hideously over that great final spectacle which is to console the Christian for the theatrical shows he has missed in this life, as he watches the tragedians writhing in the flames of Hell, with something real to howl for; the comedians twisting, more nimbly than they ever did on the stage, in the endless conflagration of Gehenna. He tells too with edification how a demon justified his entry into a woman on the ground that she had first trespassed on *his* territory —the theatre. St. Augustine mourns the tears he shed over the empty sorrows of Dido; Alcuin, watching the devils skipping about the dormitory to pinch the toes of his fellow-monks, recalls with anguish how he too had read the *Aeneid* when he should have been deep in the Psalms.

> Negant Camenis nec patent Apollini
> Dicata Christo pectora—

so St. Paulinus of Nola. Attempts were made, indeed, to exempt Virgil as the Prophet of the Gentiles, over whose grave St. Paul himself had wept. But for Odo of Cluny (tenth century) even Virgil is only 'a beautiful vase full of deadly serpents'. Medieval legend turned the Roman poet into a sorcerer: indeed one Benedictine was for prosecuting all poets as sorcerers. 'Platonem . . . Virgilium . . . Terentium . . . ceteras pecudes philosophorum', so writes the Papal Legate Leo (tenth century). And the monk in the silence of the *scriptorium* who required a pagan author would scratch his head like a dog, for pagan authors were mere hounds. Plato's dream had at least in part come true.

St. Thomas Aquinas, indeed, was rather more liberal. Recreation, he argued, was necessary to man. And had it not been revealed to the blessed Paphnutius that his companion in Heaven would be a clown?

But these are small mercies. The prejudices of the Church died hard. Remember Langland's growl:

> He is worse than Judas that giveth a japer silver.

The Reformation came, the Roman Church recoiled, but her puritanic side lived on. Ascham had no use for Malory, nor Rabbi Zeal-of-the-Land Busy for the Elizabethan stage. Even in the France of Louis XIV the actor could have neither Christian marriage nor Christian burial. Molière himself was only with difficulty laid in consecrated ground; in 1730 the charming Adrienne Lecouvreur, mistress of Maurice de Saxe, was buried in a field. Louis XIV, Louis XV, might go to Paradise; those who had toiled to amuse their royal boredom were to burn through eternity.

So the human race staggers on its way, lurching from extreme to extreme. Generations see only the pleasure-value of art, and ignore all consequences; generations care only for its consequences, and distort them grotesquely at that.

No wonder the poets hit back. No wonder the Wandering Scholars were profane. No wonder Molière wrote *Tartuffe*. But perhaps the loveliest cry of the persecuted Muse comes from the lips of Aucassin in that brilliant Provence of the twelfth or thirteenth century which Papal fanaticism was to turn into a smoking desert with the Albigensian Crusade.

'In Paradise what have I to win? Therein I seek not to enter, but only to have Nicolete, my sweet lady that I love so well. For into Paradise go none but such folk as I shall tell thee now: Thither go these same old priests, and halt old men and maimed, who all day and night cower continually before the altars, and in the crypts; and such folk as wear old amices and old clouted frocks, and naked folk and shoeless, and covered with sores, perishing of hunger and thirst, and of cold, and of little ease. These be they that go into Paradise, with them have I naught to make. But into Hell would I fain go; for into Hell fare the goodly clerks, and goodly knights that fall in tourneys and great wars, and stout men at arms, and all men noble. With these would I liefly go. And thither pass the sweet ladies and courteous that have two lovers, or three, and their lords also thereto. Thither goes the gold, and the silver, and cloth of vair, and cloth of gris, and harpers and makers, and the prince of this world.'[1]

Since then, Aucassin and his fellow-poets have

[1] *Aucassin and Nicolete*, transl. Andrew Lang (1896), p. 9.

triumphed. But they have not always known how to use their victory.

To pursue in detail the war of Puritans and poets would be intolerable tedium. A few landmarks in the controversy must suffice. But at least it is not mere antiquarianism. For this same battle still goes on. Literature still suffers under Plato's successors in the Totalitarian states.

Let us first take that Elizabethan skirmish which produced Sidney's *Apologie for Poetrie*.

One Stephen Gosson, after leaving Oxford without a degree, wrote plays, and is said to have acted himself. But in 1578, aged twenty-three, he left the theatre—because, he says, he saw the disorders it bred. Next year (1579) he attacked the stage in his *Schoole of Abuse*, followed three months later by his *Apologie of the Schoole of Abuse*. With a pretty touch of poetic justice, the players are said to have retaliated for his attacks by performing two of his own plays. In 1581 Gosson, now a clergyman, became rector of Great Wigborough; and he did not die till 1624, having lived through the full summer of that Elizabethan drama whose spring he had tried like an east wind to nip.

Though ignorant enough to fall into blunders like calling Messalina the second wife of Domitian, Gosson realized that he too was treading in Plato's footsteps. 'No marveyle,' he says of poets, 'though *Plato* shut them out of his Schoole, and banished them quite from his common wealth, as effeminate writers, unprofitable members, and utter enimies to vertue.' Yet curiously enough, this severe moralist writes himself with all the coxcombries of euphuism: 'Hee that goes to Sea, must smel of the ship; and that sayles into Poets will savour of Pitch.' However, he modestly admits *some* poets to be good and even *some* plays (including his own *Catiline's Conspiracies*). 'These Playes are good playes and sweete playes, and of al playes the best playes and most to be liked, worthy to bee soung of the Muses, or set out with the cunning of *Roscius* himself, yet are they not fit for every mans dyet: neither ought they commonly to bee shewen.'

Gosson, in short, was not very intelligent. His contribution to the wordy warfare between Puritans and Players[1] is only interesting for having provoked Sir Philip Sidney, to whom it had been dedicated without leave, into writing (*c.* 1581) his *Apologie for Poetrie*, published in 1595 and many times reprinted in the century that followed. This has become famous because it is well written, rather than because it is well argued. Sidney pleads that the oldest writers were poets (but old things need not be good); that the Romans used the same word (*vates*) for 'prophet' and 'poet', and foretold the future out of Virgil (which only shows that the Romans were superstitious); that poets create, like God (but so do forgers); and that poets can picture the righteous being rewarded, the wicked punished (but what does that signify, if life is otherwise?). His only argument of value is that creative literature, by adding emotional appeal to the finer human qualities, can do more to make men finer than the philosophers themselves. This I believe to be true; and important.

The danger with such defences of poetry was that they tended to overstress the crudely didactic element. Between Puritanism on one side and Bohemianism on the other, it was indeed hard not to be driven into the jam-and-powder view of literature. Yet one can see even in Spenser or Milton the risk that the powder may spoil the jam, and the jam the powder. Less content than Homer or Shakespeare simply to imply their values, these Puritan poets overweighted their work with ethics. Yet Spenser proved better at painting the Deadly Sins than

[1] See *Cambridge Bibliography of Eng. Lit.*, i, pp. 507-13.

any of his figures of virtue; and Milton was so far from justifying the ways of God that one can quite understand those who have objected to *Paradise Lost* as giving a gross and degraded view of religion, which children, at least, should never be allowed to read.

Dryden, as often, was better at saying, than at really knowing, what he thought. 'Delight is the chief, if not the only, end of poesy.' And yet, 'To instruct delightfully is the general end of all poetry.' And he quotes with approval from Bossu the view that the first rule for a heroic or dramatic poet is 'to lay down to yourself what that precept of morality shall be which you would insinuate into the people' (hardly, one would have thought, a very promising approach to creation, nor very much practised by Dryden in his own dramas). For once the stupid Rymer seems more to the point—'the end of all poetry is to please'; and 'some sorts please without profiting'.

Even the downright Johnson seems to fluctuate. From Shakespeare, he thought, one might collect 'a system of civil and oeconomical prudence'. And yet, he feels, Shakespeare 'seems to write without any moral purpose'; whereas 'it is always a writer's duty to make the world better'.[1] Still there is one sentence of Johnson which seems to me admirably to summarize the truth: 'The only end of writing is to enable the readers better to enjoy life, or better to endure it.' Can one say much more? (Provided one grasps that this endurance involves qualities of character.)

With the Romantic Revival, the problem receives, as might be expected, more raptures and rhapsodies, but hardly more light. In 1820 Peacock published his *Four Ages of Poetry*. He argued (having previously published four volumes of verse himself) that poets were now barbarous anachronisms, survivors from the infancy of

---

[1] For Johnson on *The Beggar's Opera*, see pp. 303-4.

mankind, 'wasters of their own time and robbers of that of others'. This he followed up by various mockeries of Scott with his Border poachers, Byron with his pirates, Southey with his Commonplace Books, Wordsworth with his sextons, and Coleridge with his tobacco-cloud of German metaphysics.

At this *jeu d'esprit* Shelley in Italy, with his passion for poetry and his total lack of humour, was naturally appalled. 'So dark a paradox may absorb the brightest rays of mind which fall upon it. It is an impious, daring attempt to extinguish Imagination, which is the Sun of life . . . impious attempt, parricidal and self-murdering attempt. . . .' And so in 1821 appeared Shelley's *Defence of Poetry*. Like Sidney, he makes the mistake of trying to defend the poets by enrolling in their ranks men whom no ordinary person would put there, such as Herodotus, Livy, Plutarch, and Lord Bacon. Even these are not enough—'all authors of revolutions of opinion are poets'. (Mussolini? Marx?).

But not only is almost everyone a poet; poets are almost everything—'the institutors of laws and the founders of society, the inventors of the arts of life'; 'the unacknowledged legislators of the world'.

Imagination, we are told, is the basis of morality; poetry develops the imagination; it is 'the record of the best and happiest moments of the happiest and best minds'. (The parting curse, for example, hurled by Catullus at his mistress as the common harlot of Rome? Villon's cry of abasement over the life he leads with his grosse Margot 'en ce bordeau ou tenons nostre etat'? The anguish of *Les Fleurs du Mal*? The burden of Leopardi's passionate despair—'Fango è il mondo'?)

'Shakespeare, Dante, and Milton', Shelley continues, 'are philosophers of the very loftiest power.' 'It is indisputable that the highest perfection of human society has ever corresponded with the highest dramatic excellence.'

(Was there really such social perfection in the England of James I, the France of Louis XIV, the Spain of Philip II?)

If literature cannot be defended better than this, it would seem wiser not to defend it. After all, it has survived pretty well without. One may question, too, whether Matthew Arnold's statement, that poetry is fundamentally 'criticism of life', has been much happier. Had he said that literature *often* embodied life's finest values, it would at least have sounded less coldly didactic. And less false. For how is life criticized by *Kubla Khan*?

In short, it is not till one reaches Tolstoy that the conflict begun by Plato two thousand years before regains reality. With Tolstoy, as with Plato, one may disagree; but at least one is not lost in a fog of banal phrases. *What is Art?* (1898) may be often fanatical, sometimes foolish; but it is always intensely sincere; and sometimes it is not easy to answer. Further, Tolstoy's tone of earnest bewilderment seems to me more sympathetic than the priggish severity of Plato.

Art, says Tolstoy, is not to be valued by its beauty or its aesthetic pleasure. Like food it must be judged by its effect, not on the palate, but on the health. (But why not, one asks in astonishment, by both? Surely pleasure-value is of some account, as well as influence-value?)

The essential of art, he continues, is its power of infection. If someone has an intense experience—say, meeting a wolf—by the mere power of words he can infect others with his own fear. Now this infectious power of art is a highly dangerous power. Better, therefore, no art at all than indiscriminate art.

Secondly, the value of art must depend on the value of the emotions it transmits; and the value of the emotions transmitted is decided by the religious attitude to life they embody. (This seems narrow. One may value, though with caution, the power to experience other men's states of mind, without necessarily wishing to adopt them

—to enter for an hour, say, into the gloom of Leopardi, without wishing to spend one's life there. For some readers, indeed, this may have a certain danger; and one may value Leopardi, fine and noble as he sometimes is, less than more balanced writers. But that is very different from banning and burning him. The song of the Sirens was dangerous; but Odysseus wished to hear it; and by his wisdom was able to hear it without getting eaten. A great deal of success in living consists in finding out how to have things both ways.)

Since the Renaissance, Tolstoy next argues, men have lost faith. Beauty has become their God. Further, a schism in society (here falls already the shadow of the Soviets) has sundered Classes from Masses. Now the art of the Classes is false. It is irreligious, affected, and monotonously limited to the themes of pride, sex, and world-weariness. Hence its growing cult of obscurity; as in Mallarmé.

This indictment seems not without serious truth. But next comes a horrific hyperbole: 'Good art always pleases everyone.' For example, the tale of Joseph and his brethren, the Parables, folk-tales, Homer, the Hebrew prophets, Sakya Muni, the Vedic hymns. It *must* please everyone, because art of this universal type is founded on religion—'every man's relation to God is one and the same'. (Surely an optimistic view in this world of warring creeds!)

Tolstoy, however, speedily contradicts himself about good religious art always pleasing 'everyone'; if it displeases some, he says, these are only the perverted few. (Which amounts to saying, 'If you disagree with me, you are perverse.' True, possibly—but unproven.)

Modern art, he pursues—less wildly—has become a sort of cone. The higher you go in it, the narrower it becomes. Its only methods are futile borrowings, naturalistic realism, appeals to brutality and pornography,

or mere intricacy of detail. Its artists are too professional
(this I believe profoundly true) and overpaid (which is
often palpably false). And it is pestered with art critics
and art schools.

Then Tolstoy goes into some harrowing arithmetic.
Say there are 30,000 painters in Paris, and 90,000 in the
rest of Europe. Add equal numbers of writers and
musicians. Suppose they each produce three works
annually; that makes over a million works of art
a year!

We can but shudder and pass on. To what? To the
ultimate arbiter of artistic excellence—the simple 'unperverted' peasant! *He* knows what true art is. 'For a
country peasant of unperverted taste this is as easy as it
is for an animal of unspoilt scent to follow the trail he
needs among a thousand others in wood or forest. The
animal unerringly finds what he needs.' (Surely not
quite so unerringly. Or why do cattle eat yew-branches?
And how is it possible—though difficult, I own—to
poison rats?)

The basis of the Greek view of life, says Tolstoy, was
the worship of Beauty, Strength, and Courage: the basis
of ours is human brotherhood. For us, then, there exist
two types of good art—one based on a religious sense of
man's relation to God and his neighbour; the other, on
those simplest feelings of common life that make us all
akin. To the first class belong Schiller's *Robbers* (an
extraordinary work to choose for this purpose), Hugo's
Les Pauvres Gens and *Les Misérables*, Dickens's *Christmas Carol*, *The Chimes*, and *A Tale of Two Cities*,
Uncle Tom's Cabin, *Adam Bede*, Dostoievsky's works,
and Tolstoy's own *God sees the Truth*. To the second
class (dealing with the simplest feelings of mankind)
Tolstoy assigns *Don Quixote*, Molière, *Pickwick*, *David
Copperfield*, Gogol, Pushkin's tales, and his own *Prisoner
of the Caucasus*.

But even these are not universal enough—not so good as the story of Joseph.

Such is good art: of bad, the price is intolerable—wasted lives of workers; an upper class drugged into satisfaction with its own unnatural existence; the bewilderment of children and the simple; the preference of beauty to goodness; the spread of superstition, patriotism, and sensuality (strange trinity!).

Therefore let us abolish the professional artist.

'Art is not,' writes Tolstoy, 'as the metaphysicians say, the manifestation of some mysterious idea of beauty or God; it is not, as the aesthetical psychologists say, a game in which man lets off his excess of stored-up energy; it is not the production of pleasing objects; and, above all, it is not pleasure; but it is a means of union among men, joining them together in the same feeling, and indispensable for the life and progress towards well-being of individuals and humanity.'

It is curious to compare Tolstoy and Plato. Both are fired with the same moral fervour, the same puritanic zeal. Both are more saint than sage. But where Plato's final arbiter is the philosopher, Tolstoy's is the peasant. Between the two thinkers stands Christianity. The meek shall now inherit the earth; babes and sucklings are wiser than the wise. This idealized peasant seems a strange resurrection of Rousseau's Noble Savage. Yet, for Tolstoy, it was a matter of fervent faith. What if peasants were lousy? Was not cleanliness itself a form of luxury? (Which did not prevent his peasant-blouses from being of fine material, and his underwear scented). Even as he breathed his last at the station of Astapovo, he is said to have murmured: 'But the peasants—how do peasants die?'

Tolstoy, indeed, was a living battlefield of conflicts, contradictions, inconsistencies. A man of great artistic gifts, driven to condemn most of his own art; a man of terrific vitality, nightmare-ridden by the horror of death; a man of intense physical passions, denouncing all physical passion, even if humanity must grow extinct—and yet inflicting on his wife no less than sixteen pregnancies. Small wonder if this violently divided personality sought refuge in return to a primitive mass-existence where the burden of personality should trouble men no more?

Yet the world cannot go back to peasantdom. Even if it were willing, it would starve. And how should it be willing? Both Tolstoy and Plato are, in fact, homesick amid the roaring onrush of our life for an older, stabler existence that has passed from us as irrevocably as childhood. Was it not perhaps really childhood itself that they hankered for, with its fixed rules, its guiding parents, its seeming immutability? But never again can we find that peace, which was most perfect in the days before we left the womb of life, till we rediscover it at last in the womb of Mother Earth. Tolstoy's accusations make, in part, a serious indictment; I do not think they should all be ignored as idealistic ravings; but his remedies seem impossibly narrow and unpractical. Further, he weakened his case by plunging into needless arguments about the pleasure-value of particular artists he happened to dislike, such as Shakespeare or Wagner. For arguments about the pleasure-value of particular works are futile; by indulging in them Tolstoy merely made it easy for opponents to treat him as an incorrigible crank, and confused the essential truth of much that he pleaded about influence-value.

Some twentieth-century writers have followed Tolstoy's views in milder form. H. G. Wells pronounced that the writer should class himself 'not with the artists, but with the teachers, the priests, and the prophets'. Mr. Bernard Shaw, as usual, had no doubts—'Art for Art's sake means merely "Success for Money's sake".'

'Good art is never produced for its own sake. It is too difficult to be worth the effort.' (And yet what artist ever imposed greater difficulties on himself, or thought less of money, than the pure artist Flaubert?)

More worth listening to is another modern writer whom some might be surprised to find in this camp— Mr. Somerset Maugham. 'The value of art is not in beauty, but in good action.' 'Little as I like the deduction, I cannot but accept it; and this is that the work of art must be judged by its fruits, and if these are not good, it is valueless.' 'Loving-kindness is the better part of goodness. . . . Goodness is the only value. I have gone a long way round to discover what everyone knew already.' As for aesthetes, 'they are no better really than drug-fiends; worse rather, for the drug-fiend at all events does not set himself up on a pedestal from which to look down on his fellow-men'. These views from Mr. Maugham's autobiography are finely embodied in one of his stories, where the wife of an 'intellectual' civil servant in Malaya leaves her husband because he has been too prudent when the hour came to be brave.

'Nothing', he pleads, 'that concerned me was at stake. Courage is the obvious virtue of the stupid. I don't attach any particular importance to it.'

But his wife's answer is implacable. 'How do you mean that nothing that concerned you was at stake? If that's true, then your whole life was a sham. You've given away everything you stood for, everything we both stand for. You've let all of us down. We did set ourselves upon a pinnacle, we did think ourselves better than the rest of them because we loved literature and art and music, we weren't content to live a life of ignoble jealousies and vulgar tittle-tattle, we did cherish the things of the spirit, and we loved beauty. It was our food and drink. They laughed at us and sneered at us. That was inevitable. The ignorant and the common naturally hate and fear those who are interested in things they don't understand. We didn't care. We called them Philistines. We despised them and we had a right to despise them. Our justification was that we were better and nobler and wiser and braver than they were. And you weren't better, you weren't nobler, you weren't braver. When the crisis came, you slunk away like a whipped cur with his tail between his legs. You of all people hadn't the right to be a coward. They despise *us* now, and they have the right to despise us. Now they can say that art and beauty are all rot; when it comes to a pinch people like us always let you down.'

This seems to me truly and nobly said. Yet it is surely fantastic to suggest judging art *only* by its power to inspire 'loving-kindness'. To ignore pleasure-value, and see nothing but influence-value, seems as exaggerated as to ignore influence-value and see nothing but pleasure-value. Why not both?

But the twentieth century appears doomed to be an age of extremes. Never has art been so anarchic, yet never so enslaved; never such an orgy, yet never such a prison. Neither Plato nor Calvin dreamed of such rigours as the Totalitarian states have made an everyday reality.

'The will to happiness', cried Herr Sieburg under Hitler, 'is lacking in us; the idea that it is possible to work and struggle for individual happiness is not only foreign to us; it is positively revolting.' And so all poetry had to become some sort of *Marseillaise*. 'So long', bellowed the *Völkischer Beobachter* of May 21, 1934, 'as there remains in Germany any unpolitical, neutral, liberal, or individualistic art, our task is not ended. There must no longer be a single artist who creates otherwise than nationally and with a national purpose. Every artist who withdraws himself from this preoccupation must be hunted as an enemy of the nation, until he gives up his intolerable resistance.'

The pseudo-Communists, less romantic than the Nazis, are no more rational. While on one side Hitler's Minister of Education shouted, 'it is no longer art for art's sake in Germany, but art for propaganda's sake', on the other the Mexican Diego Rivera proclaimed, 'art which is not propaganda is not art at all'. And while Mussolini obliterated the slim girls depicted on the walls of the Style Exhibition in Turin and instructed the Press only to accept representations of the female figure with 'fully developed bust and hips appropriate to Fascist girl and mother', Eisenstein in Russia asked: 'Where lies the difference between a play and a science lecture? Is not the mission of both to arouse inner conflict and, by its dialectical solution, to give the masses a new drive towards activity and the means for creative life?'

In effect this was only repeating Plekhanov (1857-1918): 'All views on art are an instinctive judgement of its social utility.' Art for Art's sake, Plekhanov considered, was merely the despairing cry of artists reacting against the bourgeoisie before there was hope of successful revolution.

But there is no need to multiply these barbaric yawps which seem to echo through some gathering twilight of the human mind. It is more than enough to glance at a few of the results of a system where even the dance of the Muses must toe the Party line and the artist becomes an 'engineer' of souls. The author of the following, one Kolchev, was acclaimed, it is said, as the greatest poet in the Soviet Union and enjoyed the satisfaction of having his poem printed by the million and recited in one hundred and sixty-seven languages.

> When Budyenny smiles,
>   The ice breaks on the Don;
> When Budyenny smiles,
>   The maple bloom is on.

When Voroshilov smiles,
  The sun begins to shine;
When Voroshilov smiles,
  Then spring falls into line.

When Stalin smiles,
  What might a poet dare?
When Stalin smiles,
  It is beyond compare.

And on the dictator's birthday every paper printed this, by Sergei Makhalkov:

Moscow sleeps, nocturnal city,
  Where the late stars shine on snow.
Only Stalin out of pity
  For us, sleeps not, all aglow. . . .

Stalin even hears the chatter
  Of the shepherd by the pond.[1]
Should the boy write him a letter,
  Stalin will himself respond.

In an *izba*, ill and lonely,
  You might groan 'midst Baikal trails.
Have no fear, for Stalin only
  Knows about you, never fails.[2]

After all, critical judgements become simple when, as a Moscow literary organizer explained to Mr. Koestler, 'We build up the reputations of writers whom we think useful; we destroy writers whom we consider harmful; aesthetic considerations are *petit-bourgeois* prejudice.'

And so authors like Zoschenko, musicians like Shostakovich are condemned; scientists like Vavilov are liquidated, because a rival biologist, knowing less about ears of corn, knew much more, it appears, about the ear of Stalin. 'Lenin and Stalin—these are the standards of science'; 'Socrates and Stalin are the summits of intelli-

---

[1] This, at least, seems unfortunately true.
[2] See A. Barmine, *One Who Survived* (5th ed. 1945), p. 299.

gence'; 'it is the business of the linguist and the critic to study the style of Stalin'. For unfortunately, though Plato never learnt it, when a set of men, even idealists, gain absolute power, gradually their one ideal becomes—to keep it. Yet fortunately—and without this even our battered civilization would no longer exist—the wicked seem infallibly to become also extremely stupid. For Ate is not dead.

XV

Values

TWENTY-FIVE centuries have passed since the function of the writer was first questioned; it is chastening to see what an unspeakable mess the human mind appears to have made of the answer. Against totalitarians on one side and Surrealists on the other it is equally vain —and, I think, needless—to argue. But even the serious thinkers of all these ages leave us in Babel. One propounds that art is champagne; another, that it is the bread of life; another, that it is poison; another, that it is syrup of figs; another, that it is opium; another, that it is holy water. Between those who damn its consequences and insist upon its pleasures, and those who damn its pleasures and insist upon its consequences, the truth seems to me to lie, where it so often does lie, simply in the middle. Why not consider both?

Yet to this compromise some will still object. They may argue that, though the believers in Art for Art's sake made their case grotesque by overstatement, art does remain something quite apart from right and wrong, good and evil; that its essence is aesthetic experience for that experience's sake alone. Therefore it seems only fair—and prudent—to try first to put their case as cogently as I can, even though I do not feel convinced by it. One who maintains the artist's independence of the moralist might perhaps argue on lines like this:

'Imagine a group of persons before a landscape. Among them is a farmer who is thinking of his harvest and when he will plough Ten-acre Field. There is a sports-man wondering about the shooting over there in Twittering Copse; an angler who turns towards the river, meditating on flies; a timber merchant who looks at each woodland with an imaginary axe in his hand. In Hitler's Germany there might also have been stranger figures in the group, judging by a certain Professor Freyer's idea of the soldierly aesthetics of landscape. "Now," wrote Professor Freyer (before the War), "the symphony of the country's natural riches will be systematically exploited . . . a remote corner becomes a strategic outpost; a picturesque moor, a trap for the enemy; a lovely valley-side, a sacred line of resistance."

'This, indeed, is the sort of monstrosity to which one comes by prostituting art to purpose. But in our imaginary group there may perhaps be another figure who is not calculating how to make money, or to kill animals, or to kill men. He will merely be noticing the shades of green in the woodland, the light and shade on the hill-slopes as the shadows lengthen from the west. In short, the pure artist. The Philistines always thirst to liquidate him. But why?

'Why should the glory of man's faculties—seeing for the sake of seeing, hearing for the sake of hearing, imagining for the sake of imagining—be thus despised and degraded? On the contrary, you degrade art, when you take away this disinterested joy in experience itself. Art consists in taking perception and conception as ends, not as means.

'Consider painting. No modern artist worth the name would paint a *Soul's Awakening*. He prefers a lemon on a cracked saucer. And even in the impurer art of literature, though there is no need for fantastic denials that good literature *can* be written with all sorts of purposes, how often the purpose dies and the pure art alone is left—like the golden hair upon a rotted skeleton!

'Look at the Old Testament. Much of its theology has become abominable, much of its morality outrageously immoral. And yet what poetry! Even if Jehovah became as shadowy as Baal, even if we regard Elijah as a demented dervish, the magnificence of the poetry remains—for ever that grim figure of the prophet hurls his mockeries at the priests of Baal on Carmel, or girds up his loins to run before Ahab's chariot to the gateway of Jezreel. How disgusting, again, are Donne's *Sermons*, if you think of their actual meaning—this reformed rake sadistically fishing for souls from the pulpit of Saint Paul's with his baskets of eternal worms—making the flesh of his congregations creep with visions of the infernal concentration camp where they would be tortured eternally at the fiat of the Heavenly Himmler! And yet what prose! Or *Paradise Lost*—theologically almost as odious as Donne —the Fall of the whole human race, in its unborn innocence, produced by a cabinet crisis in the celestial government—and that grotesque Heavenly Father forming an everlasting mutual-admiration society with an equally tedious Son. And yet what verse!

'Even in his own lifetime Ruskin had to lament that, while he thundered and cursed and groaned, the public just admired his style. The public (with unusual good sense) was only concentrating on Ruskin's strong point, and treating literature—as literature!

'Or look at Browning. An admirable lyric poet. But he *would* argue. And he could not argue. Contrast the vividness of *The Bishop orders his tomb at St. Praxed's*—a pure picture of a Renaissance prelate, as detached as Chaucer's Pardoner—with the weary propagandist verbiage of *Bishop Blougram's Apology*—as dull as *Piers Plowman*. Browning's arguments were broken reeds: broken reeds make scrannel music.

'Why imitate that tedious Duke in *As You Like It*, littering brooks with books and cracking stones to find sermons? How much more human was the attitude of J. M. Synge, when they pestered him to write a propaganda play on the Irish rebellion of 1598! Synge was an artist, not a propagandist. And so his proposed plot merely depicted two women—one Catholic and one Protestant—hiding in a cave from the English soldiery. They fall, however, into such an acrimonious quarrel over the merits of the Pope and Queen Elizabeth, that one prefers to leave the cave and risk ravishment rather than endure for a moment longer the abominable company of the other. Naturally, this plot with its Chaucerian irony was not greeted with enthusiasm by fanatics who wanted, not art, but a political manifesto. But are we to agree with them?

'This disinterested detachment of the pure artist from all practical aims and desires is perfectly summarized in Gordon Bottomley's poem on Helen, that eternal symbol of the beauty of the senses:

> Sackt Troy and queens at auction; if thou wert there,
> Wouldst thou buy Helen, ere her husband came?
> Passing from hand to hand so passively,
> Helen was Helen's secret, Helen's own.
> *Pass thou and gaze, she is more greatly thine.*

'So Hazlitt somewhere exults that the pictures he

went to see in rich men's houses were more his than
theirs—for true possession lay, not in purchase, but in
the power to enjoy.

'Besides, with creative literature, this is not only true,
but must grow increasingly true. Once, the poet could
be a philosopher or scientist, like Xenophanes or Par-
menides, Lucretius or Virgil; a theologian, like Hesiod,
Dante, or Milton; a politician, like Theognis, or Dryden,
or Byron. But to-day the creative writer is hunted off
such subjects by specialists and experts. Nothing is left
him but his feelings and his senses. There he remains a
specialist, an expert, still. Let him stick to his last—
look in his heart—and write as a bird sings.

> O fret not after knowledge. I have none.
> And yet my song comes native with the warmth.
> O fret not after knowledge—I have none.
> And yet the evening listens.

Or, as the Chinese wisely put it, "The rose has thorns
only for the gatherer."

'After all, one can drag purpose into everything.
Bernardin de Saint-Pierre thought melons were made
ribbed by a considerate Creator to ease their division
among families; and trees green to rest our eyes; and
fleas black to help us catch them. But to-day we see that
such attributions of purpose to Nature are ludicrous;
why, then, insist on attributing purpose to Art?'

Much of this plea seems to me true. Art, like mathe-
matics, may be pure or applied. Experience shows that
both kinds may be excellent. And, instead of being
childishly intolerant, artists who create for the pleasure
of creation, and artists who create for other purposes also,
should live and let live.

But though there can be art without purpose, there
cannot be art without result. Everything that moves
men moves them in some direction, up or down, for
better or worse. In practice the result is often so imper-

ceptible, the influence often so immaterial, that there is no need to consider it. Often; but always?

If this influence of literature, indeed, were proved always negligible, I could see no answer to Anatole France's view of critical judgements—that they are merely subjective and autobiographical. For, as already explained, absolute beauty seems to me a fiction—a projection of one's own preferences on to the Universe. The pleasurableness of art remains a matter of individual taste.

The first question, then, is how much influence can art and literature actually exert. Is it really important enough to be worth weighing? The answer is not easy.

The ordinary person seems to consider this influence insignificant—if he considers it at all. Plato, it is true, thought a new style of music could overset a state; but Plato no doubt was a visionary. Fletcher of Saltoun approved the view that 'if a man were permitted to make all the ballads, he need not care who should make the laws of a nation'; but Fletcher was an eccentric. Nor need one believe the rhapsodies of Shelley about poets being the 'unacknowledged legislators of the world'. And if Tolstoy regarded art as 'an infection'—and so potentially dangerous, still Tolstoy was given to exaggeration.

Besides, it can be argued, these are only fine-sounding generalities. If one looks more closely at specific instances, they often amount to little. Augustus banished Ovid to the Black Sea on the pretext that his *Art of Love* was a corrupt and corrupting book. No doubt it was. But who can suppose that the Empire's decadence was postponed by victimizing Ovid; or that it would have been postponed if Ovid had never lived?

Or take that example which divided eighteenth-century judgements—Gay's *Beggar's Opera*. Johnson hesitated: 'I do not believe that any man was ever made a rogue by being present at its representation.' And yet, he reflected, 'there is in it such a *labefactation* of all principles as may be injurious to morality'. But his most reasoned decision seems perfectly just: 'The play like many others was plainly written only to divert without any moral purpose, and is therefore not likely to do good; nor can it be conceived *without more speculation than life requires or admits* to be productive of much evil. Highwaymen and house-breakers seldom frequent the playhouse.'

Gibbon, on the other hand, is slightly absurd: '*The Beggar's Opera* may, perhaps, have sometimes increased the number of highwaymen; but it has had a beneficial effect in refining that class of men, making them less ferocious, more polite, in short, more like gentlemen.'

This seems dubious. Gay's opera is less likely to polish highway robbery than to loosen sexual morals. But, even so, is its influence so serious that we need break his butterfly? Surely that does involve 'more speculation than life requires or admits'. Was not Macaulay right in his sturdy good sense about expurgating the Classics?— 'a man who, exposed to all the influences of such a state of society as that in which we live, is yet afraid of exposing himself to the influence of a few Greek or Latin verses, acts, we think, much like the felon who begged the sheriff to let him have an umbrella held over his head from the door of Newgate to the gallows, because it was a drizzling morning and he was apt to take cold.'

But to this it may in turn be answered that perhaps, as so often, Macaulay over-simplified. It is not merely a matter of 'a few Greek or Latin verses', whose expurgation one might find as childish as he; it is a matter of cumulative effect. A man who objected to felling a tree, on the ground that trees affect climate, would be thought mad; yet we know what has been the effect of the reckless felling of trees, in turning whole provinces into dust-bowls. Further, we have learnt more of the human mind than Macaulay could have conceived possible.

Stekel after quoting Jean Paul's aphorism, 'Books cannot make a man good or bad, though they can make him better or worse', adds, 'I cannot agree with this view. I can confirm from my own experience that books *can* make men good or bad; and I will no less affirm that they can make them ill or well. People underestimate the influence of the printed word, which contains an enormous power of suggestion. Many books penetrate the human soul like high-explosive shells and destroy what has been laboriously built up by the labour of years.'

'Writers', says the same authority, 'are the conscience of mankind.' (Perhaps it would be better to say 'should be'.) And again: 'Whoever wishes for sound children, should take care to have only good books in his house.'

It seems clear enough that what men read can sink deeply into their unconscious minds. I have already mentioned the patient whose phobia went back to Poe's *Black Cat*.[1] Then there was the curious case of a lady doctor who found herself unable to read clinical histories to her superior, when they had red-ink underlinings. She perpetually hesitated and blushed. 'Have you ever read Hawthorne's *Scarlet Letter*?' 'No.' But, having bought the book, she recognized that she *had* read it—indeed it formed part of her father's library at home. And it will be remembered that the heroine of Hawthorne's tale is condemned to wear on her dress a scarlet 'A' for adultery. That recollection removed the symptom.

Again, a neurotic patient of Stekel's with a hatred of his father once dreamed that he was sitting within a niche in a wall beside an unknown woman (his mother). Then there came round the corner a creature with lit-up face and glowing eyes (his other self), which looked at him and said, 'O!' The patient was asked if he

[1] P. 135.

knew any poem where 'O!' was important. 'Yes, some ballad.' 'Edward, Edward.' You remember?—

> Your steed was auld, and ye hae got mair,
>   Edward, Edward;
> Your steed was auld, and ye hae got mair;
>   Some other dule ye dree, O.
>
> O I have killed my father dear,
>   Mother, mother;
> O I have killed my father dear,
>   Alas, and wae is me, O!

You look sceptical. So did I, as I read it. But the patient lets us down. For he then recollected that he had actually read this ballad aloud in his room a few days before. I only wish we were all as familiar with our English literature as this Austrian analyst in his Viennese consulting-room.

To all this it may be answered that anything whatever may embed itself in the Unconscious—its contents are as miscellaneous as those of the sea-bottom; and that the opinions of a psychoanalyst on the specially potent influence of literature remain mere opinions. It may be so. Yet if I recall my own experience, I still feel that no real person has influenced me so much as my reading of Homer and Plutarch and the best of the Greek Anthology, Chaucer and the Icelandic Sagas, Ronsard, Montaigne, and Flaubert, Johnson, Morris, Ibsen, and Hardy. You may remember that George Moore felt similarly; even though that admission was really a powerful argument against his own creed of Art for Art. I think you may also find, if or when you have children of your own, that you become far more concerned about the effect of what they read. When the issue becomes so practical and so near home, it makes quite a difference. That, at least, has been my experience.

On the whole, then, from evidence of the kind that I

have given—fragmentary though it necessarily is—I find myself believing that the influence of literature, both good and bad, can be important. Not so important as Plato or Tolstoy urged—but quite important enough—more important than most of us seem to think.

If that be so, then the complete irresponsibility about that influence shown by many modern writers, by almost all modern critics, and by a large part of the modern public, seems to me curious. It is not a matter of legal controls or censorship—these are usually the clumsiest of machinery and should, I think, be kept to a minimum. But surely it *is* a matter for more responsible consideration by writers, critics, and public.

For example, there have been sufficient indications of the effect of the cinema on children to goad the state into doing something. But, as so often, the state fumbles. Certain films are marked 'A'; yet parents or guardians (that is, in practice, any adult whatever) can take a child to them. It is not clear that, if the film is unsuitable for children, its effect will be neutralized by the magic presence of an adult in the next seat. It can, indeed, be pleaded that parents should be free to judge what is good for their own children. If all adults were grown-up, this might be true. But the real motive is, perhaps, rather that all adults have votes.

As I look back over two Wars, and that breathing-space between them which was as ignoble as it was horrible, I am haunted by one of Shakespeare's most poignant scenes. Troilus is parting from Cressida; little knowing that he is indeed parting from her for ever.

TROY: But yet be true.
CRES: O heavens: 'be true' againe!
TROY: Heare why I speake it, Love:
   The Grecian youths are full of qualitie,
   They're loving, well compos'd, with guifts of nature,
   Flowing and swelling o'er with Arts and exercise:

How novelties may move, and parts with person,
Alas, a kinde of godly jealousie,
Which I beseech you call a vertuous sinne,
Makes me affraid.
CRES: O heavens, you love me not!
TROY: Dye I a villaine then!
In this I doe not call your faith in question
So mainely as my merit: I cannot sing,
Nor heele the high Lavolt; nor sweeten talke;
Nor play at subtill games; faire vertues all,
To which the Grecians are most prompt and pregnant:
But I can tell that in each grace of these,
There lurkes a still and dumb-discoursive divell,
That tempts most cunningly: but be not tempted.
CRES: Doe you thinke I will?
TROY: No,
But something may be done that we wil not:
And sometimes we are divels to ourselves,
When we will tempt the frailtie of our powers,
Presuming on their changefull potencie.

This frailty of our powers, this changeful potency, these
unconscious influences that sweep us to do the things that
we never willed—to all of them psychoanalysis has lent
new force and meaning. We have seen in the last
thirty years plenty of 'novelties', of 'subtill games', of
'Arts and exercise'; are we so sure that they too did not
contribute to the rise of Hitler and the baseness of
English 'appeasement' and the fall of France? When we
recall the cynical sneerings of the 'twenties, the sadistic
nostalgia for savagery in D. H. Lawrence, the egomania
of Joyce, the hankerings of 'intellectuals' after medieval
obscurantism, or the 'tragic beauty' of bull-fights, the
anarchism of Surrealists, the calculated squalor of Céline,
even the exquisitely intelligent decadence of Proust—is
it so hard to read here the omens of what was to come?
I am not merely prophesying after the event. I got
myself into trouble in 1933 for saying that decadent
intellectuals were an invitation to Nazi brutes; just as I

got into trouble at the same date for writing that it
would be better for the world that the French should
occupy Berlin once every five years than that Hitler's
Germany should be allowed to rearm. But this view was
denounced as excessively brutal, just as the other was
thought excessively timid. After the events of sixteen
years I am not convinced that I was wrong. 'Sometimes
we are divels to ourselves.' It is well to remember
Augustine's friend Alypius.[1]

Of course it may be held that the literature and art of
the period were symptoms rather than causes of what
came. But it seems likelier that they were both. Swamps
can reflect rising storm-clouds; but they can also breed
malaria.

But, supposing literature can influence, what can be
said of the directions in which that influence is desirable?
If writers can affect their readers' values, what can be
said of the values? Such answers must indeed, at best,
be extremely general. There is an infinite variety in
human wishes; and so much the better, if we are to
avoid the growing menace of a stereotyped civilization of
mass-fabricated robots. Yet there may be some common
factors.

A typical Greek list of things in life worth wishing for
is contained in four lines sometimes attributed to
Simonides:

> Health is the best that Heaven sends;
> Next, to be comely to look upon;
> The third is riches, justly won;
> The fourth to be young among one's friends.

Sir Richard Livingstone in his *Greek Genius* quotes
the choice of R. L. Stevenson: '(1) Good health; (2)
two to three hundred a year; (3) *O du lieber Gott!*
friends.' Asked to give their four chief desires, his

---

[1] P. 154.

own Oxford lecture-class produced a somewhat different order [1]:

Health	54
Spiritual or Moral Excellence . . .	47
Friendship or Domestic Happiness . .	35
Intellectual Excellence	32
Contentment	29
Artistic Pleasures	15
Physical Excellence	13
Success	13
Hard Work	10
Travel	8
Wealth	8

Here Contentment seems somewhat out of place: that is surely the end, to which we are seeking the means. And Hard Work seems rash, unless one adds Congenial Hard Work. But it is interesting that the Greek desire for physical beauty has here disappeared, or at least not ventured to confess itself; and that Wealth has sunk low in the scale; but that Health still heads the list.

A similar question addressed to a Cambridge audience —'what are your four chief wishes?'—brought me in 1947 an amusingly different order of preference:

Personal Relations	232
Bodily Health	212
Mental Health	150
A Competence	134
Artistic Pleasures	78
Intelligence	70
Goodness	68
Religion or Philosophic Conviction . .	54
Creative Work	48
Travel	43
Wisdom	33
Congenial Work	32
Adventure and Experience . . .	29

[1] R. W. Livingstone, *The Greek Genius and its meaning to us* (1912), p. 126.

[310]

VALUES

Beauty	26
Humour or Gaiety	24
Social Service	22
Freedom	21
Learning or Knowledge	20
Long Life	17
Leisure	12
Pleasures of Nature	6

Courage, Humility, Peace, Food, Alcohol, Sleep, and Cricket
1 each.

From which Cambridge would appear more affectionate, but less good, than Oxford. The lower value attached to Mental (as contrasted with Bodily) Health seems to me interesting as showing how its fundamental importance is still not fully realized; but this is not surprising. That lesson the world has still to learn. For only a healthy mind, it seems to me, can be really good. The stress here laid on a Competence, without which Freedom is cramped, seems more realistic than the Oxford neglect of it; on the other hand, the place of Congenial Work (even if Creative Work is added to it) seems to me too low. As for Long Life, what use is quantity of life if the quality is unsatisfying?

But it will be noticed that in every list Health comes either first or (once) second; even if the emphasis is perhaps too much on its physical side. Nor does this choice seem unreasonable. For clearly every gift fortune can give us is wasted on those without the gift to enjoy them.

Naturally it is not easy to say exactly what is 'mental health'. Even psychoanalysts, who are concerned with this above all else, still find its definition difficult. Every living mind may show *some* scars, *some* lack of balance. But, on the whole, that person does not seem to me to have much to complain of, who is free from needless inward conflicts—especially at those less conscious levels where reason finds it impossible to cope with them; who is free also from those other parasitic passions, often unconscious also, that sap man's vitality—neurotic guilt, hate, fear, anxiety, the lust to suffer, the lust to inflict suffering; who has the power to work with all his energies unfettered; and who can love persons and things with an undivided warmth of heart. There is great truth, I think, in Alfieri's confession that the two essentials of his happiness had been 'un degno amore' and 'qualche nobile lavoro'; much truth, also, in the words of Alain—'les beaux visages sont comme des preuves de cette puissance d'oublier et de s'oublier. Je doute qu'on puisse citer un beau visage où l'on ne lise cette absence de préjugé, ce pardon à toutes choses et à soi, cette jeunesse enfin toujours jeune, qui vient de ce qu'on ne joue aucun personnage.'

This calm the best Greek sculpture often has—such calm as lives in the countenances of the men and women of the Lapithae, even amid their desperate battle with the bestial Centaurs, on that western pediment of Olympia where stands with arm outstretched above the tumult one of the noblest figures of a God that ever came from sculptor's hand—Apollo, the divinity of restraint without asceticism, the lord of light, of healing, and of art. To face reality, yet accept it; to learn from the past, without repining; to use the present, without growing unnerved by its transience; to prepare the future, without being dismayed by its inscrutability; to get the best from the people, the experiences, the work that comes one's way; to be content to be forgotten when those who once loved one shall vanish in their turn—this is as near as I can come to a rough sketch of mental health; that 'sound mind in body sound' for which alone the Roman poet thought man, even in his blindness, might dare to ask the immortal gods. And it is not only the individual that is concerned. Individually, indeed, there is little we can do for world peace; but there would be more chance of it, if more men were at peace with themselves.

Such qualities seem to me valuable alike on a desert island, in a state, or in a world-state. After all, the state is only a machine (creaking enough, at best) to enable its members to live the fullest lives possible with the maximum help, and the minimum interference, from one another. For the idea, exploited by the Nazis, that individuals exist for the state, and not the state for individuals, seems to me a demented mysticism. Only infantile minds can turn a machine into a father-substitute, a deity; as well worship the parish bull.

It can, of course, still be argued that many writers, especially in the last two centuries, have none the less been neurotic themselves. The Goncourts, in opposition to Taine, believed that this was perhaps essential and that, had they been less neurotic, their talent might have disappeared. If so, better for them perhaps if it had. Lombroso, again, regarded all genius as a sort of deranged monstrosity; but I doubt if he has many followers to-day.

On the other side it can be urged that many writers who *were* unbalanced, have yet maintained their own balance by finding an outlet for their conflicts in their art. In any case, what matters for the rest of the world is, not their private characters, but whether their works are likely to leave other men mentally healthier or the reverse. That sanity which Homer or Horace or Montaigne possessed, and which Arnold found in the Greeks and missed in many modern writers, seems to me a quality that many modern critics do not value enough. True, remarkable work may be done without it; all I suggest is that, other things equal, it is a very precious advantage. For I feel that too much art of the last hundred years deserves the judgement passed on his age by Paul Bourget: 'Avec sa littérature d'enquête, ses journaux remplis du détail de ses infamies, son art de

[313]

déformation et de laideur patiemment ramassées, ce siècle me rappelle parfois cet homme que je vis un jour, dans une visite à l'Hôtel-Dieu, tirer de son chevet une glace à main et y regarder, entre deux pansements, sa bouche dévorée d'un cancer.'

It is, of course, clear that thus to introduce considerations of health into literary values could easily be exaggerated into absurdity. I can imagine the sort of parody an opponent might compose—some caricature of a critic heavily loaded with stethoscopes, thermometers, temperature-charts, and volumes of psychoanalysis, going round a hospital ward of Immortals with the grotesquest comments: 'Heart not quite in the right place, I am afraid, Lord Byron'; 'Your temperature, Mr. Swinburne, is too high'; 'Symptoms, I regret to say, Mr. Pater, of sadism, masochism, homosexuality, and necrophily.' From such a person not even the nightingales on the trees would be safe—'You sit up too late.' All the same the possibility that this view of things could easily be exaggerated by puritans and cranks does not seem to me a reason for totally ignoring it.

As with health of mind, so with personal relations, which in one form or another stood so high in our various lists of preferences. A writer can deepen human sympathy or he can lessen it; he can increase the good will in the world, or the hatred; he can serve Brahma the creator or Siva the destroyer; he can make his readers more generous or more cynical. This does not seem to me a matter of indifference. I have already suggested that for Homer and Shakespeare, reticent as both of them are about passing judgements or uttering preachments, none the less the quality most prized in human life was, in the end, loyalty. That is hardly the impression derived from Restoration comedy or much modern fiction. And this difference, I think, makes a quite important difference in their ultimate value.

So too with the passion for human freedom that vibrates in Tacitus or Byron; the courage of the Sagas; the gay tolerance of Chaucer; the compassion of Virgil or Hardy. These writers left the world better, where others have done their best to leave it worse. It seems to me a false and degenerate type of criticism that shies away from such considerations to talk of technique, for fear of being thought to moralize.

The pure aesthete may at this point retort: 'But suppose I do not care about health of mind? Suppose I *prefer*, like Cressida, to be tempted? For that matter may not a Cressida be as "healthy" as an Imogen? You do not believe in Absolute Good any more than in Absolute Beauty—why, then, all this prate about ethics in the influence of art?'

This point was bound to come. It is, I believe, impossible to keep Ethics and Aesthetics apart. Sooner or later one leads into the other. And this very difficulty was raised only the other day in an interesting letter from three members of Girton, for which I am grateful. For unless I get letters such as I invite you to write when I fail to make myself clear, or convincing, I feel out of touch with my audience. One becomes like a goldfish swimming round and round in a glass bowl, making mouths at an inscrutable world; or, to reverse the image, like St. Anthony preaching to the fishes. And I believe such letters are far more effective, at least with an audience of any size, than attempts at verbal discussion, which too often lead only to verbiage and confusion.

The gist of my correspondents' attitude was:

'(1) We agree that taste and aesthetic standards are merely subjective and relative; (2) we agree that to be neurotic is, in itself, a drawback in literature, as in life; but (3) granted that it is stupid to ignore the influence of art, if there is no Absolute Good, how can we judge this influence? If there is no Absolute Good, whence does ethics come? What is its sanction? Does not ethics also sink to a mere matter of individual taste? Why should we not all soak ourselves in Huysmans and Dali, if we like?'

These are pertinent questions. And even to try to answer seems a heavy responsibility. Here are three young ladies asking why they should not adopt a life of crime? How shall we dissuade them?

Psychoanalysis in practice concerns itself with mental health; it is shy of ethics. Perhaps too shy. But one can see that there are prudential reasons for this reserve. Yet health and ethics inevitably merge. Though one's mental health involves primarily one's relations towards oneself, it affects all one's relations towards others; and though ethics is concerned primarily with one's relations towards others, it can intensely complicate one's relations towards oneself.

As soon as two people meet, ethics begins; and without ethics, in some form, any family or state must end. Indeed without some advance in ethics, to balance our advance in power, our world itself may end. Ethics, therefore, is hardly a whim. It is a necessity of human society—not less a necessity, because it too is subject to eternal change.

But whence did ethics come? For the religious, the answer is simple—from God. All virtues are thus ultimately reduced to one virtue—obedience.

Personally, I find myself unable to believe this; and the problem therefore becomes much more difficult. Ideas of good, like ideas of beauty, vary wildly from country to country, from age to age. You remember the story of Darius and the Greeks who burned their parents and the Indians who ate theirs. If morals are merely traditional patterns of behaviour, evolved under the pressure of circumstance, as means to other ends—often mistaken means, and often to mistaken ends—why have any morals at all? Why not be purely egotist? Even if some sort of ethics is vital for the survival of any community, why bother about the community, if one is sly enough to outwit it? If, for example, society is stupid enough to pay me for poisoning it with neurotic art, why not poison?

Great figures in history like Napoleon, or in philosophy like Nietzsche, have approximated to this consistent egotism, which sees ordinary mankind as mere game for super-Nimrods to hunt. Yet Napoleon died a prisoner; Nietzsche, mad. Not simply by bad luck. The man who sets out to loot society is not merely challenging society; he is challenging something in his own nature. He is not only declaring war on his fellows; he is declaring a civil war within himself. He is not only an individual; he is a gregarious animal; if he loses sight of that internal reality, he is liable to lose sight of external reality also— as Napoleon when he crossed the Niemen.

> Marlbrouk s'en va-t-en guerre,
> Mironton, mironton, mirontaine,
> Marlbrouk s'en va-t-en guerre,
> Ne sais quand reviendra.

When the Emperor whistled that, was it with some dim sense of the disaster he was courting? We cannot know. But we *can* know that, as we saw in the chapter on Poetic Justice, most of us have to face a court of judgement within ourselves. There speak the voices of the dead; there watch the faces that watched our earliest years. They may be unheard, unseen, by consciousness; but they are there.

The Greeks believed in the Erinyes and Nemesis. So do I. Let us take some perfectly simple, but perfectly concrete examples. There are modern young women who deliberately set themselves to flout the code of their childhood by plunging into series of unrestrained love-affairs; but not uncommonly the Unconscious retains its veto and still denies the forbidden ecstasy. The would-be Ninon de l'Enclos may find herself incorrigibly frigid. It may be argued that there are plenty who do not. To this it can be answered, in part, that the Erinyes are versatile and, as Macbeth found, have many different ways of pursuing those who defy them. They may not deny physical pleasure to those who turn life into an endless chain of amours; but they may still deny happiness. It was Ninon de l'Enclos herself who said in her old age that she had had good fortune such as few could hope for; but that, had she foreseen what life would become, she would have hanged herself.

In the period between the Wars, in particular, many married couples decided that loyalty was an old-fashioned illusion. 'Modern love' should be 'perfect freedom'. Now either they had children or they did not. If they did not, their marriages were liable to collapse. Even if they did not collapse, they had missed what can be (though, of course, it is also a dangerous adventure) one of the fundamental experiences of life. (You remember the ageing Flaubert in tears before the little girl?—'Voilà ce qu'il m'aurait fallu!') There was a play in Paris in those years—*Madame ne veut pas d'enfant*. Madame might evade children. She found it less easy to evade Nemesis.

Alternatively, people did have children, as well as love-affairs. In consequence, society became full of neurotic little creatures, split by conflicts between their parents, bewildered by jealousy of those parents' mysterious partners, by tangles of divorce and remarriage. There is no need to exaggerate. The price was sometimes very heavy indeed—and it was largely the innocent who paid.

If unconcealed freedom was bad, secrecy on the other hand was no remedy. Sooner or later the children found out; and that only made things worse. We have seen it all in *Hamlet*; and Mr. Noel Coward was able to make

a very topical drama by modernizing that tragedy as
The Vortex.

It has to be remembered, too, that not only were the
children damaged by their elders' failure to find happiness; they missed also the confidence a happy childhood
can give, its balance, its belief that happiness, even in
adult life, is not a romantic illusion, but something
that *can* exist.

I do not say it was wrong to experiment with ethics in
this way. Do what we will, the ethics of a changing
society must change. I only say it proved dangerous.
Jealousy might seem irrational; but so is human nature.
Men were trying to disregard the strength of the Unconscious both in themselves and their children. Whether
the present generation of adults is saner than that
between the Wars, I do not know. But I suspect that
something has been learnt by experience.

Families and societies, then, in the effort to adapt
themselves to reality, must impose certain codes of conduct. Often, we know, these are fantastic; sometimes
they enjoin the right thing for the wrong reason;
sometimes, as in the *Antigone*, the ethics of state and
family conflict; and never can such wide generalizations
as moral systems involve be wide and elastic enough for
all the varying situations of life. Much of Ibsen's work
was rightly devoted to stressing the need for intelligent
individuals to judge conventions and, if need be, defy
them. But, when all provisoes have been made, there
remains a good deal that is solid in the mixture of reason
and tradition that forms the moral code of civilized states.

So if it is asked 'Whence does ethics come?', the
answer seems 'From the experience of the race in its
struggle to survive.' And if it is asked 'Why should we
regard ethical codes?', the answer seems 'Because they
have become part of ourselves, largely from the influence
of parents and elders and those we admired in childhood.

It is well to think carefully before infringing them. If they do conflict clearly with our own ideas of good sense and decency, then infringed they must be. But the Erinyes may be there.'

In short, to think that ethics cannot exist without an Absolute Good, seems to me like thinking that there cannot be any law without an absolute monarch, or a totalitarian state. I have no wish to exaggerate the place of ethics in judging the influence-value of literature, or to exaggerate that influence-value itself. The Puritan, as I have said, is colour-blind. Plato and Tolstoy, for example, would have disapproved of Herrick; doubtless he was a somewhat scandalous parson. But there lives in his work such healthy, good-natured gaiety, such a freshness of country air, such a sense of natural and artistic beauty that one would not dream of sharing Southey's horror of him. The Olympians had room also for Pan and Silenus. It is not forbidden apples I object to, so much as to maggots.

Finally, if ethics cannot be kept out of aesthetics, neither can aesthetics be kept out of ethics. Here the philosophers and moralists seem to me to have been often extremely unfair to the influence-value of the creative artist. Living is itself partly an art. The creative writers have often known much more of the human heart than the thinkers. And, further, they have often been able to make emotionally alive and appealing those patterns of living which reason may indeed enjoin or moral codes may command, yet often with lifeless voices that provoke only a sense of futility or rebellion. In literature the Word is made flesh. Just as in moods of depression, when one doubts if good and evil be more than names and noises, even then faces passing in the street can bring back, by all that one reads in their lines, a passionate sense of the reality of the human qualities incarnated in them—their fineness or their squalor.

[320]

Modern psychology may know more of Madame Bovary than Flaubert himself knew, more of Hedda Gabler than Ibsen; but it also reveals how amazingly true the intuitions of these writers were; and with such artistry its own case-histories cannot compete. Without emotion of some sort our intellectual constructions remain, imposing perhaps, yet lifeless—like elaborate machinery without its electric power. All the wisdom of Solomon grows vanity of vanities without those emotions that can alone give it vitality. The Muses did not lie to Hesiod. Their gifts are twofold—not only lovely illusions, but also the truths that they make alive. Or, to return to Confucius, art contains both things that are 'perfect beauty and perfect goodness' and things that are 'perfect beauty but *not* perfect goodness'. This simple difference I think it dangerous to ignore. That is all.

XVI

Conclusion

*The longer I live, the more I value men who
are not lamed.*

TOLSTOY.

I HAVE tried to consider the ancient question of literary values—pleasure-value and influence-value— from the point of view of the critic, with elementary illustrations of the kind of help that modern psychology can give. Summaries, though often necessary, are usually boring. It may be a little less boring if I now attempt to summarize what I have said from a slightly different point of view—that, not of the critic, but of the writer. During the War the P.E.N. sent its members a questionnaire on this matter, from which it hoped to make a book. But the writers apparently failed to respond. Ignorance, indolence, reticence? I do not know. At least the book never appeared. A pity; for it might have been interesting. It would, no doubt, have shown wild differences of opinion. But why not? Some people seem to wish that we could all think the same. But what a tedious world that might make! The important thing is not to think the same, but to think.

There has, indeed, since appeared a book on the writer's function, by certain distinguished writers of to-day, to which I rushed for enlightenment. Perhaps I am blind: but I did not find much. One of them described at length an Agricultural Show at Lichfield, 'the rich smell of animals', the fowls with their 'alcoholic eyes'. After this excursion (the relevance of which escaped me), he suggested that writers should be subsidized by public committees (after being exhibited, one wondered, at Cultural Shows?). Another advocated 'disloyalty'. But do not be alarmed—he turned out merely to mean defiance of conventions. A third believed in 'Shape': 'Shape is possibly *the* important thing. Even to objectify futility is something.' And so to the book's conclusion: 'I don't think any of us feel ourselves to be unrelatable to something. We envisage, we are not passive, and we are not contributing to anarchy: that may be the most to be claimed for us.' This did not seem a very potent conclusion with which to meet the challenge of Plato or Tolstoy, Goebbels or Stalin. I was six shillings poorer and not a penny wiser. However, 'even to objectify futility is something.' That may be the purpose of much modern literature; but it is hardly inspiring.

The P.E.N. questionnaire had been a good deal more precise. I propose roughly to follow it here. First, 'What motives for writing?'

Some are obvious—influence, fame, money. But writing remains a mysterious impulse—sometimes an end in itself. Juvenal mocked it as an itch. 'C'est une ulcère', echoed Flaubert, 'que je gratte.' Lady Mary Wortley Montagu beguiled old age by writing a history of her own times, and then (strong-minded woman!) burning each quire as soon as written. Casanova spent thirteen hours a day in his library at Dux (thirteen hours, he says, that passed like as many minutes), scribbling those memoirs which he could not conceive ever being published and intended to have burnt before his eyes on his death-bed. Similarly with the journals of Pepys and Amiel. After all, birds sing without insisting on being broadcast.

Others have pursued the same passion without the same prudence. In the sardonic words of Piron:

> Ci-gît au bord de l'Hippocrène
> Un mortel longtemps abusé.
> Pour vivre pauvre et méprisé
> Il se donna bien de la peine.
>
> (Here where the Spring of the Muses bubbles,
> Sleeps one that bore long years of blame.
> To live in penury and shame
> He gave himself his fill of troubles.)

In general, the underlying motives seem complex. There is the pleasure of daydreaming; there is Narcissism; there is exhibitionism; there is also the release of putting into exact words, that one can control, the thoughts and emotions that otherwise tumble cloudy and chaotic in the brain.

> Qui chante,
> Son mal enchante.

> Klingt das Lied auch nicht ergötzlich,
> Hat's mich doch von Angst befreit.

Depression finds vent in expression. The things of time fall forgotten for a moment among timeless things. Besides, a pen can be like a diviner's twig; one never knows, till one tries to put them on paper, the things one has at the bottom of one's mind.

Then there are writers, like Flaubert or Mallarmé, bewitched by words. Having devised sounds to express their feelings, men may acquire intense feelings about the sounds themselves. Words stand for things; yet there are moods when things seem but weary children of the dust, and words the daughters of enchantment.

Sunt apud infernos tot milia formosarum—
by what hidden magic have those six words of Propertius outlived sixty thousand poems? Some psychoanalysts

will tell you that such writers are 'oral' types and that this verbal fascination is a relic of that suckling stage when love and joy centred in the infant's lips at the breast. It may be so.

Art, at all events, consists in giving form to feeling and feeling to form. The Classic stresses the form, the Romantic the feeling. That is the real basis of their long quarrel.

'The writer's relation to his public?' As we have seen, a public is not essential. Cézanne tossed his pictures over hedges. Still, he is uncommon. Reputation remains a gamble. In any case a public, like an oak-tree, is not good for much till it has lasted at least a century. Therefore no writer can live to see the only public that is really worth seeing. The dying Virgil ordered his epic to be burned. True, Horace and Shakespeare felt sure of immortality; but then so did Samuel Rogers.

Besides, the House of Fame grows now a full house; and as King Midas, that father of criticism, grows more democratic, his ears grow only larger and hairier. After all, what is a 'public'? The basest, the crudest, the most sheep-witted can find one—even Hitler, even Father Divine, even the humorous programmes of the B.B.C.

Should one write, then, for money? It will be recalled that Johnson said only blockheads wrote for anything else. But perhaps Johnson's best work was his talk; which was certainly not for money. Scott, again, unashamedly studied his sales returns. So did Trollope. So, doubtless, did Shakespeare with his box-office receipts. It is quite possible to serve both God and Mammon. But it remains a gamble; and a temptation. Perhaps it is better to write for 'les amis inconnus'. And perhaps best of all to write to serve, in the never-ending battle of ideas—though not under the flag of the state. To-day there are plenty of causes worth serving. In that phrase of Euripides, once adapted by Aristotle to justify himself:

> Base to sit dumb and let barbarians talk.

Some of you will write. I suggest that you had best, perhaps, regard your public with something of Shakespeare's good-humoured amusement at his populace—as being fantastic in their judgements; idiotic, very often, in their passions; yet full of lovable and even admirable individuals. The only vocal part of the public consists of reviewers, who are largely geese; you may have a few letters from readers (usually far more interesting than reviews); you may have the comments of friends and acquaintances—often too kind, or too jealous. The rest is silence. The readers you must respect remain hidden in the crowd. As soon as a book is finished, it is probably best to forget it and turn to the next—or to something else. Your artistic conscience must be facile, if you are content with giving the public what it wants; and your conscience likewise. A book must be left to go its way like a message in a bottle. To-day, unhappily, the sea is stiff with bottles. That is the penalty of an over-populated world. I do not believe in large communities or *Massenmenschheit*. The earth's population needs reducing by 90 per cent. Let us hope it may happen some day—painlessly, and not leaving the worst to survive. Then individuals may feel themselves more significant again and less like helpless drops in a world-ocean. For the rest, Landor has summed it in two lines:

> Neither in idleness consume thy days,
> Nor bow thy back to mow the weeds of praise.

'Relation to other writers, past and present?' For the writer, I believe dead authors are healthier company than the living. For the living, if good, may cramp his style; and if they are not good, why read them? Occasionally there have been useful 'movements'—the *Pléiade*, the

Romantics, the Pre-Raphaelites. But even these were largely matters of shouting. As writers gradually find their true gifts, their movements lose them. Hugo, Sainte-Beuve, and the other French Romantics, Rossetti, Morris, Swinburne, and the other Pre-Raphaelites, soon went their separate ways. Gregarious birds only twitter: songsters perch alone.

> Alone the sun arises, and alone
> Spring the great streams.

From too much frequenting the living a writer may catch that deadly itch to be 'in the movement' and up to date. A writer's job is to be good; if he has any personality, he will be new anyway. All individuals are unique. No good comes of an 'originality-neurosis'.

But from the dead one can learn what time has tested. No danger of being too like *them*. That fear is idle. Each age stamps its own children, however diverse, so indelibly that the future expert will be able to date our work, however much we quarrel, as 'mid-twentieth century'. No branch of art has to be more contemporary than the orator's; but it was the dead Thucydides that Demosthenes copied out five times. Yet who could mistake Demosthenes for Thucydides?

The Renaissance humanists, again, imitated the Ancients; and the bad writers among them produced only bad imitations; but they would probably have been bad anyway. Yet though Ronsard aped Pindar and Anacreon, and for a time overdid it, in the end he found himself. No one could mistake Ronsard for Pindar or Anacreon. Chatterton imitated the fifteenth century, Beddoes the Elizabethans; yet they remain quite different. Curiously enough, it is only their imitations of the dead that are still alive; their work in the manner of their own age is dead itself. Therefore I think the best masters are the dead. Literary fashion and the craving

[327]

for novelty are snares. The cry for 'contemporaneity' is as stupid as it is ugly.

'Writing as a career? The Ivory Tower?' Since Dryden, literature has tended to become a profession; but I doubt if this is the blessing most of us assume. Often it is precarious for the writer and dangerous for his writing. If he remains poor, he may pot-boil or over-work; if he grows comfortable, he may retire to some seclusion like Grasmere, or Farringford, or Box Hill, with a risk of premature interment. Wordsworth might have gained by living through another Revolution at forty; FitzGerald may well have been right in deploring for Tennyson his 'cursed inactivity'.

Aeschylus put on his epitaph where he was born, and how he fought the Persian, and where he died; but not a syllable about his plays. Perhaps that is partly why we remember them. Chaucer was too busy a civil ser-vant to finish the *Canterbury Tales*. But perhaps that is partly why we wish they had been finished. As a poet in his prime, Milton may seem a 'mute inglorious Milton' while he sits scribbling peevish propaganda for the Commonwealth; but their Latin Secretary, though he lost his eyes, kept his vision. Whereas of Southey, who turned his life into a literary concentration-camp, what survives? *The Three Bears!*

The test of a true poet, says Rilke in his *Briefe an einen jungen Dichter*, is that, if writing were denied him, he would die. But such sentimental *Schwärmerei* about art remains very modern. To a Greek this portentous fragility would have seemed worthy only of a slave; from those practical men of affairs, Shakespeare or Montaigne, it would have brought only a smile. When in 1939 some modern poets prudently withdrew to the shelter of the New World, a reviewer in the *New States-man* produced the characteristic defence that, after all, perhaps the best thing a poet can do is to save his own skin. But this would have seemed a little odd to Thucydides, or Sidney, or Cervantes, or Byron, who held that a writer was concerned with the art of living rather than of remaining alive.

Literature, like sport, can suffer from professionalism; one may write too much and live too little. Is it good enough to spend one's whole adult existence blacking paper? In normal times there have been other careers where a man could write quite enough if it was going to last, and too much, if it was not. Think only of Scott or Trollope. Even Marx, in one of his more human moments, looked forward to a future socialist society where 'the fragmentary man' would be replaced by the 'completely developed individual, one for whom different social functions are but alternative forms of activity. Men could fish, hunt, or engage in literary criticism, without becoming professional fishermen, hunters, or critics.'

An Ivory Tower in one's life, yes: but not life in an Ivory Tower.

'The writer's function in society? His purpose?' As we have seen, for many gifted authors of the nineteenth century the answer was simple—'None'. That view, though no longer shouted, remains in practice still common. In the modern Tyrant State, on the other hand, the writer becomes all purpose—a sort of nigger minstrel performing official airs under the baton of a policeman. Neither extreme seems very intelligent.

Once the creative writer was thought of as a guide to life's values. Then the philosophers, followed by the priests, accused him of meddling beyond his competence; their view has often been that men should come to *them* for wisdom and righteousness and go (if they could not be prevented) to theatre and story-teller for mere entertainment. For the writers were often corrupting in theory and immoral in practice. And yet of this superior wisdom of philosophers and creeds, after two thousand years one may be a little sceptical. Who have in fact done more to keep the world to some extent decent, or to make it decenter—Homer, Virgil, Shakespeare, and Ibsen; or Plato, Augustine, Calvin, and Hegel? For example, the poets have generally cared more about loyalty than marriage-lines. But may they not have shown in this rather more understanding of life than the respectable? Shakespeare's Antony played the fool. Shakespeare does not minimize the folly; he does not romanticize it, like Dryden. Antony's world was *not* 'well lost'. Yet Shakespeare's Antony remains a character so loyal and generous that he shames into something nobler both the Enobarbus who had abandoned him and the Cleopatra who had betrayed. That is not the sort of lesson often found in moral treatises or sermons. For these are commonly the work of meaner men. Writers *can* be, if they choose, in part 'the conscience of mankind'. Often, indeed, they are poor enough judges of ways and means; often they bungle their own lives past repair. But with the ends of living it may be different; writers may not very often discover new values; but they can make men *feel*, not merely see, the values that endure.

It remains an amazing and amusing paradox that some of the most gifted of the literary have often preferred to regard themselves as butterflies and their art as skittles; while enemies of literature like Plato, and the Nazis and the Communists have, on the contrary, regarded literature as one of the most formidable engines of the state. Men who beheld the Muses with the fish-like eyes of detectives have credited them with these enormous powers for good and evil, while the Muses' lovers have treated them too often as aimless *filles de joie*. No generation in France or England has been more guilty of this fundamental frivolity than ours; and none with less excuse. *Mein Kampf*, though hardly a classic, is still a book. Adolf Hitler, though a vulgar artist, was still an artist. Like Nero, he too might have died murmuring: 'Qualis artifex pereo.' And if the German people had possessed the sense, or the taste, to loathe his essential vulgarity instead of responding to it, a good deal more of Germany and Europe would be standing now.

My essential argument has been that the influence of literature is not to be underestimated (least of all in the light of modern psychology), merely because its effects are often so slow and so unconscious. It is like the effect of forests on a climate; and it is not only with material dust-bowls that we are threatened to-day. Because this influence is so potent, dictators try to capture it; but literature breeds ill in captivity and in harness it dies. Literature belongs to the free; but not to the irresponsible.

In antiquity the Guild of Hippocrates imposed on the new-made physician an oath never to abuse the power of his art. The writer will rightly take oaths to none. He may question, and reject, the codes of convention. But it seems to me that both writers and critics might ask themselves a little more often than they do, whether their powers are being used or abused. The twentieth century has seen too much writing that was squalid, intolerant, whimpering, or cruel; and too often the critics only comment was 'How interesting!' The Chinese had a myth that debasing playwrights suffered in Purgatory as long as their plays ran on earth. It was a sensible myth.

The future of mankind does not look at present over-bright. Quite apart from the menace of Asiatic despotism and fanaticism, in fifty years, if it continues its mad multiplication, humanity may be battling for bare food. Wisdom and courage do not look like becoming superfluous. Men cannot live on literature; but literature can help them to live. Or it can hinder. With all his exaggerations, Tolstoy seems to me a good deal wiser about the influence-value of art than the aesthetes who smile at him. Archilochus threw away his shield in battle and wrote a poem jesting at it. Yet it was not the jesting of a coward: Archilochus fell fighting. But the modern world has seen too many writers encouraging men to flee from reality into decadence. To wish poets to produce only *Marseillaises* would be stupid. But I suggest that some of us are dangerously content that art should become an opium-den. The artist, indeed, may by temperament be inclined to forget his ultimate responsibility: but the critic and public opinion have less excuse for forgetting. And Nemesis, at all events, does not forget.

Conclusion—what shall I say to my son if in fifteen years he wants to write? Something, perhaps, like this. 'If you feel the impulse, follow it. Anyway, learn how to write. To-day it is simple common sense to be master of one's pen; just as three centuries back it was simple common sense to be master of one's rapier. You never know when you may need it—even in the most practical of professions. Do not live to write, nor write to live (unless you want to be a journalist—a profession often despicable, but at its best extremely important). Most professional men of letters turn into old women or ghosts. And though brave writers have defied unpopularity, even at the cost of starvation, it seems better generalship not to get starved out at all, by making your base elsewhere.

'Difficulty of publication? Yes, I know. But persistence can do marvels. No need to start by being too proud. Even a letter to a provincial paper may be better than nothing. (Shaw trained himself in controversy by going to meetings and contradicting the speakers.) And you do not *have* to publish. You can keep a journal. A letter to a friend costs 2½d. (Most people have forgotten how to write letters. Yet Dorothy Osborne seems to me to write better prose than Milton; and what are Walpole's books to his letters?) Even conversation— another half-lost art—is a form of authorship. The rest may follow—or it may not.

'Reviewing is a good beginning. You learn. But get out of it in time. It's a poor life writing always what will be dead in a week, about books that (nine-tenths of them) will be dead in a year. And for the character it is a "dangerous trade". Periodical-writing in general can be useful; but don't get caught up in it—"fugitive things not good to treasure". If you write fiction, I hope it will not be the usual stuff, as small as common life and twice as boring. If it is poetry, I hope it will be clear and about something; not a muddy puddle in which you sit belly-aching to eternity about your private pangs. Do not join movements—they belong more to advertising than to art. The real bread of literature is generally grown from a lonely furrow. Do not get involved in learned controversies; they are mostly besieging mares' nests. Political controversies? Yes, if you have to; they *are* sometimes of use. Never answer critics, except perhaps on points of fact; "il faut laisser ces mauvaises gens dans l'incertitude." Do not write for the learned (but remember they are there): write for the intelligent —or even for the simple. Try to bring back into litera- ture some of the grace and dignity it has forgotten. And be brief—nearly all books are too long.

'Do not write for immortality. You will not read your epitaph, nor attend your centenary as an incognito cherub. (Yet write as carefully as if you hoped to.) Do not write for popularity; those who try to collect a crowd, get collected by it. Write by all means for money, if you can get it; but if you write only for that, I hope you get none. But better write because you want to; it will make life pleasanter and more vivid, but also exasperated, toilsome, often depressed. Do not let it suck your life out, like a vampire; living comes before writing—as Flaubert came to realize, too late. Do not think dead children a substitute for live ones—they are not. Some writers have been poor human beings; we may be grateful for their books; but by now the world has more books than it knows what to do with; and not enough men of good sense and good will. So write, above all, to be of some use. The dykes of civilization prove weaker than anyone dreamed fifty years ago. The little rats of decadence swarm there. And, outside, there may well wait another deluge.'

(Or will this make him go and do exactly the opposite? I shall wait and see.)

To prophesy unpleasant things is not pleasant—except for a certain unpleasant type of prophet. And it may well be that most human apprehensions turn out in the end to be idle croakings. None the less it remains quite possible that the comparative calm and comfort of the nineteenth century, which bred so many aesthetes, decadents, and other human bric-à-brac, were only an exceptional interlude—a brief fair interval in a stormy world. While men persist so blindly in spawning their kind and squandering their resources, with Asia and Africa beginning to challenge the long dominance of the white West, the dawn of the coming age looks more red than rosy. These long-term tendencies may as yet worry only a few far-sighted scientists; but we already feel the creaking of our own economy under the stresses that forerun them. I believe that the future may need from writers something more than 'objectifying futility'. I believe that it may need from literature (if it has not by then been degraded to a state-department) all its power to fortify and inspire human endurance, and from psychology all its capacity to understand and to control the infinite complexities and perversities of human character.

[334]

INDEX

A

...ing merit

The University of Michigan Press — Ann Arbor